## *The Crucible of Language*

From the barbed, childish taunt on the school playground, to the eloquent sophistry of a lawyer prising open a legal loophole in a court of law, meaning arises each time we use language to communicate with one another. How we use language – to convey ideas, make requests, ask a favour, express anger, love, dismay – is of the utmost importance; indeed, linguistic meaning can be a matter of life and death. And yet, until relatively recently, the communicative value of language was all but relegated to the margins of scientific enquiry.

In *The Crucible of Language* Vyvyan Evans explains what we know, and what we do, when we communicate using language; he shows how linguistic meaning arises, where it comes from, and the way language enables us to convey the meanings that can move us to tears, bore us to death or make us dizzy with delight. Meaning is, he argues, one of the final frontiers in the mapping of the human mind.

**Vyvyan Evans** is Professor of Linguistics at Bangor University, where he has served as Head of the School of Linguistics and English Language, and Deputy Head of the College of Arts and Humanities.

# Praise for *The Language Myth*

'A much-needed, comprehensive critique of universal grammar. Vyvyan Evans builds a compelling case that will be difficult to refute.'

David Crystal,
*author of The Cambridge Encyclopedia of Language*

'Evans' rebuttal of Chomsky's universal grammar from the perspective of cognitive linguistics provides an excellent antidote to popular textbooks where it is assumed that the Chomskyan approach to linguistic theory (in one avatar or another) has somehow been vindicated once and for all.'

Michael Fortescue,
*Professor Emeritus, University of Copenhagen*

'The Language Myth builds a compelling case that there is no innate universal grammar. Evans's work is a welcome contribution to our understanding of the origin, nature, and use of human language.'

Daniel L. Everett,
*Dean of Arts and Sciences, Bentley University*

'Highly recommended.'

Seizi Iwata,
*Kansai University*

'Is the way we think about language on the cusp of a revolution? After reading The Language Myth it certainly looks as if a major shift is in progress, one that will open people's minds to liberating new ways of thinking about language.'

*New Scientist*

'Voluminous ... completely persuasive.'

*Fortean Times*

# The Crucible of Language:

How Language and Mind Create Meaning

VYVYAN EVANS

CAMBRIDGE
UNIVERSITY PRESS

# CAMBRIDGE
UNIVERSITY PRESS

University Printing House, Cambridge CB2 8BS, United Kingdom

Cambridge University Press is part of the University of Cambridge.

It furthers the University's mission by disseminating knowledge in the pursuit of education, learning and research at the highest international levels of excellence.

www.cambridge.org
Information on this title: www.cambridge.org/9781107561038

First published 2015

Printed in the United Kingdom by TJ International Ltd. Padstow Cornwall

*A catalogue record for this publication is available from the British Library*
*Library of Congress Cataloguing in Publication data*
Evans, Vyvyan.
The crucible of language : how language and mind create meaning / Vyvyan Evans.
    pages   cm
ISBN 978-1-107-12391-5 (Hardback) – ISBN 978-1-107-56103-8 (Paperback)
1. Semantics.   2. Cognitive grammar.   3. Psycholinguistics.   I. Title.
P325.E955 2015
401′.43–dc23   2015017918

ISBN 978-1-107-12391-5 Hardback
ISBN 978-1-107-56103-8 Paperback

..............................................................................

Every effort has been made to secure necessary permissions to reproduce copyright material in this book, though in some cases it has proved impossible to trace or contact copyright holders. If any omissions are brought to our notice, we will be happy to include appropriate acknowledgements on reprinting, or in any subsequent edition.

In memory of Jim Gardner, 1937–2012, and Joseph Gardner, 1940–2013.

'Language is to the mind more than light is to the eye.'

William Gibson, *The Miracle Worker*

# Contents

# Figures

# Tables

# Preface

For much of the second half of the twentieth century, the scientific study of language assumed that syntax – our ability to construct grammatically well-formed sentences of great complexity – was the underlying hallmark of human language. The unfortunate consequence was that the study of meaning was relegated to the margins, barely getting a look-in. Yet, in our everyday world of experience, as we act and interact in the host of encounters that make up our daily lives, it is the communicative value of language – the meanings we use it to convey – that is of pre-eminence; in everyday life, how we use language and for what purpose is of the utmost importance; linguistic meaning can be a matter of life and death. And yet ironically, until recently, the scientific study of language relegated its central function – the way we use language to convey ideas, make requests, ask a favour, express anger, love, dismay – to all but the margins of scientific analysis.

In recent times, the study of meaning has returned to the fore, regaining its rightful place as the centrepiece of the scientific study of the human mind. This book tells the story of how our language, in conjunction with the vast body of knowledge about the world which we carry around with us in our heads, enables us to communicate with one another – sometimes for the better, sometimes for the worse. From the barbed, childish taunt on the school playground to the eloquent sophistry of a lawyer prising open a legal loophole in a court of law, meaning arises each time we use language to communicate with one another. *The Crucible of Language* explains what we know, and what we do, when we communicate using language; it shows how linguistic meaning arises, where it comes from and the way in which language enables us to convey the meanings that can move us to tears, bore us to death or make us dizzy with delight. And in so doing, it proffers profound insight into exactly what it is to be human. This book presents the emerging story of what we now know about *how* we mean, and how we *use* language to mean, following a cascade of recent scientific breakthroughs.

This book is the sequel to *The Language Myth*. It presents the new, exciting and radical alternative to the views of language and mind that I critiqued there. I pick up some of the themes I introduced in the earlier book; I address concepts and the mechanisms that underpin mind design, the embodied basis of the mind, the semantic basis of grammar, the evolutionary origins and precursors of language, among others. And this is because these are the bread and butter concerns of language, mind and meaning. But in this book, I approach them from a wholly different perspective, in order to illustrate my central argument: meaning arises from the confluence of language and the mind; both are central to the way we use language to communicate, and consequently to convey meaning.

That said, this book assumes no background: it matters not a jot whether you have read *The Language Myth*. I provide the necessary context in each of the chapters, outlining the issues and concerns and assuming no prior knowledge. My presentation attempts to capture the wonder and excitement at what the science of language and the mind has discovered in recent years; meaning is, in many ways, one of the final frontiers in terms of mapping the human mind. This makes the terrain new, and in parts speculative. But the tale I have to tell, and the discoveries I present here, are gripping – certainly, for those of us working at the frontier of meaning in language and in the mind, the journey has been fascinating; it is also beginning to reveal vistas that earlier generations of researchers may have thought improbable. I hope you enjoy the ride.

# Acknowledgements

A work such as this one has necessarily resulted in a great many intellectual debts. It is therefore appropriate that I single out, and thank, all those who have given up their time in reading earlier draft versions of the book, providing feedback on aspects of my presentation and the details of the story I present. In particular, I gratefully acknowledge the four anonymous reviewers for Cambridge University Press, and the following colleagues: Sarah Duffy, Gilles Fauconnier, Kevin Gould, June Luchjenbroers and Alan Wallington. And last but by no means least, I remain grateful to the editorial team at Cambridge, especially my editor Andrew Winnard.

# I

# The ineffability of meaning

What can be said at all can be said clearly; and what we cannot talk about we must pass over in silence.

Ludwig Wittgenstein, *Tractatus Logico-Philosophicus*

# Chapter 1 Unweaving a mystery

Like many other species, we are minded creatures: we store representations of the world around us, and of our own internal bodily states. But unlike other species, we also have language: an unheralded means of packaging these representations – our thoughts – and rendering them public. Sometimes we use language for the better – when we share our pearls of wisdom with a friend in their hour of need – and sometimes for the worse, and to our regret – something spoken in the heat of the moment cannot, alas, be taken back, and may not always be forgiven, or forgotten. Making thought public is the hallmark of communication. And while language may, on occasion, be an imperfect means of achieving this, it nevertheless gets the job done. But communication is dependent on something more mysterious, the seemingly ineffable elixir of communication: meaning.

Meaning presents itself in a variety of ways. The dark, menacing clouds slowly creeping by in the sky outside, as I look through my window, *mean* rain. A red traffic signal *means* stop. The 'recycle bin' icon on my computer desktop *means* that's where I place an unwanted file. And the yellow and black colouration of a droning wasp *means* danger: don't touch.

But having language raises the stakes. Think about it for a second: after all, you're currently reading marks on paper, or on a computer screen. While you could be watching dark, menacing clouds through a window, or sitting at a stop signal, or contemplating deleting a computer file, the chances are you're not. You've used the orthographic representations that I've typed – and that you've just read – to conjure up complex ideas – lowering clouds, computers, traffic signals and wasps. For creatures with language – us – meaning appears to arise, in particular and most saliently, in the liminal space between the private world of thought and the

very public shop window of language. I can use it to suggest ideas
that you might then call up from your past, such as your first pet,
or your first day at school, or your first date, or the first time you
kissed; or I can use it to prompt you to think about ideas you're not
actually experiencing in the here-and-now, such as a droning wasp
meaning danger. We can even use it to suggest imaginative flights
of fancy, such as how you might spend your millions if you won
the jackpot in the national lottery.

Meaning seems to arise when we understand the ideas conveyed
by a word, or sequences of words. But it also involves understanding what a speaker intends by the words – which, paradoxically,
might not always be the same as what the words themselves, other
things being equal, might actually convey. For instance, the
utterance 'lovely to see you!', said with a grimace by your ex after
a messy break-up as she or he bumps into you in the supermarket,
might not *mean* what it literally says.

## The commonplace view of meaning

One view, a commonplace view perhaps, takes language, in all
its kingly splendour, as the mover and shaker in our everyday
world of meaning. After all, every time we open our mouths and
converse with someone – a passer-by in the street, our ex in the
supermarket, a colleague over a drink after work, or even a lover
during a breathless dinner date – we are performing one of the
most remarkable feats that can take place between people; we use
language, all the time, to gossip, persuade, seduce; to argue and to
make up. Our use of language to communicate – and this is by
no means restricted to the spoken variety – might seem, on the
face of it, all there is to meaning-making. Words, whether spoken,
written, typed or signed, *carry* meanings. And as we have learned
what 'our' words mean at mother's breast, scarcely before we can
remember remembering, we can join them together in sentences
and in larger chunks of discourse, and almost effortlessly when
listening to others, or reading a text, unpack their internal

residue. And in so doing, we *understand* the meaning inlaid in their symbolic essence.

But a moment's reflection reveals this appealingly intuitive view of meaning to be unsatisfactory. For one thing, the self-same word can *mean* many different things on different occasions of use. Take the verb *to kill*, in the following line from Shakespeare's Henry IV, part II: *The first thing we do, let's kill all the lawyers.* This is uttered by Dick the butcher. And his utopian resolution is to murder all of England's lawyers.

While this sentiment may resonate with some contemporary readers – lawyers narrowly follow bankers and politicians among those some of us most distrust – *kill* doesn't always, paradoxically, *mean* 'to kill'. *She dressed to kill,* or *That joke killed me,* clearly don't beckon death – at least, one hopes for something rather different. Nor is *a lady-killer* normally taken to betoken a murderer of women, save perhaps in the Ealing Studios black comedy *The Ladykillers* (1955). We can *kill time,* or say that too much garlic or chilli *kills a meal.* We can *kill* (switch off) *an engine,* or *the lights*; we can *kill (off) a bottle of brandy,* or we can complain that a new pair of shoes is *killing me,* or that fatigue from overwork *kills your love life* and potentially, over time, *the relationship.* A long hike can *kill us,* or rain can *kill plans* for a barbeque. Clearly, each of these different uses of *kill*, and there are many others, seem to be related somehow. But only the first, from Shakespeare, explicitly relates to death.

So, what are we to make of this variation in the meanings associated with a single word? At the level of language, this reveals meaning not to be an all-or-nothing affair. It shakes us out of our commonplace assumption that words neatly package a single discrete meaning and that somehow, during the process of language comprehension, we unpack it, thereby revealing the meaning folded up inside, in much the same way as we might open a suitcase and remove our neatly arranged clothes after a trip.

But variation in meaning can also come in more complex forms. Someone can *buy the newspaper.* Here your gut response might be that *newspaper,* the word, refers to the printed item you or I purchase from a newsstand, perhaps on our daily route to work. But if you were a tycoon, it could *mean* the publishing company that employs journalists, and produces and prints the daily tabloid we purchase. This second meaning, however – referring to a company, rather than an item of printed text – sounds and feels a little bit more abstract. And this is because *this* meaning draws upon our knowledge of the world – that certain types of companies produce newspapers. This background knowledge – knowledge about how newspapers are produced, and by whom – enables us to use the word *newspaper* to refer, somewhat paradoxically – at least on the face of it – to a type of company, rather than an item of paper, with print, reporting the news. To understand the meaning behind this second use of the word *newspaper*, we have to know that there is a direct relationship between a particular type of publisher and the physical newspaper we buy in a newsagent, or subscribe to online. And in so doing, the physical entity that we might read is, in some sense, standing, in our mental gymnastics, for the newspaper publishing company. But here the meaning is not, apparently, coming from the word itself, but rather from what we know about the world. It relies upon something other, or more, than language.

And this begins to get to the heart of the matter. Language is but the tip of a meaning-making iceberg. Of course, it floats above the surface, and sails into plain view. It is there in front of us, every day, when we interact with strangers, our children, friends, colleagues or lovers. Language is such an impressive feat that some scientists have attributed to it near-godly powers in elevating the human mind – essentially built on the brain-plan of an African ape – to a rarefied state of cognitive splendour, unmatched by the mental capacities of any other earthly being, present or past.

But let's not beat about the bush. In terms of meaning-making, language is indeed but the tip of the iceberg. It is, self-evidently, the visible portion: we hear language around us every time we step outside our front doors and we see it each time we boot up our computers, or switch on our tablets and open an email, or respond to a text message. And, consequently, we might be forgiven for assuming that it *is* language that *carries* meaning: that it *is* language that clinches the deal – *enabling* communication.

In this book, I will show you that there is a large infrastructure supporting the creation of meaning, one that's less easily glimpsed beneath the murky surface of the whys and wherefores of words and their complex semantic webs. Language works extremely well because it is part of a larger meaning-making complex. It's dependent upon a suite of other capacities – in particular, a repository of thoughts and ideas that we carry with us, in our minds – upon which language draws each time we open our mouths to speak. Language, together with this mental apparatus, co-conspires to produce meaning, enabling effective communication.

## And the word is ... meaning

In fact, *meaning* – the word – itself provides clues as to what this meaning-making complex might amount to. Words, like people, families and nations, have histories – good and bad, unremarkable and momentous, attractive and downright ugly. A word's timeline can provide clues from the past that are relevant for the present, and specifically what the nature of meaning might amount to, and how it might arise. The noun, *meaning*, was derived in the late Anglo-Saxon period from the pre-existing verb *to mean*. Old English was spoken in England roughly until the invasion of England by William the Conqueror of Normandy, in 1066, after which it gradually morphed into the Middle English of Chaucer. While contemporary dictionaries often list 'intend' or 'to make known' as definitions of *to mean*, the Anglo-Saxon verb *mænan*, '*to mean*', probably comes from the far earlier Indo-European root *\*men*, '*think*'. And this would have given rise to the Indo-European form: *\*meino* 'intention/opinion', both forms suggested on the basis of historical reconstruction – there's no hard evidence these word forms actually existed, as Indo-European was spoken sometime in the region of 9,000–6,000 years ago, way before the advent of written records.[1] But assuming something like these ancestral words existed, this reveals the following. The modern English word, *meaning*, derived, in its distant past, from the idea of 'thinking' and 'thought'. While we doubtless use language to help us think, thinking itself is something done by a mind – as implicitly acknowledged by the very real frustration we may feel, on occasion, at our seeming inability to adequately articulate a deeply held feeling, thought or complex idea via language. Everyday, hackneyed expressions point to this: 'I can't quite put it into words', 'My words fail me', 'I'm at a loss for words', and a host of others. Meaning, on this evidence, seems to have *at least* as much to do with thought, and the minds that produce thought, as it does with language.

In this book I explore, on the face of it, a simple idea: meaning arises from the confluence of language and mind. Yet trying to figure out its essence – how this confluence gives rise to meaning – has remained, until relatively recently, one of the greatest scientific mysteries of the cognitive and behavioural sciences; after all, trying to figure out its ineffable essence goes to the heart of the scientific study of language, the mind and brain and human behaviour.

While our species, *Homo sapiens*, has an unprecedented capacity for meaning, a reasonable account of the nature of meaning, the respective roles of language and mind in producing it and its evolutionary origins appeared to lie beyond the capability of contemporary science. But over the past couple of decades, things have begun to change. Exciting new discoveries about the mind, language and the way they work together in producing meaning now offer the prospect of a science of meaning. Meaning is central to our lives, and to what it means to be human. And the story of how we create meaning is one of the most fascinating, challenging and even perplexing in the contemporary science of language and mind.

# Chapter 2    The alchemist, the crucible and the ineffability of meaning

Dr John Dee (1527–1608 or 1609), was renowned as one of the most learned men of Elizabethan England. While still in his twenties, he was invited to lecture on algebra at the University of Paris. He was a widely respected mathematician and astronomer. He was also one of the age's leading experts on navigation: he trained those who led many of the English voyages of discovery to the Americas. During his lifetime, he amassed one of the greatest personal libraries in all of England. Moreover, his intellectual prowess brought him into the orbit of the court of Elizabeth I, whom he served as scientific advisor.

But John Dee was also a scholar of the occult: his compass included the realms of both science and magic, in a time, before the Age of Enlightenment (1650–1800), when the two were still not clearly separated or distinguishable. Dee was an expert in the mysteries of alchemy – the pseudoscientific study of the essences of materials. His investigations drew on the mystical, such as Hermetic philosophy, which attempts to tap into cosmic consciousness, and primordial wisdom. And in his final years, his research increasingly focused on an attempt to commune with divine beings, including angels, seeking to uncover a universal 'language of creation'.

For Dee, all his research endeavours nevertheless formed part of a coherent intellectual quest to uncover the divine forms that undergird and infuse the visible world of corporeal experience. Dee was, in an important sense, representative of a tradition of mediaeval scholars whose scholarly pursuits both presaged and led to the later development of scientific thought, theory and practice, based on observation rather than divination and the occult.[1]

The ostensible goal of alchemy was the transmutation of material form into perfection. One example of this was the quest for the 'philosopher's stone', a substrate that would work on base materials, transmuting them, via a chemical process, into more noble metals, such as silver or gold. In terms of the human form, the search for an 'elixir of life' was meant to transmute the human body, providing youth and longevity.[2] While alchemy dates back to antiquity, it was still widely practised during the mediaeval period, and even into the Enlightenment.

Alchemy was, perhaps, the paradigmatic example of a proto-science: one that incorporates pseudoscience with more rigorous, analytic elements; and it paved the way for the modern discipline of chemistry. Its practitioners pioneered laboratory techniques and an experimental method which led to the emergence of chemistry: the terms *alchemy* and *chemistry* were used interchangeably as late as the seventeenth century.[3]

For instance, Robert Boyle (1627–1691), the Anglo-Irish philosopher and scientist widely credited as the father of modern chemistry, dabbled in alchemy. He was instrumental in the successful repeal of the 1688 Royal Statute which had prohibited the alchemist's attempt to manufacture gold and silver.[4] And his background in alchemy informed his views and methods in developing a more rigorous scientific method based on experimentation and observation.

In contemporary popular culture, the physical symbol of alchemy is the crucible: a vessel manufactured from a refractory material like porcelain or ceramic. Alchemists used a crucible to subject materials to very high temperatures, combining admixtures of different substances in their experiments. The practice was both informed by and, in important ways, sought to reveal aspects of the transcendental.

But the search for the philosopher's stone, as well as John Dee's quest to understand the language of creation, were doomed affairs. They were doomed because they amounted to a search for the ineffable: the genuinely unknowable. Until recently, the prevailing view among scientists was that, like the transcendental mysteries that infused alchemy, meaning too is ineffable, and its study made little sense from the perspective of 'science'. The case of alchemy, for my money, provides an interesting and illuminating point of comparison with some of the intellectual psycho-drama surrounding the study of meaning in the recent past in the history of ideas.

## The ineffability of meaning

During the twentieth century, new disciplines emerged that pioneered, in important and often startling ways, the scientific discovery of the human mind and human behaviour – making strides in charting some of the last great frontiers of the human psyche. The scientific study of language – linguistics – emerged, during the course of the century, as a rigorous and mature academic discipline, offering great insight into the nature of this most complex of human behaviours. Today linguists know how social life gives rise to variation in language use, leading to language change; they have amassed a huge amount of knowledge about how languages diverge and the cultural, experiential and psychological factors that lead to this; they have made great strides in understanding the way the mind processes language when we speak and understand, and, when it goes wrong, some of the reasons why; and, although the debate is still sharply divided, there is an emerging sense of how language is organised in the mind, and the way young infants learn their mother tongue – in *The Language Myth* I intervened in this debate, weighing the various claims for nature versus nurture in giving rise to language.

But as we saw in the previous chapter, in terms of meaning, as it's such a slippery beast, there has been a feeling among many experts that it almost defies scientific analysis. Indeed, despite the advances elsewhere concerning other facets of language and the mind, for much of the twentieth century the scientific study of language swept the study of meaning under the carpet – out of sight is out of mind. One of the twentieth century's truly great linguists, Roman Jakobson, tellingly observed that, in the first part of the last century, 'semantics, or the study of meaning, remained undeveloped, while phonetics made rapid progress and even came to occupy the central place in the scientific study of language'.[5] And for much of the second half of the twentieth century, the scientific study of meaning was again marginalised – this time in favour of the somewhat different study of linguistic form, especially the analysis of the rule-governed behaviour for generating sentences. This branch of language science, often referred to as 'syntax', is most closely associated with the pioneering research of arguably the world's most famous twentieth-century linguist, Noam Chomsky.

Beginning in the 1950s, Chomsky proposed that sentence form – or syntax – and meaning are separate and, indeed, autonomous types of knowledge. While meaning is nebulous, like a butterfly – difficult to pin down, and hence unsuitable for objective scrutiny – a science, in contrast, *can* be built on the close analysis of the grammatical rules that govern sentence structure. Syntax, it turns out, is much easier to study, and to say precise things about. The ineffability of meaning, it seemed, was simply too daunting; like John Dee's search for the universal language of creation, it was too mysterious and too unknowable to say anything concrete about.

Consequently, separating sentence structure – observable patterns in word order – from its meaning enabled professional linguists, perhaps somewhat ironically, to study form without having to be overly concerned with meaning – with *what* the sentence forms actually *do*, and *how* they are actually *used*, when we open our mouths and converse with one another.

But since the 1970s, and with gathering momentum ever since, the study of meaning has steadily returned to the fore.[6] Another famous linguist, Ray Jackendoff, writing at the turn of the twenty-first century, spoke for many when he proclaimed meaning to be 'the "holy grail" not only of linguistics, but also of philosophy, psychology and neuroscience ... Understanding how we mean and how we think is a vital issue for our intuitive sense of ourselves as human beings. For most people, meaning is intuitively the central issue in the study of language – far more important than understanding details of word order [aka syntax]...'

But the challenge, of course, is a significant one. How do words, and other units of language, come by their meanings so that we understand what others are saying to us? And how do we make sense of the sort of variation we witnessed with the verb *kill* in the previous chapter? *What* do I know, and *how* do I know it, when I understand *Kill all the lawyers* to refer to death, but *She dressed to kill (me)* to refer, hopefully, to something else entirely? In short, what are the mysterious mechanics of meaning? What part does language play? And what unseen actions do concepts perform?

An early proposal, in the 1970s, by the philosopher Jerry Fodor, suggested that we might be born with what he likened to a 'language of thought'.[7] We enter the world ready-equipped with a rudimentary set of ideas or concepts, which form the bedrock of our meaning capability. We can use these to build other, more complex ideas. Moreover, we learn the meanings of words by matching particular words to the innate concepts – our internal language of thought – which words, in essence, are merely labels for. The idea is brilliant: we learn to mean, not because we actually *learn* anything, but because meaning was *there* all along – we didn't have to *actually* learn anything to begin with. We come ready-equipped with meaning, and just have to map word forms – determined by the culture we grow embedded in – onto the meanings we're born with. For instance, in England, and the rest of the English-speaking world, the word-form *cat* gets mapped onto the same internal concept, in the mind's language of thought, as the form *chat* in France and Quebec, or *Kätze* in the German-speaking nations.

But this approach, to my mind, is very much akin to the transcendental mysticism invoked by John Dee in his version of alchemy. Because a problem is hard to explain, our first course shouldn't be to invoke magic: we should reserve that for a position of last resort when all else fails. To assume we're born with meaning already more or less in place is very much like an appeal to magic. It removes the problem in one fell swoop: we don't know where meaning comes from, so let's just assume it was there all along.

While invoking magic, in one sense, is always deeply satisfying – who doesn't want to be entertained, intrigued and mystified – in another it's deeply frustrating. There's a time and a place for magic, of course: the circus, the magician's parlour or the illusionist's stall at the fairground – not the research laboratory. It's frustrating because it means giving up on the challenge almost before we've begun. And it's also deeply unscientific: positing an innate sets of meanings – concepts – fails the 'good science' test – it cannot be proved one way or another; contemporary science is based on the litmus test of 'falsifiability'. Hence, any scientific account must justify its entry by paying the price of, at least in principle, the capability of being shown to be false. But claiming that meanings are imprinted in the brain by genetics amounts to a biological claim – one that can never be disproved, at least not given the current state of what we know about the brain. If we really want to understand something, we need to take a more rigorous route and move, as Boyle did, away from alchemy and into the enlightened world of chemistry, and the more rational method offered by science.

Today, we're in a position to do far better than appeal to magic. Since the 1970s, significant progress has been made across a diverse range of scientific fields, and there are new methods and techniques, including some that didn't even exist until relatively recently – cognitive neuroscience being a case in point, which now allows direct and indirect study of what the brain is doing when we produce meaning. We use language in and during acts of meaning. But meaning itself is not a thing, in the way that tables or chairs are, out there in the world, with shapes and forms. It's an act of creation and interpretation, involving people of flesh and blood who interact with others, in their everyday world of sense-perception. And people come equipped with minds, and knowledge of a particular language system, and create and interpret meaning in particular settings and contexts of language use, embedded in specific cultural milieus, which shape a linguistic system in the process.

In this book I focus on two of the prime ingredients in meaning-making: language and concepts. Ideas and concepts in the mind's 'conceptual system' derive not from innate prescription but through experience, both with our own bodies and with the world around us. We have a range of learning mechanisms that give rise to these 'embodied' concepts. Moreover, language provides our species, alone, with a means of harnessing these during the course of meaning-making: elaborating, nuancing and combining them in complex ways. The evolutionarily far more ancient conceptual system didn't evolve for communication, but for learning about, recognising and categorising the entities, events and situations around us, and this system ensured the survival of our forebears in the sometimes perilous, challenging and ever-changing world of quotidian threat and opportunity; but, enhanced and engaged by language, our repository of concepts – the conceptual system – can be harnessed to provide enormous expressive power, unlocking its otherwise mute meaning potential.

This feat enables us, in the absence of telepathy, to engage with other similarly minded bodies and develop, through coordinated co-action, a rich material and ideational culture and a cooperative mode of living. The two systems form a linguistically coordinated concept-complex – a recent invention of our evolutionary lineage: *Homo*. And, working in tandem, the linguistic and conceptual systems make meaning, and communication, possible: they bring us together.

Returning to another aspect of the analogy from alchemy, the creation of meaning can be likened to an admixing of these essential ingredients, in order to produce the seemingly mystical blend of the two – the admixture of language and concepts, each poured in, in sufficient quantity, together co-conspire to produce meaning. This entails investigating the nature of the mind's conceptual system, in order to understand how language interfaces with concepts when we think, and externalises them each time we open our mouths; or gesture, in the case of sign language; or, indeed, press letters on a keyboard, constructing the words that make up our utterances. And in so doing, this will reveal what language brings to the table in terms of meaning-making – my claim will be that language itself constitutes a system of concepts that are qualitatively distinct from those in the conceptual system. 'Linguistic concepts', I will show, bring the know-how to meaning construction; they coordinate the richer concepts in the mind's conceptual system, directing proceedings. Like an orchestral work, the musicians require a conductor to coordinate the performance. Language and concepts work in tandem, very much like this, fulfilling distinct, complementary and equally essential roles. In the nexus of the two, language nuances and tweaks concepts, enabling them to serve an evolutionary far more recent function: meaning-making, and linguistically mediated communication.

Another consequence of trying to get to grips with the seeming ineffability of meaning is that it enables far greater insight into the nature and status of language than was available to previous generations of scientists. If language is just part – albeit a significant part – of a more complex suite of meaning-making capabilities, this leads to a reanalysis of the relative contribution of language to the cultural efflorescence that has been the hallmark of our species for at least 50,000 years.

Our species is like no other in that it possesses language: we have evolved a means of using linguistic symbols to co-create and hence externalise thought. The interaction between language and our conceptual system, in creating meaning, is one that is unparalleled in any other known species. Over the last couple of decades, exciting new findings and theories have led to a new scientific turn in the nature of meaning-making, imagination and creativity. This now makes it feasible, arguably for the first time, to begin to get to grips with the respective role of language and the mind in co-creating meaning. It reveals the way in which both language and concepts, as well as our uniquely human instinct for cooperation – which, as I shall argue, led to the development of language – have produced our capacity to mean. I present evidence revealing how language co-conspires with our meaning-ready minds to create meaning: meanings that can make us laugh or cry, breathless and dizzy with delight. Moreover, beginning to harness this power enabled our early hominin ancestors, collaboratively, to resolve the challenges of the ecological niche they inhabited over 2.8 million years ago, as well as allowing our species, *Homo sapiens*, to surmount new ones.

## Language as a window on the mind

In 2009, *The Guardian* newspaper reported the following:

> [British Prime Minister] Gordon Brown made a 'slip of the tongue' when he said the world was in a depression, a Downing Street spokesman said today.[8]

In 1901, Sigmund Freud brought the phenomenon of slips of the tongue to the forefront of popular consciousness. Freud argued that linguistic errors of this type revealed people's true thoughts, feelings and emotional states. Former Prime Minister Brown's famously dour Scottish personality seemed to be revealed to all by his 'Freudian' slip – he meant, of course, to say, 'recession'. But instead, he revealed something about his own outlook. Since the work of Freud, popular culture has embraced the idea that the language we use sheds deep and revealing insight into everything from our hidden desires and motives to our mental health, and even our intelligence.

For instance, the mangling of the language by another political leader, former US President George W. Bush, led to some doubting his mental acuity. Bush famously demonstrated his talent for grammatical atrocity with the words: 'They misunderestimated me'.[9] He revealed his ability for decidedly odd phrasing still further when, in decrying the demise of gynaecologists in the United States, he declared that 'Too many OB-GYNS aren't able to practice their love with women all across this country'.[10] The mind boggles.

While Bush's intelligence, as measured by an IQ test, is perfectly normal – he scores 120, the same as his one-time democratic rival for the Presidency, John Kerry – it's been claimed his misuse of language points to a psychological condition. According to psychologist Keith Stanovich, Bush exhibits a thinking disorder that makes it difficult to form beliefs, and to examine one's beliefs for internal consistency. This condition, which Stanovich dubs 'dysrationalia', is independent of intelligence.[11] And, it has been claimed, it's revealed by the linguistic gaffes – the 'Bushisms' – for which George W. Bush became so (in)famous.

The point of these examples is that language has the power to reveal important aspects about individual minds. It provides a way of understanding different temperaments, and even whether particular individuals think rationally, or not, as the case may be. In some ways, of course, this isn't news at all. After all, we use language every day to convey our thoughts and ideas: we put our thoughts into words in order to communicate with others, to tell them what we think, what we feel, whether we agree or disagree, are angry or sad. In short, it's a truism that language reveals the landscape of an individual mind to us because, in a non-trivial way, that's the job of language; language provides us with a ready means of facilitating communication: what we use it to communicate are thoughts, ideas, feelings. And whether we like it or not, language *does* often seem to reveal our temperament, personality, motives and motivations, even whether we have internally consistent belief systems. While language, perhaps self-evidently, reveals the thoughts of an individual, in this book I will seek to persuade you that language can also do more than this. I argue that it reveals fundamental aspects of mind design: features of the human mind that are universal to us all.

This provides us with the first of two major themes that runs through the book: by examining the nature and role of language in facilitating meaning-making, we gain a direct vista into the nature and mechanics of the human conceptual system, upon which language depends for its semantic prowess. Language reveals the structure of thought: it is a window on the mind.

But a word of caution is nevertheless in order. Language cannot reveal the structure of thought alone – it is an imperfect window. After all, not all thoughts are, or indeed can be, reflected in language. Consider, for instance, the place on your face above your top lip and below your nose; this is the place, if you are an adult male, where a moustache can be grown. There is no word in English for this part of the face – yet this doesn't mean that you can't think about it and have a concept for it. I shall argue in this book that words are not the same as concepts – the latter being the bedrock of thought – although words can and do provide clues as to the nature of concepts.

Language provides an important line of evidence for building up a picture of the nature of the human mind. But it's just one line of evidence. Another type comes from behavioural studies, such as those conducted in the psychology lab. Behavioural experiments allow the psychologist to infer thought processes, by observing how human subjects behave in certain situations. And a third line of evidence comes from studies on the human brain, such as neuroimaging – images of the functioning brain – and electrophysiological studies – measurement of the electrical signals produced by the functioning brain. Language can be used, in conjunction with findings from other brain and behavioural sciences, to develop a more complete picture of the human mind.

A further note of caution is in order. Language is a system in its own right – this can limit its purview, as it may run on principles that are different from other aspects of mind; indeed, earlier researchers have claimed that language is an encapsulated mental 'module', distinct from other dimensions of mental function.[12] However, the evidence from language itself seems to suggest that this position isn't quite right – language appears to reflect more general properties of the mind, as revealed by behavioural evidence from psychology, and studies of the brain from cognitive neuroscience.[13]

A further complication is that it's becoming clearer that different languages both reflect and can lead to slightly different cognitive realities: language has the power to transform minds in different ways. The classic formulation of this issue concerns the principle of 'linguistic relativity'. At one time controversial, there is now compelling evidence that the different languages we each speak do influence aspects of thought, ranging from how we perceive colour,[14] to our conceptualisations of time, to our ability to navigate in space.[15] This means that the relationship between language and mind is a dynamic one: while language can serve as a window on the mind, it also plays a role in shaping the way we think.

Despite these caveats, language *is* the visible portion of our meaning-making iceberg: it allows us to glimpse the mental architecture that lies beneath. No one's ever actually seen a mind – the cognitive processes that constitute our mental life. Yet we hear and see spoken and written language every day: language provides the backdrop to our lives, and the glue that maintains social cohesion. Recent breakthroughs in the discipline of linguistics now provide a means of examining in some detail the nature of mind design by using language.

## The body in the mind

The second theme of the book, and a truly startling finding, is that the human body is central to the way in which knowledge is represented in the human mind.[16] Our thoughts and concepts arise from having the kinds of bodies we have, coupled with the way that we act and interact in the world around us – it is not that the human mind is a crucible of pure disembodied reason – the mind *is* embodied. In recent years, findings from linguistics have led to trailblazing insights into the ways in which our bodies influence and shape the structure of thought.[17]

In a non-trivial sense, that the mind is embodied is undeniable. The nature of our bodies determines the kinds of creatures we are: our bodies determine not only *how*, but *what* we experience. One obvious way in which our embodiment affects the nature of experience is in the realm of colour. The human visual system has three kinds of photoreceptors, or colour channels. In contrast, other organisms, such as squirrels, rabbits and possibly cats, make use of two channels. Still others, like goldfish and pigeons, have four channels. Having a different range of colour channels affects the experience of colour in often dramatic ways, not least in terms of the accessible portion of the colour spectrum. Some organisms, such as rattlesnakes, can see in the infra-red range. Rattlesnakes, which hunt prey at night, can visually detect the heat given off by other organisms. Humans are unable to see in this range. As this simple example demonstrates, the nature of our visual apparatus – one aspect of our physical embodiment – determines the nature and range of our visual experience.[18]

Similarly, the nature of our biological morphology – the kinds of body parts we have, for instance, arms rather than wings – together with the nature of the physical environment with which we interact, determines other aspects of our experience.[19] While gravity is an objective feature of the world, our experience of gravity is determined by our bodies and by the ecological niche we inhabit: hummingbirds – which can flap their wings up to a remarkable fifty times per second – respond to gravity in a very different way from humans. In order to overcome gravity, hummingbirds are able to rise directly into the air without pushing off from the ground, due to the rapid movement of their wings. Moreover, due to their small size, their experience of motion is rather different from ours: hummingbirds can stop almost instantaneously, experiencing little momentum. Compare this with the experience of Usain Bolt at the end of a 100-metre race: a human cannot stop instantaneously, but takes a number of paces to come to a standstill.

The nature of our species-specific embodiment leaves an indelible mark on the nature and structure of the human mind. Imagine a person in a locked room. A room has the structural properties associated with a container: it has enclosed sides, an interior, a boundary and an exterior. The consequence of these properties is that the locked room has the additional functional property of containment: the person is unable to leave the room. Although this seems rather obvious, observe that this instance of containment is partly a consequence of the properties of the locked room, and partly a consequence of the properties of the human body. Humans cannot pass through tiny crevices like gas, nor crawl through the gaps under doors like ants. This reveals that containment is a meaningful consequence of a particular type of physical relationship that we experience, on a daily basis, in our interaction with the external world.

The concept of containment represents one of the ways in which bodily experience gives rise to meaningful concepts. While the concept of containment is grounded in the directly embodied experience of interacting with bounded landmarks such as locked rooms, and many others, the human conceptual system – our repository of concepts – can also give rise to more abstract kinds of meaning. To show you what I mean, consider the following everyday examples:

> He's *in* love. We're *out of* trouble now. She's *coming out of* the coma. I'm *slowly getting into* shape. He *entered* a state of euphoria. He *fell into* a depression.[20]

Examples such as these are licensed by the structuring of particular sorts of abstract states – love, trouble, physical fitness, and so on – in terms of the concept of containment. In short, meaningful structure from bodily experience gives rise to concrete concepts like containment. And these, in turn, structure more abstract conceptual domains like states. In this way, human concepts are embodied, and language reveals this to us.

To begin to get a sense of this, consider the following linguistic examples:

> Christmas is *fast approaching*. The price of shares has *gone up*. Those two have a very *close* friendship.

While each of these sentences is, on the face of it, banal, they nevertheless point to something fundamental about the way we *all* think. These examples relate, respectively, to the abstract conceptual domains of TIME, QUANTITY, and AFFECTION – a conceptual domain being a body of knowledge within our conceptual system which contains and organises related ideas and concepts (when I refer to a whole domain – a system of concepts – rather than a more specific concept within a domain, I'll typically use small capitals). For example, the conceptual domain of TIME might relate to a range of temporal concepts including *Christmas*, which is a temporal event. But in each of these sentences, the more abstract concepts – *Christmas, price (of shares)*, and *friendship* – are understood in terms of conceptual domains relating to concrete physical experiences. For instance, Christmas is conceptualised in terms of physical motion (*fast approaching*), the price of shares in terms of vertical elevation (*gone up*), and friendship in terms of physical proximity (close). Clearly Christmas, and other temporal concepts, cannot literally be said to undergo motion. Yet – and here's the point – although we use language relating to motion, neither you nor I get confused. If I were to say: *Christmas is just around the corner*, no one in their right mind would expect to turn the street corner and see Father Christmas, Rudolph, my granddad dressed as a Christmas tree, or whatever, standing there. When we use language in this way, we, with seeming effortlessness, automatically understand that Christmas is *close* in time – rather than in space. And space, it seems, appears to provide the informational structure that supports our understanding of a number of more abstract domains of experience, as we shall see.

One of the major findings to have emerged from studies into the human conceptual system is that abstract concepts are systematically structured in terms of conceptual domains deriving from our experience of the behaviour of physical objects, involving properties like motion, vertical elevation and physical proximity. It seems, then, that the language we use to talk about temporal ideas, like Christmas, provides powerful evidence that our conceptual system organises abstract concepts in terms of more concrete kinds of experiences, which helps to make abstract ideas more readily accessible.

But again, a word of caution is nevertheless in order. Language only imperfectly reveals the nature of human embodiment, and throws up puzzles in what it does reveal. The abstract domain of TIME is a case in point. We shall see that language suggests that our concepts for time are constructed, in part at least, from our embodied experience of acting and interacting in a spatial environment. But time also reveals a paradox. Recent findings relating to how the brain processes time show that at the neurological level time is not structured in terms of space; time is a foundational domain of experience, and in fact, may be more foundational than space: we rely on time to facilitate our perception of spatial experience.[21] So, time highlights a puzzle in terms of our mind's design.

## Meaning is the Holy Grail

Meaning is unarguably the Holy Grail of all the disciplines in the brain and cognitive sciences, including linguistics. Yet, until relatively recently, many researchers considered meaning to be the hard problem of language and cognitive science: how does meaning arise? What mechanisms produce it? And what are the respective roles of language and concepts, severally and collectively, in producing meaning? The nature of meaning-making, so it seemed, was a mystery.

A number of leading psychologists – including those who would broadly support the argument that the mind is embodied[22] – and even some linguists have claimed that language doesn't directly contribute to the construction of meaning. To be sure, so their admonition goes, language contains words, as well as a system of rules allowing us to combine these words. But meaning, so the argument goes, does not arise from language per se.[23] The nature of semantic content – that elusive *sine qua non* – resides in the mind's concepts, in the conceptual system, which words unlock. Words themselves can point to the concepts. But it is the concepts – and not language per se – which possess the raw semantic material from which meaning arises.

In contrast, I will seek to convince you that language involves semantic material that *is* independent of non-linguistic concepts. Words encode meanings – I'll refer to these in later chapters as 'parametric' concepts – which add to, and are qualitatively distinct from, full-blown concepts – the concepts that reside in the mind's conceptual system. Take, for instance, the distinction between the words *red* and *redness*. On the face of it, they point to the same concept: our experience of what it means to be red, extracted from our quotidian experiences with all things red. This includes red in all its glory and diversity: from Gwyneth Paltrow's truly red lipstick to the dun red of a fox being pursued in the landed gentry's fox-hunting.

But words do something more than simply *point* to a particular concept: 'all things red'. In addition to activating our concept of 'what it is to be red', the words frame how we interpret the concept of 'what it is to be red'. The word, *red*, relates to a property of a thing. In contrast, the word, *redness,* relates to a thing in and of itself. Another way of saying this is that *red* is an adjective, and *redness* a noun. But the *meaning* of adjectives is that they tell us we are dealing with a property – of a thing – while the *meaning* of a noun is that we are dealing with a thing – rather than a property. And this follows, perhaps confusingly, because properties can be things, as in the case of *redness*.

For instance, when following an instruction for a skin medication, the choice of *red* versus *redness* alters the meaning in subtle, yet important ways. When we say: *Apply to the redness*, versus, *Apply to the red area*, in the first sentence, *redness* refers to a skin condition. But *red area* refers to skin that is discoloured in a particular way. *Red* and *redness* may be referring to exactly the same type of colouration: the same concept. Yet they nuance how the concept gets activated in our minds in slightly different ways: they provide distinct ways of construing, and so understanding, the concept of redness.

This simple demonstration illustrates that language encodes semantic content that is distinct from embodied concepts – concepts that language nevertheless helps harness. It also reveals the following. The way in which language allows us to subtly package concepts for purposes of communication has, in evolutionary terms, provided our species with an enhanced potential for meaning-making. The co-occurrence of a sophisticated conceptual system *and* language provides our species, uniquely, with a previously unheralded design feature for meaning and communication.

To be sure, many of the mechanisms involved in creativity are not linguistic in nature – and I also explore these. For instance, meaning construction involves hidden mental networks that integrate often bewilderingly complex webs of ideas, enabling new conceptions to see the light of day. I also probe, later in the book, the mechanisms that facilitate the genesis of creativity.

Nevertheless, meaning arises from an interplay between the parametric meanings encoded by language and the rich, 'analogue' concepts – as I shall refer to them – inherent in our conceptual system: meaning construction arises in the mix between the two systems. The evolutionary advantage of language is that it harnesses the conceptual resources that our forebears possessed, for purposes of meaning-making.

Any species more complex than, say, the earthworm, has a conceptual system. And many species have fairly complex conceptual systems: a system of concepts that allows them to categorise objects, to find their way in space and to otherwise act and interact in an ever-changing environment. But humans have additionally developed a linguistic system, bringing with it a new level of sophistication and representation, one unseen in other species. This set of semantic representations – unique to our species – has allowed humans to control, and thus bootstrap, the evolutionarily much older conceptual system, for purposes of meaning-making. Meaning does not reside in language, nor in the mind's concepts: it arises in the intersection between the two. But with language, our species is provided with the means to massively amplify the meaning-making potential of our conceptual systems. While a cat can miaow, seemingly plaintively, it can't tell you that it is moved by a pale moon on a clear still night. There are some ideas that only language can help express.

## Meaning in mind, meaning in language

In this book, I take you on a tour of findings that have emerged within the context of the scientific study of language: linguistics.

Over the past couple of decades, a revolution has taken place in our understanding of the way in which language and the mind co-conspire to create meaning. Scientists now know that language reflects key features of mind design. And as such, language can be employed in order to study the nature and structure of our minds, and of thought: language provides us with a window on the mind. The major discovery has been that meaning arises from the symbiotic coupling of the two, of language, in conjunction with our human repository of concepts. In the pages to follow, I survey some of the most significant claims and findings that shed light on the respective roles of both language and the mind, separately and collectively, in enabling the creation of meaning. So, to whet your appetite, here is the range of issues that I explore in each of the chapters to follow.

The discussion takes place in two parts. In the next part of the book, Meaning in Mind, I consider the nature of mind design, focusing on the nature and structure of the conceptual system, processes of concept formation and creativity. In the subsequent part, Language in Mind, the focus turns to language, how it interfaces with the conceptual system, and its precursors and origins.

## Meaning in Mind

### Patterns in language, patterns in the mind

How are concepts organised in the mind? Patterns in language reveal that much of our everyday meaning-making is based on 'conceptual metaphors': systems of stable links that enable us to structure more abstract systems of concepts in terms of more concrete experiences, gleaned from our everyday interactions in the world. I can talk about the *power* of love, for instance, because I, you and all competent users of English draw upon a system of metaphors in our minds which enables us to structure and so make sense of love, in terms of a physical force. But this is only the tip of the iceberg. In the next chapter, I explore the nature of the mind's metaphor systems – as revealed by language. And I chart their role in everyday meaning-making, as well as poetry and public discourse.

### Time is our fruit fly

Time is not something that is tangible: we can't touch it in the way we can tables, chairs or trees. But we nevertheless sense its passage in the ageing of our bodies, and when we close our eyes, we sense its transient presence. In Chapter 4 I ask, what is time? Using language, as well as findings from the psychology lab and the brain sciences, I explore how meaning-making in the domain of time proceeds: what is the nature of this abstract realm, time? And what does it reveal both about the way our minds are structured and how language interacts with our conceptual systems in enabling us to find and create meaning in this most abstract of domains?

### Concepts body forth

In Chapter 5, I consider the nature of our embodied cognition: the way in which our mind's concepts are directly grounded in our action and interaction with our daily world of experience. After all, concepts are the raw materials that, in part, allow us to deploy language, and to create rich, powerful meanings. I deploy language to shed light on the embodied nature of concepts, as well as findings from a range of disciplines, especially the interdisciplinary project known as cognitive science. I ask: what are concepts like? How does language shed light on their embodied nature? And, how do concepts underpin the meaning-making process?

### The concept-making engine (or, how to build a baby)

In Chapter 6, I take you on a tour of what we now know about the way in which concepts grow in the mind of a child, beginning from birth (perhaps even before). My focus is on the development of the most rudimentary concepts we know of – 'image-schemas' – from baby's first breath onwards. These very basic types of conceptual representations emerge very early in the life-span. Moreover, by around the first year of life, their complexity is able to support an emerging linguistic system, and the range of increasingly sophisticated behaviours in which a young infant engages. The chapter considers the significance of this sort of rudimentary concept for the meaning-making process.

### The act of creation

An outstanding question in the study of meaning concerns how language and the mind interact in giving rise to novel and sophisticated ideas: feats of imagination. In Chapter 7, I explore the processes involved in the act of creation: for instance, the way in which we imaginatively construct instruments of thought and reason. These include, but are by no means limited to, joke-telling for humorous effect and imagining scenarios that don't in fact exist, but which enable us to draw conclusions about likely outcomes that help us make sense of our everyday reality.

### *Meaning in Language*

### Webs of words

Of course, language is integral to our human meaning-making capacity. In Chapter 8, I explore the nature of words, and their contribution to the meaning-making process. Here, I investigate the way in which words shift their meanings in different contexts of use, and the way they are organised in the mind. I ask: what are word meanings? What role do they play in meaning-making? And what does our mental inventory of words look like?

### Meaning in the mix

While earlier chapters focused, separately, on the nature of either the conceptual system or the linguistic system, in Chapter 9

I bring the two together. Our unique capacity to create exquisitely sophisticated meaning arises from an intersection between the two. The types of representations – meanings – in both systems is qualitatively distinct. But together they intersect, enabling us to use language to encode and externalise concepts for purposes of linguistically mediated meaning. While language provides the scaffolding, affording our meaning-making capability its structural outline, the rich representations from the conceptual system fill out the details. Chapter 9 tells the story of how this happens.

### The cooperative species

But our meaning-making capacity is not just about language and the mind; it arose from an evolutionarily older 'cooperative intelligence', enabling language to emerge in the first place. Chapter 10 explores the nature of our cooperative intelligence, and how it has enabled meaning-making to flourish.

### The crucible of language

And finally, I explore the evolutionary melting pot that forged language and our unprecedented capacity for meaning. Based on recent discoveries in the field of paleoarchaeology, as well as what we now know about the trajectory of language evolution and change, I examine the seeds of meaning-making, showing how our cooperative intelligence led to the emergence of language and the development of a grammar system. And this enabled ancestral humans to employ language to bootstrap concepts in the evolutionarily older conceptual system, allowing our uniquely human meaning-making ability to see the light of day.

### Epilogue: The golden triangle

While my focus in this book is on thought and language, and how the two intersect in symbiotically creating meaning for purposes of communication, there is a third, critical ingredient within and through which meaning unfolds: culture. And in this sense, meaning is more than simply an act of communication; it is also an act of social cohesion. I liken language, thought and culture to points in a golden triangle, which exhibit a complex interplay, giving rise to meaning.

Of course, this selection of topics is necessarily partial, not least to avoid a book far weightier than the present one. But I've selected these topics precisely because they reveal the roles of both language and mind, separately and collectively, in facilitating meaning-making. My presentation includes research areas to which I've made major contributions, in particular the discussion of time in Chapter 4, the findings relating to word meaning in Chapter 8 and the nature of meaning-making in Chapter 9. I've also drawn extensively upon the many important insights arising from the research of other leading anthropologists, archaeologists, linguists, neuroscientists, philosophers and psychologists. That said, my account of the human capacity for meaning-making is not necessarily the way others would present it; it is, inevitably, a presentation as seen through my eyes. But what is remarkable, I think, is that, for arguably the first time, we are now at a stage in the language and cognitive sciences where we can realistically glimpse the way in which the admixture of language and concepts, composed and burnished by the mind, produce meaning; we are beginning to have a much clearer understanding of how creativity, imagination and meaning-making more generally are achieved, and how language and our conceptual systems grow and develop in the mind of a human infant; we also have an emerging sense of how our meaning-making capacity may have evolved, built upon an evolutionarily more ancient pro-social impulse. And so, perhaps for the first time in the history of ideas, we can begin to tell the story of what enables us to mean, and where this unique meaning-making prowess comes from.

The American poet, Mark Amidon, has said that 'Language is the means of getting an idea from my brain into yours without surgery'. In slightly different terms, the Greek playwright Aristophanes said 'By words the mind is winged'. And Oliver

Wendell Holmes describes the relationship between language and thought in this way: 'Language is the blood of the soul into which thoughts run and out of which they grow'. While these quotations provide striking, even haunting imagery, what I hope to show, in this book, is that the idea they get at is essentially correct. Recent advances in linguistics provide us with a methodologically con-strained means of using language to probe the structure of thought. And in the process, we shall see that language is more than a mere window; it also shapes the thoughts it helps reveal, enabling us to produce and express complex, subtle meaning, every day.

# II

# Meaning in mind

Perhaps what is inexpressible (what I find mysterious and am not able to express) is the background against which whatever I could express has its meaning.

Ludwig Wittgenstein, *Culture and Value*

# Chapter 3    Patterns in language, patterns in the mind

**Gillian** What people want to know, whether they ask it directly or not, is how I fell in love with Stuart and married him, then fell in love with Oliver and married him, all within as short a space as is legally possible. Well, the answer is that I did just that. I don't especially recommend you try it, but I promise it's possible. Emotionally as well as legally.

I genuinely loved Stuart. I fell in love with him straightforwardly, simply. We got on, the sex worked, I loved the fact that he loved me – and that was it. And then, after we were married, I fell in love with Oliver, not simply at all, but very complicatedly, entirely against my instincts and my reason. I refused it, I resisted it, I felt intensely guilty. I also felt intensely excited, intensely alive, intensely sexy. No, as a matter of fact we didn't 'have an affair', as the saying goes. Just because I'm half French people start muttering *ménage a trois*. It wasn't remotely like that. It felt much more primitive for a start. And besides, Oliver and I didn't sleep with one another until Stuart and I had separated. Why are people such experts on what they don't know about? Everyone 'knows' that it was all about sex, that Stuart wasn't much good in bed, whereas Oliver was terrific, and that while I might look pretty level-headed I'm a flirt and a tart and probably a bitch as well. So if you really want to know, the first time Oliver and I went to bed together he had a serious attack of first-night nerves and absolutely nothing happened. The second night wasn't much better. Then we got going. In a funny sort of way, he's much more insecure in that area than Stuart.

This passage, from the novel *Love etc.* by Julian Barnes, is about Gillian falling in and out of love. Love is one of the most majestic and humbling of human experiences. And it can be as painful when we are loved as it is when our love is rejected. Those of us who have suffered from unrequited love can attest to this. Love can also be intensely amusing, as is evident from the passage: especially as we watch the hapless lover(s) writhing in the painful, complex bliss of love, pinned and snared, helpless to escape, but not wanting to in any case.

But this passage also reveals something very interesting about how we speak about love. And how we speak about love reflects how our concept of love is structured in our minds. While LOVE is a relatively abstract domain of experience – there is nothing in the world that can be pointed to and identified as love: love is not a physical thing in the way a chair or a table is – we nevertheless use language relating to concrete sorts of experiences, experiences relating to physical experience, to talk about love. We commonly speak about being *in* love, as Gillian does in the passage above. But love is patently not a physical container that we can literally be *in*, unlike, for instance, a room. We can be in a room. And an object can be in a container such as a box or a drawer. In what sense, then, can we be *in* love?

Moreover, Gillian speaks of *refusing* and *resisting* love. We normally reserve words like *resist* to speak about physical forces and to describe our exertions against them, such as the pedestrian's attempt to maintain his or her balance when walking into a strong wind. It is also common to talk of *resistance* when we speak of the physical force of others. For instance, when referring to military force – a particularly salient type – we speak of *resisting*, or *overcoming resistance*.

Moreover, the pattern exhibited by the *language of love* is repeated across the board: we deploy the language of physical experience and force dynamics to talk about more abstract ideas and experiences in general. For instance, we speak about states, including emotional states, as if they really *are* physical locations that we can be *in, on* or *at*:

> James is *in* trouble. We are *in* debt. The management is *in* a state of panic. The army is *on* red alert. The blouse is *on* sale. She's *on*

the verge of madness. The country is *at* war. Those two are *at* loggerheads again!

We also speak of states as if they *are* actually physical forces:

> She couldn't *resist* his love. His charm *overpowered* her. Her
> jealousy *made* her *lose control*. John was *forced into* a life
> of petty crime by his drug habit. He felt *pinned down* by his debts.

Why is it, then, that we so naturally talk about love – and other emotional states – in terms of physical location, and in terms of physical force?

Every day we use language to tell others whether we are happy or sad, to convey whether we are angry or bored. We use it to make requests and demands, to signal our wishes and desires, and to say whether we prefer our coffee with or without sugar. Language is indispensable in making public our thoughts – or at least those that we choose to make public. But while we use language to get our thoughts across, does the way language is patterned in expressing these thoughts provide us with insight into the very nature of our minds?

Language reveals how we think. More than that, language can illuminate, to the scientist, the way in which thought is structured. It reveals underlying features of mind design. To begin to get to grips with the nature of meaning-making, in this chapter I consider how thought is structured, using language as our window. I do so by examining the nature of abstract thought, and the systems of knowledge that enable us to construct abstract conceptual domains – love, emotion more generally, time. These sorts of knowledge systems, as we shall see, are systematically structured in terms of more concrete experiences: physical transfer, force, motion and space. We'll look at the way in which these patterns in language reveal hitherto hidden aspects of the way our minds are designed. And we'll begin to see that these knowledge systems, in our minds, provide us with a foundational base of knowledge which gives grist to the meaning-making mill.

## Patterns in language

In language, using one expression in order to understand something else is commonly referred to as metaphor. When Jane says: *My debts are weighing me down*, she is comparing her debts to a physical force: one that makes it more difficult to remain upright. In one of the most resonant theoretical developments of late twentieth-century linguistics, linguist George Lakoff and philosopher Mark Johnson have shown that metaphor is not just a mere matter of language.[1] The patterns that show up in language are, in fact, a matter of thought. In order to emphasise this, they employ the term 'conceptual metaphor' to identify the patterns in the mind that motivate the language we use.

So what then is a conceptual metaphor? It involves a series of links in the mind: between ideas belonging to different types of knowledge. The links are known as 'mappings', as they map or project information about one idea onto another, in order to better understand it.

To get a better sense of how this works, I want to begin with an example I discussed more briefly in *The Language Myth*: our understanding of love in terms of a journey. Consider some, on the face of it, unremarkable, everyday expressions, in which we talk about love *in terms of* a journey:

> Look *how far* we've *come*. We're at *a crossroads*. We'll just have to *go our separate ways*. We can't *turn back* now. I don't think this relationship is *going anywhere*. *Where* are we? We're *stuck*. It's been *a long, bumpy road*. This relationship is *a dead-end street*. We're just *spinning our wheels*. Our marriage is *on the rocks*. This relationship *is foundering*.[2]

These sentences ostensibly relate to journeys of various sorts. But, in the context of a tête-à-tête with one's lover, no one is confused. If you were to suggest that 'This relationship is a dead-end street', you can be sure that your partner would quickly get the drift, and would soon become your ex. We effortlessly understand that an expression like this has very little to do with a literal car journey.

The expressions above are all motivated by an entrenched pattern in our mind: a conceptual metaphor. The conceptual metaphor can be stated as LOVE IS A JOURNEY. It's made up of a fixed set of well-established mappings. The mappings are fixed in the sense that there is a set number of them. They are well established in the sense that they are stored in our long-term memory. Moreover, these mappings structure ideas belonging to the more abstract domain of LOVE, *in terms of* concepts belonging to the more concrete domain of JOURNEY – a domain being a large-scale, coherent body of knowledge in the mind.

In the domain of LOVE, we have a number of different concepts. The sorts of concepts we must have concern knowledge that there are lovers, the sorts of activities that lovers engage in, the problems that sometimes arise in a relationship, as well as the attempts made to resolve difficulties. We might also have concepts for the relationship goals, both shared and separate, as well as choices that lovers face in a romantic relationship: for instance, whether to move in together, whether to get engaged and, at particular pressure points, whether to call it a day.

And by the same token, we also hold in our minds a raft of concepts concerning the domain of JOURNEY. These will certainly include concepts for the travellers themselves, and the means of transport used. Other concepts concern the direction and route, as well as the sorts of impediments to travel we often experience – delayed flights, traffic congestion on the roads – leading to journey delays, missed connections and so on.

To be able to use language that literally refers to journeys, to talk and think about a romantic relationship, points to an entrenched pattern in our minds: the conceptual metaphor, LOVE IS A JOURNEY. And the conceptual metaphor encompasses a number of specific mappings: concepts from one domain – the domain of JOURNEY – systematically structuring concepts from the domain of LOVE. For example, in the expression *We're at a crossroads*, the use of *We*, while literally referring to travellers, is taken to refer to lovers. This provides evidence that the concept of lovers in the domain of LOVE is being structured, by the metaphor, in terms of travellers, from the domain of JOURNEY. Similarly, obstacles that face travellers in the domain of JOURNEY, such as being *stuck in a rut,* or *on the rocks,* are mapped onto the concept for obstacles in the domain of LOVE. What this all points to is that the expressions above provide evidence for a systematic pattern, a conceptual metaphor. We systematically structure, and so understand, the various concepts that populate our domain of LOVE in terms of concepts drawn from the domain of JOURNEY. And it is language that furnishes us with the evidence for these patterns in our minds.

> I've summarised the mappings for the conceptual metaphor LOVE IS A JOURNEY in Table 3.1. Concepts in the domain of JOURNEY are found in the left-hand column, while concepts in the domain of LOVE are on the right. The arrows capture which concepts map onto which. For example, the concept for lovers is structured in terms of content drawn from the concept for travellers. And the consequence is that a conceptual metaphor is composed of a series of mappings, whereby pairs of concepts have cognitive links which are established between them.

A further consequence of a conceptual metaphor is that the mappings exhibit a directionality. While we can talk and think about love in terms of a journey, we don't, and indeed can't, think

Table 3.1 *Mappings for* LOVE IS A JOURNEY *(after Evans 2014)*

| JOURNEY (SOURCE DOMAIN) | Mappings | LOVE (TARGET DOMAIN) |
| --- | --- | --- |
| TRAVELLERS | → | LOVERS |
| VEHICLE | → | LOVE RELATIONSHIP |
| JOURNEY | → | EVENTS IN THE RELATIONSHIP |
| DISTANCE COVERED | → | PROGRESS MADE |
| OBSTACLES ENCOUNTERED | → | DIFFICULTIES EXPERIENCED |
| DECISIONS ABOUT DIRECTION TO | → | CHOICES ABOUT WHAT TO DO |
| DESTINATION OF THE JOURNEY | → | GOALS OF THE RELATIONSHIP |

of a journey in terms of love. I can describe two newlyweds as learner drivers – indeed, it is common, at least in the United Kingdom, for 'brides-to-be' to wear learner 'L' plates when out on a hen party – and be understood to be referring to the challenges of adapting to a new marital relationship, which, like learning to drive, also requires a 'licence' – a marriage licence. But in contrast, I can't describe a learner driver as a newlywed and be understood to be referring to someone taking driving lessons.

This patterning in language points to a fundamental design feature of conceptual metaphors, and hence our minds: the mappings are asymmetric, as represented by the arrows in Table 3.1. A conceptual metaphor provides us with a series of cognitive links which map information relating to ideas *from* the domain of JOURNEY *onto* concepts in the domain of LOVE, but not vice versa. Hence, we can think of the domain of JOURNEY as being the 'source' domain – knowledge is borrowed from this domain. In contrast, the domain of LOVE is the 'target' domain – the knowledge from the source domain is borrowed by the domain of LOVE.

An important consequence of this *borrowing* process is that what is borrowed in fact constitutes a permanent loan. And, importantly, what is borrowed is 'inferential structure', rather than what we might think of as literal structure. What I mean here is that it is the conceptual metaphor that guides us in drawing inferences relating to a physical crash and its consequences, and applying these as relevant to marriage. A crash imperils the physical well-being of the vessel and the crew. It can threaten to end the ship's journey. The inferential structure projected by the conceptual metaphor, as it relates to marriage, involves the emotional, and perhaps also the social and financial, well-being of the married parties. It might also concern the threat to the continued existence of the love relationship.

## Patterns in the mind

One of the most intriguing issues arising from the existence of conceptual metaphors relates to their origin. Where do they come from? It turns out that conceptual metaphors like LOVE IS A JOURNEY are built from more basic associations in the mind. These are known as 'primary' conceptual metaphors. Primary metaphors form part of the bedrock of the human mind. They arise from our most fundamental experiences of acting and interacting in the world, and our response to these interactions. Moreover, primary metaphors emerge early in the life-span, prior to the onset of language, from around 12 months of age onwards – as we shall see in more detail in Chapter 6. They provide the human mind with the building blocks for the construction of complex meaning. Complex conceptual metaphors like LOVE IS A JOURNEY are built from these more basic primary metaphors.[3]

In order to see what primary metaphors are and how they form, let's begin by first considering the domains of TIME and SPACE. These conceptual domains are, perhaps, self-evidently fundamental to human experience. In terms of SPACE, being able to represent objects and places and navigate our way between and around objects and locations is crucial to our ability to successfully function in the world. But in addition, this ability involves a complex set of brain mechanisms which harvest and process perceptual information from a complex range of sensory streams of information. These sensory streams include our ability to see, our ability to hear, our sense of touch, our sense of balance and our awareness of the internal movements of our limbs and body parts so that we know where different parts of our bodies are in space at any given time.

In terms of TIME, we're aware of different dimensions of temporal experience: the result of a complex interplay of different brain mechanisms and structures. For instance, we experience and represent duration, simultaneity, the present, past, the future, event sequences and so on, as we shall see in more detail in the next chapter. Without our time sense, we wouldn't able to understand – let alone interpret – schedules and timetables, and to coordinate a whole range of interpersonal behaviours that rely on our ability to co-time action. In short, both spatial and temporal experience is multifaceted and, crucially, phenomenologically real.

In contrast to the complex metaphor LOVE IS A JOURNEY, which involves a number of distinct, albeit related, mappings between sets of concepts, a primary metaphor brings together a single 'source concept' and a single 'target concept'. The source concept derives from experience of the world *out there*. This involves information that's harvested from perceptual experience via one – or more – of the sensory streams I mentioned earlier (e.g. visual experience). In contrast, the target concept concerns a concept deriving from the world *in there*. This relates to information that is subjective in nature: body-based responses to externally derived perceptual information.

To show you what I mean, consider the primary metaphor NOW IS HERE. This involves an association between two relatively simple, albeit directly experienced, concepts. The metaphor is stated such that the target concept, Now, appears first, and the source concept, Here, follows.

A feature of primary metaphors is that the target concepts, while relatively abstract – in the sense of not being straightforward to apprehend – are subjectively real. They are, in some sense, subjective evaluations or responses. For instance, our experience of the present (Now) arises in the course of perceiving events and situations. It is a subjective response to external events. Yet, the provenance of the domain of TIME – from which Now derives – is internal in nature. Moreover, we experience Now in a very real sense. If that weren't the case, we wouldn't be able to distinguish past from future as mediated by the present. Accordingly, primary target concepts, such as Now, consist of a conscious awareness of a real – albeit subjective – experience. But this experience arises as a response to an external stimulus.

The source concept in a primary metaphor relates to more concrete experience types. These come from sensory–motor (i.e. perceptual) experience. The concept Here, for instance, derives from the domain of SPACE. It arises from a perceptual stimulus that is external to us, and which we evaluate and respond to – in part by the formation of a primary target concept. Accordingly, primary metaphors link fundamental and universal experience types, like Now and Here. And in so doing, they provide us with linked structures that combine a subjective response or evaluation on the one hand, and an external stimulus that gives rise to the evaluation on the other.

The evidence for primary metaphors comes, in the first instance, from language. For instance, in the expression: *The time for a decision is finally here*, we understand that the decision is something that cannot be put off any longer. It is *located* in the present. In this example, the word *here* doesn't literally mean 'here'. Native speakers of English unfailingly, and effortlessly, interpret an expression such as this as relating to the present moment. The point is, of course, we must have the NOW IS HERE primary conceptual metaphor stored somewhere in our heads. If not, it's unclear why it should be that this expression, and count- less others that relate to our current location, are taken to refer the present moment – rather than the spot where you or I are standing.

But if primary metaphors are responsible for more complex metaphors, like LOVE IS A JOURNEY, what causes primary meta- phors to form in the first place? Why do the primary target and primary source concepts come to achieve permanent links in the human mind, as in the case of NOW IS HERE? And moreover, why is this a feature of humans the world over, regardless of sex, culture and geographical region? The answer, it turns out, relates to the nature of human experience.[4]

Primary conceptual metaphors involve concepts which are universal across our species, and fundamental to the human experience of reality. Consequently, they form part of the infra- structure of our thought process. Primary target and source con- cepts arise from recurring and inevitable co-occurrences in our interactions in and with the world. For instance, our experience of Now just *does* co-occur with our experience of Here. Whenever we experience the present, it inevitably happens at our present location. Now always co-occurs with Here.

On first blush this finding seems to be so obvious that it barely seems to qualify as a finding at all. But, of course, it is spotting the obvious that often leads to great leaps forward in our scientific understanding of ourselves and the world around us. Isaac Newton's genius, for instance, was not in noticing that the apple fell downwards from the tree. The directionality of gravity is something so obvious that we don't see it as anything but normal. Babies the world over spend months incessantly dropping items from high chairs – or other perches – and watching to see what happens. We all start out as apprentice physicists, and each of us has to learn about the force dynamics that govern our environment anew.

In a sense, Newton's observation was barely remarkable at all, a point that Douglas Adams, with typical hilarity and acute observation, makes clear in his 1988 Dirk Gently novel, *The Long Dark Teatime of the Soul*:

> 'Sir Isaac Newton, renowned inventor of the milled-edge coin and the catflap!'
> 'The what?' said Richard.
> 'The catflap! A device of the utmost cunning, perspicuity and invention. It is a door within a door, you see, a . . .'
> 'Yes,' said Richard, 'there was also the small matter of gravity.'
> 'Gravity,' said Dirk with a slightly dismissive shrug, 'yes, there was that as well, I suppose. Though that, of course, was merely a discovery. It was there to be discovered.' . . .
> 'You see?' he said dropping his cigarette butt, 'They even keep it on at weekends. Someone was bound to notice sooner or later. But the catflap . . . ah, there is a very different matter. Invention, pure creative invention. It is a door within a door, you see.'

But, while gravity was indeed a discovery, it nevertheless takes an occasional intellectual giant to spot the obvious and ask 'Why?', as Newton did. Wondering why the apple falls downwards rather than up may seem, on the face of it, perverse. But it led to one of the greatest of discoveries in physics: gravitation.

The *discovery* of primary metaphors, and their genesis in inevitable associations in everyday experience, is, to my mind, one of the most significant in the contemporary study of mind. The idea, then, is this. Relatively simple, phenomenologically real responses, such as our experience of the present (Now), *just do* co-occur with other relatively simple but concrete perceptual experiences, such as our physical location (Here). The co-occurrence *just is* a consequence of the way we, as humans, experience the world. This correlation between two experiences gives rise, in our brains, to a co-activation of the neurons that are responsible for registering and recording our experience of particular sorts of experiences. The primary metaphor arises, therefore, because what fires together, in neuronal terms, wires together.[5]

Of course, not everything that is experienced as co-occurring gives rise to a primary conceptual metaphor. The experience types have to be of the right kind: they must be phenomenologically real, relatively simple and involve the asymmetry apparent in the disjunction between subjective responses – and the primary target concepts they lead to – and external perceptual experience – and the primary source concepts they lead to. The upshot is that, by early in life, human infants have a foundation of primary conceptual metaphors. These, then, in part at least, support language and a range of other higher-order cognitive behaviours, including reason, choice and categorisation.

## All about events

So how do primary metaphors give rise to more complex conceptual metaphors such as LOVE IS A JOURNEY? To better illustrate this, consider a set of primary metaphors that provide us with the means for conceptualising events no matter how abstract. This set of primary metaphors gives rise to the kind of structure that we attribute to events. These so-called Event Structure primary metaphors are listed, with linguistic examples, in Table 3.2.[6]

In each of these primary metaphors, part of an abstract event – for instance Change, a Caused Event or a Long-term Purposeful Activity – is structured, and so understood, in terms of a more concrete aspect of sensory–motor experience, such as Motion,

Table 3.2 *'Event Structure' primary metaphors*

Metaphor: STATES ARE LOCATIONS (BOUNDED REGIONS IN SPACE)
Example: *John is in love*
Metaphor: CHANGE IS MOTION (FROM ONE LOCATION TO ANOTHER)
Example: *Things went from bad to worse*
Metaphor: CAUSES ARE FORCES
Example: *Her argument forced me to change my mind*
Metaphor: ACTIONS ARE SELF-PROPELLED MOVEMENTS
Example: *We are moving forward with the new project*
Metaphor: CAUSED EVENTS ARE PHYSICAL TRANSFERS
Example: *David Beckham put a lot of swerve on that ball*
Metaphor: PURPOSES ARE DESTINATIONS
Example: *We've finally reached the end of the project*
Metaphor: MEANS ARE PATHS (TO DESTINATIONS)
Example: *We completed the project via an unconventional route*
Metaphor: DIFFICULTIES ARE IMPEDIMENTS TO MOTION
Example: *It's been uphill all the way on this project*
Metaphor: EVENTS ARE MOVING OBJECTS
Example: *Things are going smoothly in the operating theatre*
Metaphor: LONG-TERM PURPOSEFUL ACTIVITIES ARE JOURNEYS
   (ALONG A PATH)
Example: *The government is without direction*

Physical Transfer and Travel along a Path, respectively. Hence, each of these metaphors pair phenomenologically simple aspects of subjective evaluations – or responses – with external experience types. We thereby understand the nature of a crucial aspect of what an event is in terms of, in some sense, more readily apprehended perceptual content.

For instance, in the sentence *David Beckham put a lot of swerve on that ball*, no one gets confused: not for a second does anyone really think that Beckman actually takes a lump of *swerve* out of his pocket and places it on the ball, whatever that might mean. Rather, the primary metaphor: CAUSED EVENTS ARE PHYSICAL TRANSFERS allows us to understand an event's cause *in terms of* inferential structure recruited from our experience of

Table 3.3 *The composite primary metaphors for* LOVE IS A JOURNEY

| |
|---|
| Expression: We're *at a crossroads* in our relationship |
| Metaphor: STATES ARE LOCATIONS (BOUNDED REGIONS IN SPACE) |
| Expression: We went *from* being total strangers *to* lovers in 3 days flat |
| Metaphor: CHANGE IS MOTION (FROM ONE LOCATION TO ANOTHER) |
| Expression: *The wedding preparations are moving forward* |
| Metaphor: ACTIONS ARE SELF-PROPELLED MOVEMENTS |
| Expression: Their love followed *an unconventional course* |
| Metaphor: MEANS ARE PATHS (TO DESTINATIONS) |
| Expression: We can never seem to *get to where we want to be* in our relationship |
| Metaphor: PURPOSES ARE DESTINATIONS |
| Example: Throughout their marriage George's infidelities had continually *got in their way* |
| Metaphor: DIFFICULTIES ARE IMPEDIMENTS TO MOTION |
| Expression: *Things are going smoothly in their love life* |
| Metaphor: EVENTS ARE MOVING OBJECTS |
| Expression: Their marriage had been *a rather strange journey.* |
| Metaphor: LONG-TERM PURPOSEFUL ACTIVITIES ARE JOURNEYS ALONG A PATH |

a physical transfer. The causal event involves David Beckham using a well-rehearsed technique such that he strikes the ball with his foot in such a way as to cause a swerved trajectory as the ball moves through the air. We understand this causal event *as if* it involves physical transfer.

Let's now return to the experience with which we began the chapter, namely love, and specifically the conceptual metaphor LOVE IS A JOURNEY. Each of the following everyday expressions is motivated by a specific primary metaphor, as represented in Table 3.3.

> We're *at a crossroads* in our relationship. We went *from* being total strangers *to* lovers in 3 days flat. The wedding preparations are *moving forward*. We can never seem to *get to where we want to be* in our relationship. Their love followed *an unconventional*

*course*. Throughout their marriage George's infidelities had continually *got in their way*. Things are *going smoothly* in their love life. Their marriage had been *a rather strange journey*.

What Table 3.3 reveals is that LOVE IS A JOURNEY is a 'complex' conceptual metaphor: it consists of a number of more primary metaphors. Collectively, these provide different and complementary ways of understanding aspects of LOVE in terms of our knowledge relating to JOURNEYS.

Primary metaphors are fundamental to the way knowledge is organised in the mind. They provide the mental infrastructure which supports fundamental associations between distinct experience types. Moreover, due to recurring correlations in human experience, they are probably also universal across all human languages and cultures.

## Computers behaving badly, and reluctant lovers

One of the most surprising things to emerge from the research on conceptual metaphors is just how ubiquitous they are: we use them on a daily basis. They are equally liable to crop up in high literature as they are in everyday discourse. They show up, for instance, at the shopping mall, and in our daily newspapers. Consider the following which appeared in *The Guardian* newspaper. The excerpt is from a column by the journalist and humourist Charlie Brooker, in which he is commenting on the launch of a new Microsoft computer operating system.

> Recently I sat in a room trying to write something on a Sony Vaio PC laptop which seemed to be running a special slow-motion edition of Windows Vista specifically designed to infuriate human beings as much as possible. Trying to get it to do anything was like issuing instructions to a depressed employee over a sluggish satellite feed. When I clicked on an application it spent a small eternity contemplating the philosophical implications of opening it, begrudgingly complying with my request several months later.

It drove me up the wall. I called it a bastard and worse. At one point I punched a table.[7]

Many of us will no doubt be able to relate to Brooker's frustration, having experienced at first hand a computer appearing to run at double-slow time. Much of the humour, in this excerpt, comes from the very human properties and qualities Brooker attributes to his laptop computer. He likens it to a depressed employee, and communicating with it as being akin to talking to someone over a sluggish satellite feed. He attributes to it deep philosophical contemplation, which has the unfortunate consequence of slowing down its performance by – what feels like – several months. He abuses it, and punches the table in fury. But while a description such as this, and the humour which ensues, is the result of a highly skilled practitioner of the English language, the excerpt nevertheless provides us with evidence of a very common way of thinking and speaking about inanimate entities such as machines.

In point of fact, the conceptual metaphor, MACHINES ARE PEOPLE, is one of the most commonplace conceptual metaphors there is. Expressions such as: *My car hates me. It just won't start*; *My computer is refusing to boot up*, and so on, are so common that it is only when the conceptual metaphor is accentuated by a professional journalist that it becomes apparent. On an almost daily basis, we attribute intentionality to otherwise inanimate entities such as cars, computers and the host of other machines that we interact with in our daily lives. And of course, a car can't literally *hate* us, just as a computer can't actually *refuse* to do anything. Cars and computers don't have thought: refusal presupposes an intentional state, something that machines like cars and computers don't possess, except in the realm of science fiction.

But what this excerpt *does* reveal is this: by conveying his computer's operation in terms of human intentionality, Charlie Brooker is more effectively able to communicate his extreme frustration. Brooker invokes ideas from our knowledge of people to explain how his computer is *deliberately* winding him up. The actions and the intentional states of other human beings are among the things we know most about. We can often *read* the mental states and intentions of others from people's faces, from their body language, gestures and expressions. Such 'intention reading' is essential if we are to recognise friend from foe and, in evolutionary terms, to ensure our survival.[8]

By virtue of borrowing inferential structure from the domain of human intentionality, this allows us to make sense of what a machine is doing when it fails to *comply* with a request we make, such as to start up. After all, a *refusal* to start by our car can be detrimental: it can hold us up, make us late for work and be potentially harmful, due to missed appointments, to lost business and even, potentially, to losing one's job. In short, the conceptual metaphor allows us to make sense of the lack of appropriate functionality associated with an inanimate entity, such as a computer or a car, by reducing the otherwise complex operations and consequences of the operations to human scale, an issue to which I'll return in Chapter 7. By conveying his computer's operation in terms of human intentionality, Charlie Brooker is able to construct a humorous narrative in which his computer is behaving badly on purpose, justifying his extreme frustration.

Conceptual metaphors are not just instruments of thought that are reserved for quotidian matters, like the operation of computers and cars. Conceptual metaphor is also central to high art forms such as literature. Consider the following excerpt from a poem by Andrew Marvell, the seventeenth-century metaphysical poet. In the poem, Marvell is addressing his coy mistress, attempting to induce her to succumb to his – less than coy – advances:

> But at my back I always hear
> Time's winged chariot hurrying near;
> And yonder all before us lie
> Deserts of vast eternity.
> Thy beauty shall no more be found,
> Nor, in thy marble vault, shall sound
> My echoing song; then worms shall try

That long preserv'd virginity,
And your quaint honour turn to dust,
And into ashes all my lust.

In the excerpt, Marvell implores his mistress to put aside her coyness. After all, he says, virginity and honour are worth nothing in death. And so he hopes to seduce an otherwise reluctant lover. But the way he does this invokes conceptual metaphors. In the second line, for instance, he talks of *Time's winged chariot*. Time, here, is being personified. But as we have seen in the excerpt by Charlie Brooker, bestowing human qualities on non-human entities is extremely common. Time itself is an agentless dimension of our experience. By attributing to it human characteristics, we can understand a non-causal event – time – as if it were an agent that can bring about changes of various sorts – for instance, death. And in so doing, we better understand it.

In the poem, Time's winged chariot arrives from behind: *But at my back I always hear/Time's winged chariot hurrying near.* These lines draw on the primary conceptual metaphor KNOWING IS SEEING. We commonly say *I see what you mean* to mean *I understand you*. We systematically structure the concept of Knowing in terms of Seeing, which is why we can say things such as *We need a leader with vision,* and not be misunderstood as bemoaning the fact that our political leaders need frequent eye-sight tests.

Given the physiology of our human bodies, our eyes are situated at the front, rather than the back. One consequence, then, of structuring the concept of Knowing in terms of visual experience is this: we know quite a lot about what is in front of us. A related consequence is that what is visually inaccessible, because it is behind us, is, by virtue of the metaphor, unknown. We often don't know about what we can't see. The poet takes advantage of this conceptual pattern: Time's winged chariot is at the poet's back. It arrives unexpectedly – he can't see it, after all – only entering awareness when it is close by, and perhaps, when it is too late to do anything about it.

And finally, in lines 3 and 4, Marvell describes the *vast deserts of eternity*. These lie ahead of us, he says. This description takes advantage of the conceptually entrenched pattern in which we understand time as a path across which we move, as I'll discuss in more detail in the next chapter. This conceptual metaphor allows us to conceptualise events as locations, with the future located in front and the past behind. As the state of death is yet to come, it is metaphorically located in front of us. From this perspective, it makes sense to describe death as a vast desert located ahead.

While the images evoked by Marvell are complex, the ideas are readily accessible to us all. Indeed, even those of us forced to read Marvell's *Ode to his coy mistress* as less than willing schoolchildren grasped the ideas. The idea of time's winged chariot appearing from behind, and vast deserts of eternity lying ahead, don't bewilder or confuse. Even the young readily make sense of the ideas being conveyed. And the reason for this is that the conceptual metaphors that Marvell invokes in his verse are the very patterns we each carry around with us in our heads. We acquire these patterns early in infancy. While the average school-age pupil may not quite recognise it, Marvell's ode to his reluctant lover is a stunning example of metaphysical period verse.[9] What makes great literature *great* is the ability of its peerless exponents to exploit the run-of-the mill conceptual resources we all have access to, in order to produce the extraordinary.[10]

## Foundations of meaning

The uncovering of conceptual metaphors proffers even more, however, than better insight into the ways our minds are organised. The mind's conceptual metaphor systems provide us with the foundations of meaning: when we think and speak, we often draw upon conceptual metaphors, enabling us to convey abstract and complex ideas, making use, metaphorically, of more concrete realms of experience.

The old cliché 'the pen is mightier than the sword' relates to the idea that we can use language to *do* things; language has the power to change fundamental aspects of the world. We can cause someone to fall in (or out of) love with us using language. Our politicians beguile us into trusting them through their honeyed words. And it is the language used by advertisers that persuades us to part with our hard-earned cash. Language is a powerful tool which allows us to influence others and get what we want – and sometimes don't. But part of the reason for this – the power of language to win friends and influence people – is precisely that language is built upon a web of conceptual metaphors. These patterns in our minds provide us with an infrastructure that facilitates, in part, our thoughts and our decision-making. It is through language that we can tap into conceptual metaphors, using them to create rich meanings.

For instance, one of President Obama's first acts as President of the United States was to change the language used by American civil servants and military planners. He banished the use of the expression *war on terror*. The term introduced by the Bush administration was *Global War on Terror,* or GWoT for short. President Bush had, of course, famously pronounced that the Global War on Terror 'will not end until every terrorist group of global reach has been found, stopped and defeated'.[11] But Barack Obama quietly banned its use in his government. In its stead, he preferred the term *overseas contingency operations.* This (admittedly far blander) term was much more than a mere linguistic symbol of his break from the neo-conservative policies of his predecessor.

A number of experts and politicians have argued that the phrase *war on terror* has done more harm than good. One military expert has put it this way: 'Declaring war on a method of violence was like declaring war on amphibious warfare'.[12] The phrase *war on terror* suggests a battle, not against a specific ideology or even a human individual, nor a specific group, but rather against a type of violence. A war on terror is incoherent. And as such, it is a war that can never be won.

Another potential difficulty with declaring a war on terror is that it suggests there is a military solution. It does so because it frames the resistance of those who are against terrorism in terms of warfare. But by evoking the metaphor of warfare, this commits all those who subscribe to it to a single approach. And herein lies the power of conceptual metaphor, as enacted through language: it influences not just thought, but policy and strategy. If there is a war on terrorism, this then entails tanks, bombs and soldiers, casualties and sadly, collateral damage – civilian deaths. These things are all consequences of the framing provided by this particular metaphor: OPPOSING TERRORISM IS WAR. By subscribing to the conceptual framing, to the conceptual metaphor, we subscribe, however reluctantly, to the consequences of the metaphor. The conceptual metaphor leads, incontrovertibly, to the conclusion that opposing terrorism becomes war. We view terrorism not as a criminal activity engaged in by criminals, or even as a type of social delinquency; but rather, terrorists become elevated to the status of 'combatants' in a war. As George Lakoff has argued, conceptual metaphors can be a matter of life and death. They can kill or save lives.[13]

Obama's blander expression, then, provides greater flexibility. The language – and the metaphor system upon which it draws – doesn't restrict in the same way. It provides a smarter choice of words and ideas, allowing a wider range of options, including military ones. And it does so while not disallowing alternative approaches to countering terrorism. Conceptual metaphors are powerful instruments of thought. They can restrict choice, as in Bush's GWoT, or provide more choice.

Another fundamental way in which conceptual metaphors influence our thinking comes from their role in hiding and highlighting. A metaphor can highlight one aspect of an idea or experience while at the same time hiding another. Combining my discussion of war with my earlier analysis of metaphors for love, I'll illustrate using the conceptual metaphor LOVE IS WAR. This metaphor allows us to think about love in terms of a fight, as in the utterance *He fought for her love*, or as a conquest: *He conquered her.* But in so doing, the metaphor highlights certain aspects of my – and your – experience of love, while hiding others. For instance, the conceptual metaphors LOVE IS MAGIC (e.g. *She cast a spell on him*), LOVE IS HUNTING (e.g. *He ensnared her*) and LOVE IS FOOD (e.g. *He drank from her lips*) highlight (and hide) different aspects of the domain of LOVE. And, in so doing, they provide you and me with different ways of conceptualising the love experience. One consequence of this is that evoking different conceptual metaphors can induce different ways of thinking and, hence, different actions, and so, real-world consequences.

## Meaning in mind

The use of language to promote – or defend – one course of action over another invokes conceptual metaphors. It allows us all to manipulate conceptual metaphors for our own ends. As such, language provides us with perhaps the clearest of windows onto the human mind's meaning-making apparatus. In psychology departments at many of the world's most famous and prestigious universities and research institutes, there are labs containing hundreds of thousands and even millions of pounds worth of expensive equipment. These include sophisticated brain-imaging scanners which, some claim, provide the key to unlocking hitherto hidden aspects of the way the brain computes the mind: physicalists claim that the mind can only be understood by locating where and how it is produced in and by the brain. And advances in both equipment and techniques have taught us an immense amount compared to the state of the art even a decade ago. But the truth is this: language still provides us with arguably a better means of probing the hidden recesses of our thoughts than any of the neuroimaging techniques presently available.

Abstract concepts like Love, Death, Time and Events appear to be organised, at least in part, in terms of structure borrowed from more concrete sensory–motor experiences. We say things like *I'm in love*, precisely because we conceptualise love as having, in part, the topology of a container: love is hard to *get out of*. We say things like *He's passed on* when speaking of death because we conceptualise death as *a journey*. We say that *David Beckham put swerve on the ball*, even though David Beckham didn't actually take anything out of his shorts to place on the ball. We understand causal events in terms of physical transfers. And we conceptualise time as a landscape across which we move, with the past behind us and the future ahead. It is precisely because of this that Andrew Marvell, in addressing his coy mistress, could refer to eternity as a physical location which stretches out ahead: *And yonder all before us lie/Deserts of vast eternity*. In fact, the very same patterns of thought that structured the minds of seventeenth-century poets are still in evidence in our twenty-first-century heads.

But while striking, the discovery of conceptual metaphors doesn't mean, of course, that all is resolved, in terms of figuring out the nature of our meaning-making capabilities. In some ways we have barely begun to scratch the surface. There is far more to the human mind than conceptual metaphors. While language provides us with a window onto the mind, there are important and clear divergences between the nature of language and the nature of thought. These are issues to which I shall return later in the book. But for now, we need to consider in more detail the psychological reality of conceptual metaphors. So far we have been relying solely on language to provide us with evidence for their existence. But in relying on language alone, can we be really sure that the conceptual metaphors I've been discussing do in fact reside in our heads? Do they really exist?

# Chapter 4    Time is our fruit fly

The sorts of experiences that we use to structure abstract ideas, according to Lakoff and Johnson, arise from our interaction in the world. They come from our experience of moving about in space, from picking up and putting down objects, and by bumping into things. They derive from giving objects to others, and from receiving things in return. It is these sorts of spatial experiences, they claim, that provide us with the inferential structure that makes up our understanding of abstract states like love, death, time and countless others. The truly radical idea at the heart of Conceptual Metaphor Theory is that abstract thought arises from our sensory–motor systems – our eyes, ears, pressure exerted on the skin, our felt sense of movement, our sense of balance, and so on. In short, so the claim goes, our experience of the spatial world provides the basis for the range of abstract concepts that comprise our conceptual systems, and which, accordingly, enable fundamental aspects of our meaning-making capacity – for instance, our ability to think about and externalise, in language, the range of abstract concepts that we express on a daily basis. In this chapter, I investigate this issue – whether more abstract concepts and domains are *created* by importing structure from our experience of space – by considering the domain of TIME. And in so doing, this will enable us to get a handle on the nature and origin of abstract concepts, with implications for our ultimate objective: to understand our human capacity for meaning. After all, my contention is that the human conceptual system – our repository of concepts, structured in part by conceptual metaphors – provides the basis for what language can be employed to encode and express in our everyday acts of meaning-making.

The reason for selecting time is that it amounts to the paradigmatic example of an abstract domain – time is presumably as abstract as you can get. We seem to *experience* time; yet there is nothing physical or concrete in the world, like stones and trees, that you or I can point to and identify as time. We sense its presence: we anticipate the future, which is distinct from the present we inhabit, and our recollection of the past. We even feel its effects on our own bodies as we age. The psychologist Daniel Casasanto observes that '[T]ime has become for the metaphor theorist what the fruit fly is for the geneticist: the model system of choice for linguistic and psychological tests of relationships between metaphorical source and target domains'.[1] As time is so obviously an abstract domain, it represents the perfect arena in which to probe, in more detail, the claims made by Lakoff and Johnson.

Lakoff and Johnson claim that time exists for us *not* because it is something we actually perceive. Time, they suggest, may not exist as a distinct entity, a thing unto itself. In fact, it appears to be *created* by conceptual metaphors. We conceptualise and understand time, they say, because time is essentially a metaphorised version of events undergoing motion. When we say: *Christmas is approaching*, we recruit knowledge relating to motion through space to understand the imminence of a temporal event: Christmas. In short, we must first understand space, and structure time in terms of motion events in space, before we can conceptualise time. And once we can conceptualise it, only then can we experience it. But time, from this perspective, is very much a second-class citizen. It is a cognitive achievement, parasitic on spatial experience: time is not, in fact, a fundamental aspect of human cognition. If Lakoff and Johnson are right, however, then this entails the very strong claim that our thought – and in particular abstract thought – is largely, perhaps almost entirely, structured, and made possible, by conceptual metaphors. But is this right? The answer to this question will help better pin down the nature of abstract thought – part of the conceptual knowledge upon which our capacity for meaning-making presumably depends.

Another reason for examining time, in the context of attempting to understand the conceptual underpinnings of meaning, is this.

Time, like the more concrete sensory–motor realm of space, is intuitively a foundational domain of human experience, and indeed knowledge. Language itself, in most if not all of the world's languages, appears to reflect the primacy of space *and* time, with the distinction between nouns – which prototypically denote physical entities – and verbs – which prototypically denote actions that evolve through time – although I'll nuance these characterisations of nouns and verbs later, in Chapter 5. So, is our intuitive sense of the foundational nature of *both* space *and* time wrong?

## It's only Tuesday

WASHINGTON DC – After running a thousand errands, working hours of overtime, and being stuck in seemingly endless gridlock traffic commuting to and from their jobs, millions of Americans were disheartened to learn that it was, in fact, only Tuesday.

'Tuesday?' San Diego resident Doris Wagner said. 'How in the hell is it still Tuesday?'

Tuesday's arrival stunned a nation still recovering from the nightmarish slog that was Monday, leaving some to wonder if the week was ever going to end, and others to ask what was taking Saturday so goddamn long.

'Ugh,' said Wagner, echoing a national sense of frustration over it not even being Wednesday at the very least.

According to suddenly depressed sources, the feeling that this week may in fact last forever was further compounded by the thought of all the work left to be done tomorrow, the day after tomorrow, and, if Americans make it that far, possibly even Friday, for Christ's sake.

Fears that the week could actually be going backwards were also expressed.

'Not only do Americans have most of Tuesday morning to contend with, but all of Tuesday afternoon and then Tuesday night,' National Labor Relations Board spokesman David Prynn said. 'If our calculations are correct, there is a chance we are in effect closer to last weekend than the one coming up.'

Isolated attempts to make the day go faster, such as glancing at watches or clocks every other minute, compulsively checking email, hiding in the office bathroom, fidgeting, or reading a boring magazine while sitting in the waiting room, have also proven unsuccessful, sources report.

The National Institutes of Standards and Technology, which oversees the official time of the United States, is flatly denying that it has slowed or otherwise tampered with Tuesday's progression.

This excerpt is from the American-based satirical web magazine *The Onion*.[2] It captures the familiar feeling, for many, of the working week. We approach Monday with dread. The working week brings crammed buses and trains, or the tortuous stop–start drive along congested roads to the office. And at work, we have to contend with full email inboxes – messages, inevitably, all marked urgent – endless meetings, being patronised by superiors, dealing with bad-tempered colleagues, snatched lunches, and so it goes on. And having navigated Monday, many of us will relate to the feeling of frustration that it's still only Tuesday.

But this piece also reveals something else, something quite remarkable about our experience of time. Time can go faster or slower; it can even stand still. And sometimes, it can even feel as if it is going backwards. Moreover, this isn't just our imagination playing tricks on us. Scientists have demonstrated that time can indeed speed up or slow down, as I shall explain.

But first, let's look at some examples. Imagine the drive to work on the first day in a new job. The journey might take just around 20 minutes. But as you pay attention to the details of the route, and follow with care the instructions from your SatNav device, the car journey most likely feels as if it is lasting much longer. This is what psychologists refer to as 'protracted duration': time feels as if it's going more slowly than normal. Then, after a couple of months in the job, one morning you'll marvel that the car *drove itself to work*: you arrived, seemingly, in no time at all, and can barely remember the details of the route. This is referred to as 'temporal compression': time feels as if it's passing more quickly than normal.

Protracted duration and temporal compression are real phenomena. The social psychologist Michael Flaherty has documented subjects' experiences of both. In one interview, a young woman vividly describes her very real experience of time slowing down during a motor-car accident:

> My first thought was, 'Where did that car come from?' Then I said to myself, 'Hit the brakes.'. . . I saw her look at me through the open window, and turn the wheel, hand over hand, toward the right. I also [noticed] that the car was a brown Olds. I heard the screeching sound from my tires and knew . . . that we were going to hit. . . I wondered what my parents were going to say, if they would be mad, where my boyfriend was, and most of all, would it hurt. . . After it was over, I realized what a short time it was to think so many thoughts, but, while it was happening, there was more than enough time. It only took about ten or fifteen seconds for us to hit, but it certainly felt like ten or fifteen minutes.[3]

The apparent slowing down of time appears to arise in contexts when the subject is experiencing extreme emotions, as in a near-death experience such as a car crash. Protracted duration also occurs when we're unfamiliar with a new task, such as learning the drive to a new place of work. A third cause appears to be what might be dubbed *empty* intervals. In the following excerpt, a survivor from a concentration camp during the holocaust describes their experience of time while in captivity:

> The days passed with a terrible, enervating, monotonous slowness, the tomorrows blending into weeks and the weeks blending into months. 'We were about a year in Auschwitz,' says Menashe, 'but in Auschwitz, one day – everyday – was like 10 years'.[4]

Being imprisoned fails to give rise to significant or memorable events. On the contrary, in so-called empty intervals, one becomes preoccupied with self and situation, such that, compared to an event with a normal event contour, the interval feels longer than it otherwise is – at least as measured by a clock. Indeed, we can all relate to the expression: *Time drags when you're bored.*

In contrast, time seems to proceed more quickly in different kinds of situations. When the daily drive to work becomes routine, it flies by. This suggests that familiarity through repetition can lead to the opposite: time goes more quickly. Moreover, novel situations which are exciting, such as a dinner date with someone we find attractive, witty and intelligent – the perfect combination – can lead to us losing ourselves, becoming absorbed in the event. Similarly, letting off steam by playing a new computer game can lead us to *losing track* of time, and time *flying by*. Situations such as these seem to go hand in hand with temporal compression.

Flaherty has argued that time appears to *slow down* in particular contexts when we are paying greater attention to self, and the situation in which we find ourselves. In both near-death experiences and situations when we are bored, we experience a heightened focus on the self. And this leads us to process a greater amount of information, making it *feel* as if time is proceeding more slowly. In contrast, when our attention is not absorbed by self and situation, for instance in tasks that we can do standing on our heads, time *feels*, in retrospect, as if it's zipped by.

Other research has confirmed that time proceeds more slowly in empty intervals, and speeds up when episodes are crammed with activity. In one study, participants were confined to a sensory isolation unit and were instructed to estimate the time of day at various intervals throughout a 60-hour period. The results showed that without access to temporal cues, participants tended to underestimate the elapsed time, with the average subjective hour being judged at 1.12 hours in real time.[5] In another study, Michel Siffre, while assuming the roles of both experimenter and subject and exhibiting remarkable dedication to science, confined himself to an underground cave. When he emerged from the cave after 58 days he underestimated the duration of his sojourn as having lasted 33 days.[6]

The perceived duration of shorter time intervals can also be distorted. In one study, participants watched a 30-second videotape of a bank robbery, full of activity and danger. They were later asked to estimate the duration of the event. The results showed that, on average, participants overestimated the event as having lasted 150 seconds – five times longer than in reality.[7]

But is this all not just a trick of the imagination? Can time really fly, or drag by? As it turns out, it seems that time really can. In the 1930s, a psychologist named Hudson Hoagland discovered, almost by accident, that how we experience time is closely related to bodily function. Hoagland's poorly wife was suffering from a fever, and her high temperature appeared to be affecting her sense of time. With commendable detachment in the pursuit of scientific enquiry, he temporarily set aside his nursing duties, testing her as her fever varied in temperature. He observed that the higher the temperature, the more her perception of time appeared to speed up. Hoagland had his wife estimate time's passage by counting up to sixty – a 'subjective' minute – where each count corresponded to what she felt to be a second. He found that at higher temperatures, his wife's seconds became shorter, while they were longer at lower temperatures. For instance, at 98 degrees Fahrenheit, Hoagland's wife judged a minute as corresponding to around 52 seconds. However, at 101 degrees Fahrenheit she judged a minute to be equal to about 40 seconds. In other words, the higher the fever, the more Hoagland's wife misjudged time's passage: for his wife, her subjective minute was getting shorter.

Hoagland explored this observation further by subjecting his students to temperatures of up to 65 degrees Celsius by placing heated helmets on their heads – how times have changed: today's experimental psychology professors would far less readily obtain ethical approval for torturing their long-suffering grad students. Nevertheless, Hoagland found that an increase in body temperature can speed up our experience of time by up to a remarkable 20 per cent.

This finding has since been replicated using different stimulants: amphetamines, nitrous dioxide (aka laughing gas) and even large quantities of very strong coffee appear to cause our experience of time to be overestimated – time actually goes by faster. In contrast, anything that *depresses* vital functioning appears to lead to time being perceived as going more slowly – we underestimate time's passage. In one experiment, divers were submerged in the sea off the west coast of Wales in March, when sea temperatures are around 4 degrees Celsius – about the same temperature as your average fridge. The divers were asked to count up to 60 seconds before and after the dive. While beforehand their counting fairly accurately matched clock-time, afterwards their counting was slower, with a subjective minute being judged as corresponding to around 70 seconds.[8]

So what does this reveal? Our experience of time is directly tied to the functioning of our bodies, as well as the types of situations in which we find ourselves. It arises internally, an experiential by-product of how we interpret and process events. If this is the case, then this calls into question Lakoff and Johnson's claim that time is primarily *created* by conceptual metaphor: that time doesn't exist as a thing unto itself.

## A clock in the brain

Early research on temporal awareness tried to locate the brain's central timer. But scientists have been unable to find any such central clock: there is no Greenwich Mean Time in the brain. In fact, the brain seems to have many different timers. These take the form of different sorts of temporal codes or rhythms. They last from fractions of a second up to a temporal code with an outer limit of around 2–3 seconds. The purpose of the brain's temporal timers is to enable it – and so us – to integrate information. This in turn allows us to make sense of the ongoing flux of sensory experience we are exposed to in our daily lives. Without internal timing mechanisms, the brain would simply not be able to perceive events, to coordinate action – from chewing food to running a race – or even to being able to produce coherent speech. Imagine trying to dance with a partner with no internal sense of time. And more intimate activities, also involving a partner, would be harder still.

The way we perceive entities in the world is made possible by the brain's temporal codes. Consider the example of eating a piece of fruit. When you pick up a pear, and bring it to your mouth and take a bite, you have the distinct sense of a single entity: a pear. You feel its weight, you perceive its size, shape and contour, and you feel its texture in your hand. If you bring it to your nose you detect its distinct smell. And upon first bite, you appreciate the taste of pear – unmistakable.

Yet, while you perceive the fruit as a single entity, this is not how the brain sees it. Different parts of the brain process these different aspects of perceptual experience. Nevertheless, we do perceive a single entity: a single piece of fruit. How does the brain achieve this?

Until recently this so-called binding problem remained a mystery. Neuroscientists were unclear how the brain performed the trick of presenting, as a single percept, sensory information produced in different corners of the brain's cortex. It turns out that this is achieved via timing mechanisms. The brain doesn't integrate information into a *where*, but rather a *when*. The neurons responsible for perceiving the fruit's various qualities, in different brain regions, oscillate in synchronised fashion.[9] This coordinated oscillation enables the perception of the piece of fruit to emerge. In short, the brain produces experience not using physical integration of information, but by a process of temporal binding. Coordinated temporal rhythms allow us to *create* our experience, and integrate various sensations into a single entity.

Temporal processes involved in the formation of a single percept, such as a piece of fruit, take place within fractions of a second. And that being so, we are not aware of them. More important for conscious experience is the temporal rhythm that occurs within the 2- to 3-second range. This is known as the 'perceptual moment'.[10] This temporal interval allows us to update our awareness of our environment: every 2–3 seconds our felt sense of *now* is updated. And crucially, many important aspects of our ongoing experience are thereby made possible.

To be perceivable, ongoing activities must occur within this 3-second outer window. For example, the reversal rate of ambiguous

**Figure 4.1.** Ambiguous figure (after Tyler and Evans 2003)

figures (see Figure 4.1), lies within this window: every 2–3 seconds the image will switch from a vase to two faces, and vice versa.

The basis of spoken language is the 'intonation unit'. According to the discourse analyst Wallace Chafe, these are distinguished on the basis of prosodic criteria. These include 'breaks in timing, acceleration and deceleration, changes in overall pitch level, terminal pitch contours and changes in voice quality'.[11] The following transcription, which comes from Chafe's work[12], illustrates the way in which discourse is segmented in this way. Each individual intonation unit is placed on a separate line of the transcription. Different speakers are indicated as (A), (B) and (C):

(A) . . . Have the.. animals,
(A) . . . ever attacked anyone in a car?
(B) . . . Well I
(B) well I heard of an elephant,
(B) .. that sat down on a VW one time.
(B) . . . There's a gir
(B) .. Did you ever hear that?
(C) . . . No,

(B) ... Some elephants and these
(B) ... they
(B) ... there
(B) these gals were in a Volkswagen,
(B) ... and uh,
(B) ... they uh kept honkin' the horn,
(B) ... hootin' the hooter,
(B) ... and uh,
(B) ... and the.. elephant was in front of em,
(B) so he just proceeded to sit down on the VW.
(B) ... But they.. had.. managed to get out first

Each intonation unit conveys one new idea. And as an intonation unit always occurs within a 2- to 3-second range, this means that the perceptual moment provides the requisite window enabling new content to be introduced, and processed, during ongoing conversation.

Other evidence for the existence of the perceptual moment comes from poetry and music. Common to both are the notions of rhythm and metre: both of these can only be experienced if there *is* a temporal *window*, one that allows a rhythm or a metre to emerge. If the temporal window is too short there can be no pattern. But if it's too long, working memory can't perform the necessary integration. In terms of music, the world's most ubiquitous rhythm is the so-called 3+2+2 structure. It consists of three strokes and five rests: x – – x – – x–. This rhythm is found in almost all of the world's musical traditions, and was first recognised by the ancient Greeks, who termed it the 'dochmaic' pattern. It is processed within the 3-second outer limit of the perceptual moment. By way of example, next time you listen to Elvis Presley's *Hound Dog*, focus on the bass line. It consists of the 3+2+2 pattern: the backing band echo the pattern with handclapping. If you time the rhythm using a stop-watch, you'll see that it always comes in under three seconds.

The poetic line is another example. It has been claimed that all of the world's poetry traditions fall within the 3-second window.

This window facilitates the temporal processing within which a poetic line can be integrated.[13] Perhaps the most famous poetic line of all is that of blank verse, the line of choice in the plays of Shakespeare. In the stage-play world of Elizabethan England, actors had to learn their lines very quickly, with a high turnover of plays. The pattern of blank verse was the ideal vehicle to aid memorisation. Each line consists of ten syllables, made up of five pairs of unstressed–stressed syllables. The unstressed–stressed pattern provides a rhythm that aids memorisation. Indeed, ten syllables appears to be the perfect number: it ideally fits within the brain's temporal processing window – the 3-second perceptual moment.

Following decades of research, the neuroscientist Ernst Pöppel summarises the situation as follows: '... conscious activities are temporally segmented into intervals of a few seconds, and ... this segmentation is based on an automatic ... integration process establishing a temporal platform for cognitive processing.'[14] In short, timing mechanisms in the brain up to an outer limit of around three seconds provide the cognitive glue[15] that allows us to categorise and perceive objects and other entities in our environment. The perceptual moment allows conscious experiences to arise. These include the production and comprehension of 'spontaneous speech, movement control, vision and audition, also short-term memory and even cultural artefacts in music and poetry'.[16]

These findings appear to further contradict the strong position taken by Lakoff and Johnson. Our awareness of time, far from being created by conceptual metaphors, appears to be fundamental to how we function as human beings. From unconscious processes involved in percept-formation, to conscious processes such as language, poetry and music, time is essential. And in some respects, time is more fundamental than space and sensory–motor experience more generally. It allows us to process the perceptual stimuli deriving from our spatial world: temporal codes in the brain facilitate our ability to perceive objects and other entities to begin with.

## The many faces of time

In ancient Rome, Janus was the god of beginnings, transitions and endings. As a consequence, his image appeared on gates and doorways. Perhaps unsurprisingly, he came to be associated with time. In the Julian calendar, the month of January – a beginning, and in certain respects an ending – was named after Janus. Indeed, being the god of both past and future, Janus had two faces, looking both forward and back. And time does indeed have more than one face.

Language provides evidence for the ways in which time is structured in the human mind. One important finding is that time is not, in fact, a single idea. We often thing about time as a commodity, as when we say *A waste of time, Her time is so expensive*, or even in management-speak when terms such as *effective time-management* are bandied around. But in literature and rhetoric, as we saw with Marvell's poem in the previous chapter, time is often personified: represented as a causal agent of change. The following examples are both striking and representative:

> Time is the great physician [Benjamin Disraeli]
> Time is the greatest innovator [Francis Bacon]
> Time, the avenger! [Lord Byron]
> Time, the subtle thief of youth [Milton]
> Tempus edax rerum [Ovid]
> 'Time the devourer'
> Time is a great teacher, but unfortunately it kills all its pupils. [Louis Hector]
> Time is the justice that examines all offenders. [Shakespeare]
> Threefold the stride of Time, from first to last: Loitering slow, the Future creepeth – Arrow-swift, the present seepeth – And motionless forever stands the Past. [Friedrich von Schiller]

Language also provides evidence for a range of different conceptual metaphors for time – these point to quite different cognitive strategies for fixing events in time. The first is the Time Orientation Metaphor.[17] In this conceptualisation, there is a stationary

PAST            PRESENT        FUTURE

**Figure 4.2.** The Time Orientation Metaphor

Observer – what we might think of as a human centre of experiencing consciousness. The location of the Observer corresponds to the present. The space in front of the Observer, the direction in which the Observer is facing, corresponds to the future. And the space behind the Observer corresponds to the past. This I represent diagrammatically in Figure 4.2.

The reason for thinking that English-speakers do indeed have such a representation in their heads comes from language:

> The emotional upheaval of the divorce is *behind* him. *Here we are* in the twenty-first century and employment prospects look bleak. More economic uncertainty *lies ahead*.

In these examples, the expressions in italics, *behind*, *here we are*, and *lies ahead* all derive from the domain of SPACE. Yet we understand these expressions as relating not to SPACE, but to TIME. Moreover, they convey particular temporal notions; as we saw in the previous chapter, when you or I talk about the space in front of us or someone else, we understand this to mean, metaphorically, the future. We understand the speaker's physical location to designate the present, and the location behind the speaker to relate to the past. In short, you and I appear to use the human observer as a reference point, and the division of space with respect to the observer relates to temporal notions.

The representation in Figure 4.2, then, is an attempt to capture this understanding. We divide locations in space, relative to the inherent front/back asymmetry of the human body. And we understand these locations in temporal terms. After all, when you and I talk about events being *behind* or *ahead*, there is no confusion. We automatically understand that what is being referred to *is* something which took place in the past, or that *will*

Table 4.1 *Mappings for the Time Orientation Metaphor*

| Source domain: SPACE | Mappings | Target domain: TIME |
|---|---|---|
| THE LOCATION OF OBSERVER | → | THE PRESENT |
| THE SPACE IN FRONT OF THE OBSERVER | → | THE FUTURE |
| THE SPACE BEHIND THE OBSERVER | → | THE PAST |

take place in the future. Moreover, even the term for the present is grounded in the notion of physical space. The English word *present* is closely related to words such as *presence* and *to present*. These both relate, in slightly different ways, to spatial co-location.

According to the Time Orientation Metaphor, we map the location in front of the observer, in the domain of SPACE, onto the concept of future in the domain of TIME. And according to Lakoff and Johnson, it is because of this mapping that we effortlessly understand expressions such as *ahead* or *in front* to refer to the future. Similarly, you and I map the observer's location onto the present and the location behind the observer onto the past. Table 4.1 summarises these mappings which make up the Time Orientation Metaphor.

Lakoff and Johnson argue that the Time Orientation Metaphor combines with our understanding of motion through space. This gives rise to two further conceptual metaphors for TIME. The first of these is the Moving Time Metaphor.[18] In this conceptualisation there is, again, a stationary Observer whose location corresponds to the present. The Observer faces the future, with the space behind corresponding to the past. In this, the Moving Time Metaphor inherits structure from the Time Orientation Metaphor.

The aspect of the Moving Time Metaphor which is novel derives from our understanding of the motion of objects through space. In the Moving Time Metaphor, events are thought of in terms of objects that undergo motion. Moreover, the events move from the location in front of the Observer, in the future, towards

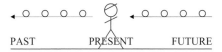

PAST          PRESENT         FUTURE

**Figure 4.3.** The Moving Time Metaphor

and then behind the Observer, disappearing into the past. This understanding is presented in Figure 4.3.

In Figure 4.3, events are represented by small circles. Motion is represented by the arrows. Events move from the future towards the Observer, and then behind into the past. The reason for thinking that speakers of English store this in their minds again comes from language:

> Christmas is *approaching*. The time for action *has arrived*. The concert *is getting close*. The summer just *zoomed by*. Christmas *dragged by* this year. The end-of-summer sales *have passed*.

As revealed by examples such as these, we employ the language of motion to refer to the passage of time. As with the Time Orientation Metaphor, the regions of space in front of, co-located with and behind the Observer correspond to future, present and past. In addition, we understand motion to relate to time's *passage*, as is clear by the use of *approaching* in the first sentence. The relative proximity of the entity, as in the expression *getting close*, relates to how *close* in time the event's occurrence is. And the rapidity of the motion relates to the nature of the durational elapse. For instance, an event that *zooms by* is understood in terms of a short duration, while one that *drags* has a long durational elapse.[19] The series of mappings that allow us to understand these different aspects of the motion of objects in terms of TIME are captured in Table 4.2.

In addition, Lakoff and Johnson claim that the Time Orientation Metaphor also combines with our understanding of human motion, giving rise to a combined conception in which we understand TIME in terms of the motion of an Observer along a path. In this conceptual metaphor, which we can think of as being a

Table 4.2 *Mappings for the Moving Time Metaphor*

| Source domain: MOTION OF OBJECTS | Mappings | Target domain: TIME |
|---|:---:|---|
| OBJECTS | → | TIMES |
| THE MOTION OF OBJECTS PAST THE OBSERVER | → | THE 'PASSAGE' OF TIME |
| PROXIMITY OF OBJECT TO THE OBSERVER | → | TEMPORAL 'PROXIMITY' OF THE EVENT |
| THE LOCATION OF THE OBSERVER | → | THE PRESENT |
| THE SPACE IN FRONT OF THE OBSERVER | → | THE FUTURE |
| THE SPACE BEHIND THE OBSERVER | → | THE PAST |

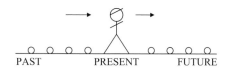

**Figure 4.4.** The Moving Observer Metaphor

reversal of the Moving Time Metaphor, TIME is conceived as a static *timescape*, with events conceptualised as specific and static locations towards which the Observer moves and then passes. This complex conception is dubbed the Moving Observer Metaphor, and is diagrammed in Figure 4.4.

As previously, events are represented by small circles in Figure 4.4, which are specific locations on the temporal landscape. Motion is represented by the arrows. In this case, it is the Observer, rather than the events, which is in motion. Here, we understand the passage of time *in terms of* the Observer's motion: the Observer moves across the temporal landscape towards and then past specific events, expressed as fixed locations in space. Lakoff and Johnson again point to evidence from language for this conceptualisation:

Table 4.3 *Mappings for The Moving Observer Metaphor*

| Source domain: MOTION OF OBSERVER | Mappings | Target domain: TIME |
|---|---|---|
| LOCATIONS ON OBSERVER'S PATH | → | TIMES |
| THE MOTION OF THE OBSERVER | → | THE 'PASSAGE' OF TIME |
| THE LOCATION OF THE OBSERVER | → | THE PRESENT |
| THE SPACE IN FRONT OF THE OBSERVER | → | THE FUTURE |
| THE SPACE BEHIND THE OBSERVER | → | THE PAST |
| DISTANCE OF OBSERVER FROM LOCATION | → | TEMPORAL 'DISTANCE' OF EVENT |
| RAPIDITY OF MOTION OF OBSERVER | → | IMMINENCE OF EVENT'S OCCURRENCE |

> They're *approaching* crisis point. The relationship *extended over* many years. He left *at* 10 o'clock. We're *getting close to* the end of term. We're *fast approaching* decision time.

Utterances like these show that language relating to the Observer's motion is ascribed to time's passage. Time is being likened to a static landscape, as can be seen from expressions like *extended over*. Moreover, the use of *at*, as in *He left at 10 o'clock*, demonstrates that specific locations in the static landscape correspond to temporal events. The relative spatial proximity or distance of the Observer corresponds to temporal proximity or distance of the event, as shown by the expression *getting close*. And the relative rapidity of the Observer's motion corresponds to the relative imminence of the event. I represent the mappings for the Moving Observer Metaphor in Table 4.3.

All of the examples above relate to English. And many other languages seem to have similar conceptual metaphors. Languages as diverse as French, Japanese, Spanish, Mandarin, Hindi and the West African language Wolof all exhibit these patterns.[20]

Nevertheless, there are some languages that conceptualise time in strikingly different ways. One such example is Aymara, an indigenous language spoken by around two million people in the Andean region of Bolivia, Peru and Chile. In Aymara, the future is conceptualised as located behind, and the past as in front: the Time Orientation metaphor is organised in reverse fashion to English. Evidence for this, in the first instance, comes from language. The word for past is *nayra pacha*, which literally means 'front time'. The word for future is *qhipa pacha,* which literally means 'back/behind time'. More recently, a study of Aymara gestures has provided further evidence for this. When Aymara speakers refer to the past they point in front of them. When they refer to the future they point behind them.[21]

Another language that does things quite differently is Amondawa. Amondawa is also an indigenous South American language spoken by a small tribe of around 115 people located in remote western Amazonia[22]. Official contact was not made until 1986. However, since that time there has been reasonably extensive field work with the Amandowa, and detailed studies of the language. Although the Amondawa have a rich lexicon and grammar of space, and have lexical resources to import space into time, they don't appear to have conventionalised metaphors to ascribe space to time. For instance, there is no evidence from Amondawa for the existence of the Moving Time and Moving Observer conceptual metaphors. Moreover, the Amondawa don't have native time-reckoning or calendar systems.

Nevertheless, it would be a mistake to conclude from this that the Amondawa don't have an awareness of time. In fact, researchers who have worked with the Amondawa have found that they can be coaxed to represent temporal ideas using space. In one so-called dinner plate installation task, circular paper plates were used to represent temporal sequences, such as seasons. The Amondawa were able to represent a temporal sequence by placing paper plates in a linear order. The task demonstrated that the Amondawa can indeed produce spontaneous linear ordering of events in a temporal sequence. Moreover, many of the Amondawa are now bilingual speakers of Portuguese; they have no trouble acquiring Portuguese, nor using Portuguese cultural artefacts such as clocks and wrist watches for measuring time – Portuguese is much like English in terms of its space-to-time conceptual metaphors.

All in all, time is a complex and multifaceted system of concepts. Language – and indeed other types of symbolic representations, such as gesture – from the domain of space, and motion through space, can be deployed to facilitate representations of time. However, spatial representation appears not to be essential for an understanding of time.

## How similar are time and space?

A common misconception is that space is important for structuring temporal ideas because time is, in some fundamental way, space-like. As we shall see, time is in fact quite different from space.

There are a number of ways in which we can compare space and time. The first concerns how much *stuff* there is of something. In terms of space, the stuff in question is matter. Matter, broadly speaking, comes in two varieties: discrete entities, such as objects, and mass entities, such as fluids. Indeed, many languages encode this basic distinction in their grammars. For example, English makes a grammatical distinction between count nouns and so-called uncountable or mass nouns. A noun such as *desk* can be preceded by the indefinite article: *A desk is useful for writing*. A mass noun such as *water* cannot: *\*A water covers three quarters of the planet* (the preceding asterisk is used by linguists to indicate that a sentence is ungrammatical).

Matter can be *cut up* into different amounts. The amounts relate to the property of extension. Extension manifests itself in three distinct ways, a consequence of the three-dimensionality of space, which I discuss below. Space's extension involves length, as

Table 4.4 *A comparison of magnitude across space and time*

| Domain | SPACE | TIME |
|---|---|---|
| **Stuff** | Matter | Action |
| **Property** | Extension | Duration |
| **Divisions** | Count vs. mass | Bounded vs. unbounded |

in a length of a piece of wood. It can take the form of an area, such as the extension of a playing field. Finally extension can be measured in terms of volume, such as how much water it takes to fill a bath.

In contrast, in the domain of TIME, language reveals that time's *quantity* relates not to matter, but to action.[23] Action can be subdivided into *stuff* that is bounded or unbounded – this broadly reflects the distinction between count and mass in matter. Again, language provides evidence for this distinction. The grammatical encoding of 'aspect' in a language such as English captures this. A sentence like *John ran* encodes perfective (or bounded) aspect. In contrast, a sentence like *John is running* encodes imperfective (or unbounded) aspect. Note that tense and aspect are different grammatical notions: aspect relates to the *shape* of an event, while tense encodes *when* it occurs relative to now.

In terms of time, the property exhibited by action, and hence the means of *cutting up* action into amounts, is duration rather than extension. While duration can, self-evidently, be quantified using measurement systems involving material artefacts such as clocks, duration – of relatively short periods – can be estimated without the need for measurement systems such as these. As we saw a little earlier, where I discussed estimations of the 'subjective minute', we are amazingly adept at gauging how long a particular event lasted. Table 4.4 summarises these differences.

The second way in which time and space can be compared relates to their dimensionality. In terms of space, entities can occupy and proceed along three dimensions. These are the lateral (left/right), sagittal (front/back) and vertical (up/down) planes. In contrast, in the domain of TIME, the units of action – namely events – take place along one dimension – succession. Put another way, when we discuss the sequence of service in a five-course dinner, there is a sequential relation that holds between the starter (or appetizer), the main course, the dessert, the cheese and biscuits and the coffee. In short, in a formal dinner event, the subevents that constitute it are related in terms of the sequential relations that hold between them. When I say that the starter comes before the main course, no one thinks that this relates to a spatial relation on the sagittal plane. On the contrary, time deals in a single dimension: succession.

The third factor in our comparison concerns the relative symmetry of the two domains. Space is symmetrical: it is possible to proceed in any direction, forward or back or from side to side.[24] In contrast, time is asymmetric. One of the most celebrated forms of its asymmetry relates to the thermodynamic property of matter, exhibited by the dispersal of energy (aka entropy): all things being equal, a cup of coffee cools down, and cannot subsequently, and spontaneously, heat up again. The asymmetric nature of time, particularly at the macroscopic level of matter, led the British astrophysicist Sir Arthur Eddington (1928) to coin the term 'the arrow of time'.[25] However, this is not the only form of time's *arrow*. The philosopher Robin Le Poidevin[26] has argued for three 'arrows' of time. The first might be termed the thermodynamic arrow, proceeding from lower to higher entropy. The second relates to what I call the psychological arrow, moving from the anticipation of events (future), to the perception of events (present), to the recollection of events (past). The third is a causal arrow, involving an asymmetry between causes and their effects: causes must, of necessity, be sequenced prior to their effects.

Finally, space and time can be distinguished in terms of transience.[27] Transience concerns the phenomenologically real experience of a ceaseless change in human experience; this amounts to the ephemeral experience of one moment being replaced by another, which in turn gives way to another, and so on. In more figurative terms, it concerns a present ceaselessly reborn, but each moment being unique, never the same as the one gone before. As I sit writing these words, I'm gazing out of the window of my study, watching leaves swirl in the wind out on the driveway. Someone passes beyond the garden wall, walking by in the road. I hear a clock ticking somewhere in the house. I feel an itch on my skin. And in all of this, I *feel* the passing of time. The most apt evocation of transience, to my mind, comes from Saint Augustine's *Confessions* written in the fourth century CE: 'If you do not ask me what time is, I know; if you ask me, I know not'. And while time exhibits transience, space does not.

One way of thinking of transience is that it represents a convergence of the three different aspects of time that I've been discussing. Duration is a type of transience that concerns the felt experience of elapse. Succession is a type of transience that relates to the felt experience of events proceeding as a sequence, a progression, with events thus exhibiting an order in the sequence. Finally, the psychological arrow of time relates to another kind of transience: the felt distinction between the present, future and past, with the future becoming the present, before becoming the past. Together, these ways in which time differs from space – in terms of magnitude, dimensionality and asymmetry – amount to transience as we experience it. And transience is entirely absent in the domain of space. Transience *is* the hallmark of time.

## Time is our fruit fly

Now I return to the issue of conceptual metaphor, and more specifically conceptual metaphors for time. I do so to begin to unravel the various issues that I've been discussing.

Conceptual Metaphor Theory begins with evidence from language. Time, in language, draws upon space, and motion through space. This leads to the hypothesis that mappings recruit from the domain of SPACE to provide structure for the domain of TIME. The first question is this. Do conceptual metaphors really exist in our minds? That is, how do we know that they have psychological reality?

This issue has been investigated by psychologists using behavioural experiments: experiments that expose individuals to certain types of stimuli. This often involves getting people to read sentences or looking at images on a page or on a computer screen. The subjects are then asked to perform some judgement task in response. This might mean making a particular choice between two images, for instance, or confirming when they have read and understood a further sentence or passage. The experimenter can then use the response provided by the subjects to ascertain how they reasoned. Behavioural tasks, then, allow the psychologist to infer the thought processes at work. They enable researchers to investigate patterns in the mind by observing how people behave in response to particular, carefully selected, types of stimuli.

One behavioural task designed to investigate the psychological reality of conceptual metaphors is the Metaphor Consistency Paradigm. If conceptual metaphors are real, then once a particular metaphor is activated, linguistic utterances which are consistent with the activated conceptual metaphor should be comprehended more quickly.

This works as follows.[28] Human subjects are asked to read sentences on a computer screen, for instance: *The time for a decision is fast approaching.* Once they understand the sentence, the subject again presses any button on the keyboard. This time the first sentence disappears and a second appears. About half the time, the new sentence, while different, is motivated by the same conceptual metaphor, for instance the Moving Time Metaphor *Christmas is getting closer.* This is the 'consistent condition'. However, about 50 per cent of the time the new sentence relates to a different conceptual metaphor, the Moving Observer Metaphor: *We're approaching Christmas.* This is the 'inconsistent condition'. The subject again presses any keyboard key after understanding the second sentence. The computer then records the time delay it took to read and understand the second sentence.

If conceptual metaphors really do exist in our heads, then sentences that are consistent with the metaphor should be processed more quickly than inconsistent sentences. After all, if a particular conceptual metaphor has been activated by virtue of a particular expression in language, then the mental processing of a second sentence, one that makes use of the same conceptual metaphor, should take less time to be understood than one which requires the activation of a different conceptual metaphor. In a series of experiments using this paradigm, a team of psychologists did indeed find that conceptual metaphors for time appear to exist in the minds of human subjects.[29]

But this then leads to a second issue. Lakoff and Johnson make the further claim that conceptual metaphors are asymmetric. While structure is recruited from the domain of space and mapped onto time, the reverse doesn't happen. We can talk about *a long time*, or *a long kiss*, and be understood to mean that *long* refers to duration, rather than spatial extension. But we can't normally talk about a *2-minute length* and be understood to mean that the expression refers to spatial extension, rather than duration. In short, we appear to be highly adept at applying spatial ideas to convey temporal notions, while the reverse is not the case.

In a series of experiments, psychologist Lera Boroditsky sought to ascertain whether time and space are asymmetric in the human mind in the same way. If the prediction made by Conceptual Metaphor Theory is right, then spatial cues should prompt for temporal reasoning, but temporal cues shouldn't be able to prompt for spatial reasoning.

In one experiment, Boroditsky investigated whether spatial cues primed for a temporal reasoning task. The first prime – labelled prime a) in Figure 4.5 – involves a picture of a person in motion, towards two objects. This is signalled by the arrow. The furthermost object is a potted plant. Underneath the prime is the sentence: *The flower is in front of me.* This serves to emphasise the directionality that the experimenter means the image to convey.

The second prime – b) in Figure 4.5 – depicts a person sitting down, watching a conveyor belt moving towards them. A hatbox and a box of tissues are depicted as being located on the conveyor

(a)

The flower is in front of me.

(b)

The hat-box is in front of the Kleenex.

**Figure 4.5.** Spatial primes (after Boroditsky 2000; reprinted with permission)

belt. The hatbox is ahead of the tissue box, and hence is closest to the stationary person.

Boroditsky designed her two spatial cues with care. She wanted her primes to be spatial analogues of the Moving Time and Moving Observer Metaphors proposed by Lakoff and Johnson. Recall that the Moving Observer Metaphor involves understanding time in terms of *our* motion along a path. It is this understanding that Boroditsky attempts to emulate with spatial prime a). In contrast, the Moving Time Metaphor involves a conceptualisation in which the motion of objects towards a stationary Observer is mapped onto our experience of time. The spatial scenario depicted as prime b) in Figure 4.5 is Boroditsky's attempt to emulate this, in spatial terms.

In the experiments, subjects were exposed to one of the spatial cues, but not both. After exposure, subjects were then asked to perform a temporal reasoning task: they had to respond to the following ambiguous question:

Q. Next Wednesday's meeting has been moved forward two days. Which day is the meeting now that it's been moved?

The question is ambiguous as there are two possible answers. The meeting might have been moved *forward* to either Monday or Friday. Go out into the street and ask English-speakers this question. You'll find that about half the people you stop will tell you the meeting has been moved to Friday. However, the other half will reply that the meeting is now on Monday.

But why are Monday and Friday each selected about half the time? Conceptual Metaphor Theory predicts that, without any form of priming, people make use of *either* the Moving Observer *or* the Moving Time conceptual metaphors. If people use the Moving Observer Metaphor, then their response to the ambiguous question will be Friday: in this conceptualisation it is the Observer who is in motion across a static temporal landscape – in this case, the days of the week. In contrast, if subjects use the Moving Time conceptualisation, then their response will be Monday. This is because, in this metaphor, it is temporal events – the days of the week – that are in motion: *they* are in motion towards the stationary observer, from Wednesday to Monday.

If space is used to structure time, as predicted by Conceptual Metaphor Theory, then subjects should reason about time in a prime-specific way. This means that Figure 4.5a) should prime for the Moving Observer Metaphor with the response: Friday. In contrast, subjects exposed to Figure 4.5b) should be primed to select Monday as the correct answer. Boroditsky found that her subjects did indeed respond in a prime-consistent way. This confirms that space appears to influence temporal reasoning.

Next, in order to confirm the asymmetry relation, Boroditsky repeated the experiment in reverse: she examined whether temporal cues can influence a spatial reasoning task. Her temporal primes were linguistic sentences which made use of the Moving Observer and Moving Time conceptual metaphors respectively:

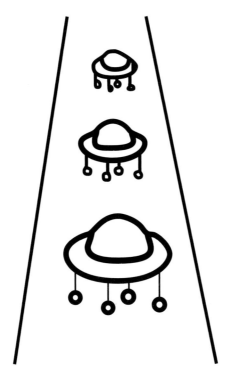

**Figure 4.6.** Ambiguous moving widget task (after Boroditsky 2000; reprinted with permission)

Prime a) *On Thursday, Saturday is ahead of us* (Moving Observer)

Prime b) *Thursday comes before Saturday* (Moving Time)[30]

Boroditsky reasoned that as each of these sentences makes use of a conceptual metaphor for time, then exposing a subject to a given sentence should activate the underlying conceptual metaphor. Subjects were then exposed to an ambiguous spatial image, depicted in Figure 4.6. This image consisted of a series of what she termed 'widgets' – vehicles without an inherent front or back. The widgets were sequenced on a path. Underneath the image, there appeared an instruction to circle the widget judged to be ahead. Just as with the ambiguous temporal reasoning task, without priming, Boroditsky found that about half the time people judged the uppermost widget on the page as being ahead. The other half of the time it was the lowermost widget.

The widgets were designed so that they appeared, to all intents and purposes, to be perfectly symmetrical. This meant that subjects couldn't determine their direction of motion from visual cues associated with the widgets. Boroditsky reasoned that if people conceived of themselves in motion, then they would *see* the widgets in motion *up* the page, in a direction away from their current location. This interpretation, which is analogous to the Moving Observer Metaphor for time, would be expected, she thought, if time does indeed prime for space, and subjects were exposed to a Moving Observer prime (e.g., *On Thursday, Saturday is ahead of us*).

In contrast, she reasoned that if subjects assume they themselves are stationary in space, then the widgets will be interpreted as moving *down* the page towards them. This interpretation is consistent with the Moving Time Metaphor for time, and is to be expected if time primes for spatial reasoning.

However, subjects were barely influenced by the temporal primes when reasoning about space. Boroditsky's experiments appeared to demonstrate, and for the first time, that while space influences how we reason about time, our spatial reasoning is far less likely to be influenced by time.

One potential drawback of the experiments just described is that they involved language, in the guise of the primes and the reasoning tasks. If we really want to examine the psychological reality of conceptual metaphors, then language needs to be removed from the experimental set-up completely.[31] Building on Boroditsky's work, the psychologist Daniel Casasanto did exactly this.

Casasanto developed a Growing Lines paradigm. He designed a computer programme so that a line would *grow* across the screen. The line would grow for a predetermined length at different speeds. This meant that the line would grow for a particular spatial extent across the computer screen and, crucially, for a predetermined duration. Moreover, the computer was programmed so that subjects were exposed to many growing lines, one after the other, each line varying in terms of both spatial extent and duration. Hence, lines could end up being long or short, and growing for longer or shorter periods of time. Once the line had finished growing, it would disappear again. At this stage, and only at this stage, subjects were told whether they needed to evaluate the spatial or temporal extent of the line. The subject then had to draw the extent of the line by using the computer mouse, or holding the mouse key down for the length of time the line had grown for.

What Casasanto found was this. Lines of the same duration were adjudged as lasting for a longer period of time if they had a longer length, but for a shorter period of time if they had a shorter length. However, lines of the same length were judged as having exactly that, the same length, no matter whether they grew for a longer or shorter period of time. In essence, Casasanto found that when people are asked to make judgements concerning the duration of a line's growth, they are influenced by, and indeed are incapable of ignoring, spatial information. If a line is longer (in space), people also believe that it lasted longer (in time). But if the line is shorter (in space), they judge it as also lasting for a shorter period of time. In contrast, when making judgements about spatial extent, temporal information doesn't influence their judgement at all.

This finding shows that spatial cues influence temporal reasoning, while time is far less influential in spatial reasoning. This corroborates the results of Boroditsky's tasks involving language; as predicted by Lakoff and Johnson, concrete experiences derived from our spatial environment structure a more subjective, abstract conceptual domain such as TIME. The relationship between space and time is, indeed, asymmetric.

## Time in hand (and ear)

But wait. Close your eyes and listen; you are still aware of time. Might the previous experiments have relied too much on the visual modality? In fact, in more recent experiments, it turns out that time may in fact be just as useful for understanding space as space is for time: space may not structure time in an asymmetric fashion after all. In one study, psychologist Zhenguang Cai blindfolded subjects and asked them to feel sticks of different lengths using their hands.[32] At the same time, participants heard a note which lasted for different periods of time. The experimenters found that the judgements about stick length, based on touch, were influenced by how long the note lasted: a note of greater duration influenced subjects to judge a stick to be longer. Notes of shorter duration provided the reverse effect.

In another study, Alex Kranjec replicated the growing lines experiment.[33] But rather than participants seeing the lines grow, the subjects *heard* them. Kranjec played sounds to subjects that lasted for varying durations of time. The sounds were digitally manipulated so that they were perceived as being closer to, or further away from, the experiment's participants. Kranjec found that subjects judged longer sounds as being further away from them than sounds of shorter duration. Thus, in the modality of sound, time is *as good* at influencing judgements about space as space is at influencing time.

These two sets of experiments relating to touch and sound reveal the following: if we strip away visual cues, our perception of spatial and temporal extent are mutually contagious – they influence each other in a symmetric way, not the asymmetric pattern predicted by Lakoff and Johnson.

And when you actually look at it, language does in fact provide evidence for an asymmetric relationship between space and time – notwithstanding the claims regarding conceptual metaphors for time I discussed earlier. For example, I am equally able to respond to the question: *How far is London from Bangor?* with *three and a half hours* as with *about 250 miles*. Moreover, the grammatical organisation of English reveals their asymmetrical interdependence. We can describe temporal notions, *John called her on the phone*, as if they were physical objects, *John gave her a call*, where a telephone call is conceptualised as a physical transfer event, in which John, metaphorically, *gave* the call. But analogously, physical acts can be conceptualised as if they were actions, with a temporal contour. For instance, *Jane removed the pit from the olive* can be expressed as *Jane pitted the olive*.

More tellingly, neuroscientists have discovered that temporal experiences are processed by brain areas which are entirely distinct from those brain regions responsible for sensory–motor experiences.[34] If time were largely constructed, at least at the level of thought, in terms of space, and motion through space, then we would expect to see some overlap between brain regions responsible for processing the relevant experiences that underlie our concepts for time and space. But this is not the case.

One aspect of temporal perception relates to our felt sense of duration. While the brain has a wide array of time-keeping mechanisms, in general terms, duration at sub-second intervals appears to be processed in specific regions beneath the human cortex – the outermost and most evolutionarily recent region of the brain. The regions implicated are the cerebellum and basal ganglia. In contrast, temporal intervals at the supra-second interval, up to the 3-second outer limit of the perceptual moment, are processed in the cortex. The brain regions involved seem to be the supplementary motor area and left inferior frontal and superior temporal cortical structures.[35] Timing mechanisms that underlie larger-scale circadian rhythms, ranging from the menstrual cycle to the so-called master circadian rhythm – the human wake–sleep cycle – are located in the hypothalamus.[36] A notable side effect of the wake–sleep cycle being out of sync with the local time zone is, of course, jet lag.

The brain regions implicated in thinking about the past and future seem to involve a *core system* centred on the medial prefrontal cortex, the medial parietal cortex, lateral inferior parietal cortex and medial temporal lobe structures. While not strictly speaking perceptual, it nevertheless seems to be the case that the basis for thinking about the past and future is grounded in brain regions that dissociate from those directly associated with sensory–motor processing.[37]

A final piece of evidence, one that weighs against Lakoff and Johnson's asymmetric view of time and space, comes from patients suffering from brain trauma. Some English words, such as prepositions, *in*, *over*, *through* and so on, have multiple, related meanings grounded in the domains of both TIME and SPACE. For instance, the preposition *at* has a spatial meaning (e.g. *at the bus stop*) and a temporal meaning (e.g. *at 1.30pm*). In tests on four brain-damaged patients with trauma in the left perisylvian region, the neurolinguist David Kemmerer found the following. Two of the patients could correctly process the spatial concepts of the preposition but not the temporal concepts. In contrast, two of the patients could correctly process the temporal but not the spatial concepts. This provides a line of evidence suggesting the temporal and spatial representations that underlie language can be, in principle, dissociated at the neurological level. This should not be possible if temporal concepts are dependent on content from the domain of SPACE, as claimed by Lakoff and Johnson.

## So where does this leave us?

Conceptual metaphors for time appear to exist: they are mental structures that have psychological reality for us – we use them to think and reason. And in so doing, we import knowledge about space, and moving around in space, to draw inferences about time. But while this asymmetry appears to be particularly prevalent in the visual sphere – as demonstrated by Casasanto in his growing lines experiment – it is less clear that other sensory domains structure time in terms of space in an asymmetric way.

Why, then, would time be structured asymmetrically by space in the visual field, but not in terms of other sensory domains such as hearing? While both primate vision and audition evolved in the context of a spatial field, vision provides faster and more accurate spatial information. The eye's retina preserves spatial relations in early representations, while the cochlea (in the ear) doesn't.[38]

Moreover, humans are less adept at locating where an entity is, using sound information than they are using visual experience.[39] In part, this may be a consequence of the different types of perceptual information involved. By its very nature, sound is transient. When we converse with someone, the words fade but the person remains, even in the pauses between our words and the silences that punctuate our conversation. For these reasons, space appears to be more tightly coupled with time in (human) visual experience than in other sensory experiences, such as touch and sound.

So, the difficulty for Lakoff and Johnson is this: they take this asymmetric relationship in visual experience, and conclude that time must be parasitic on space; it is only by structuring time in terms of space that time can be conceptualised and experienced. This implies that an abstract domain such as TIME may in fact be, at least partly, *created by* the conceptual metaphors: time doesn't exist – at least in large part – before it obtains structure from the domain of SPACE.

But much of the evidence I've reviewed in this chapter points to a slightly different conclusion. Research from neurobiology suggests that time is essential to facilitate perceptual processes, and conscious behaviours including language, and artefacts of culture such as music and poetry. Linguistic evidence also indicates, for example in the case of Amondawa, that while humans can experience time, they don't inevitably represent it in terms of conceptual metaphors. So where does this leave us?

In all likelihood, Lakoff and Johnson's conclusion is too strong. There *are* conceptual metaphors – no one, least of all me, disputes this. And these conceptual metaphors most probably facilitate the way in which we represent an abstract domain such as TIME. But it is probably too strong to conclude from this that the conceptual metaphors thereby bring our concepts for time into being – and this *is* what Lakoff and Johnson appear to claim.[40] Temporal processes and temporal awareness are as fundamental to human experience as space. Our conceptualisations for time are, in part at least, structured in terms of these purely temporal experiences: part of what we understand by time is literal time, time unadorned by our representations of space, which nevertheless help clothe it.

Albert Einstein, most famous for claiming that time is relative, once made the following quip: 'The only reason for time is so that everything doesn't happen at once.' And in fact, this throw-away remark actually gets to the heart of the matter. Temporal mechanisms, even those that we are aware of – such as the 2- to 3-second perceptual moment – facilitate our perception of, and interaction in, the socio-physical world which we inhabit. Temporal experience enables us to process change, precisely because things don't happen all at once. But as a consequence, temporal experience is in fact an artefact of perception and action. Time arises not as the focus of perception and action, but as a consequence of it: time is the *how* of perception while space is the *what*.

A number of researchers, myself included, have suggested that as temporal awareness is not the focus of perception and action but a consequence of it, it may be less well connected to the representational centres of the mind.[41] For purposes of symbolisation in language, gesture and so on, time is not easy to encode and externalise, which is anecdotal evidence to support this view. Time may therefore require the recruitment of the spatial content with which it is correlated during perception in order to enable it to be represented in language. Put differently, time is structured in terms of space not because it is somehow less foundational to human experience, or because it doesn't exist as a thing unto itself. Time is structured in terms of space to enable it to be encoded and externalised in gesture, language and in other forms of symbolisation.

## The mystery of time and its implications for meaning

Time remains one of the most fascinating yet perplexing areas of study. For many, time remains a mystery: intangible and unknowable, as strikingly illustrated by John Langone:

> Of all the scientific intangibles that shape our lives, time is arguably the most elusive – and the most powerful. As formless as space and being, those other unseen realms of abstraction on which we are helplessly dependent, it nonetheless affects all material things . . . Without it we could barely measure change, for most things that change on this Earth and in the universe happen in time and are governed by it. Stealthy, imperceptible, time makes its presence known by transforming our sense of it into sensation. For though we cannot see, touch, or hear time, we observe the regularity of what appears to be its passage in our seasons, in the orchestrated shift from dawn to dusk to dark, and in the aging of our bodies. We feel its pulsing beat in our hearts and hear its silence released in the precise ticking of a clock.[42]

However, we have seen in this chapter that time, a familiar stranger,[43] has its basis in our neurological and cognitive functioning. It plays a crucial role in a host of mental functions, and through language we can reflect on it. One way of thinking of the function of temporal processing is to employ a computer-as-mind analogy; time is like a computer operating system: it allows other programs to come to the fore. And for this reason, it remains only partially seen. But with the assistance of the sorts of experiences it helps to create – our perceptions of space and motion – time is, perhaps paradoxically, brought into view. Time is foundational to our experience of almost everything, including our own self-awareness. And yet, ironically, some scientists have for too long doubted that it even exists.

So, in terms of our quest to uncover the conceptual foundations of meaning, where does this leave us? Humans, like other species, must be able to compute not only *where* objects and other entities are located in the world, and *what* those objects and entities *are doing*; in addition, they must also be able to judge *when* events are happening, *in what order*, and for *how long*. At the level of human experience, time concerns, at the very least, understanding the distinction between now and not-now, duration and succession. Without the capacity for perceiving and responding to the *flow* of events and the ability to judge the duration of an event, even the most basic of endeavours would become impossible. Everyday activities, ranging from the ability to tell the time to interpreting a train or university timetable, would become impossible – these self-evidently presuppose an understanding of the nature of time. But even many of our most basic capacities which we take for granted, such as language, and our ability to coordinate motor actions – upon which a host of behaviours depend, such as lifting and setting down objects, walking, running, and so on – are dependent upon temporal processing that, psychologists now know, is fundamental to the way in which the brain coordinates and regulates our bodies. Time also appears to be fundamental to our ability to perceive sensorimotor activity – such as motion – in our external, spatial environment. In short, both space *and*, crucially, time appear to be among the foundational domains of human experience. While they are combined in the guise of conceptual metaphors, which provide our minds with a fundamental organisational principle for knowledge representation, it is overly simplistic to conclude from this that our experience and, indeed, knowledge of time is thereby created. Conceptual metaphors for time, importing structure from our understanding of space, enable us to consciously reflect on time and externalise our conceptions in language, for purposes of meaning-making. But in no sense does this mean that for us, time isn't real, or foundational.

# Chapter 5    Concepts body forth

Any account of the human mind has to grapple with the nature of concepts, the subject of this chapter. After all, concepts are the foundation of our mental life, and play a central role in our meaning-making capacity.[1] For without concepts that could be no thought; moreover, language would have nothing to express. Love, Freedom, Peace, and even Superman are all concepts. A considerable amount of ink has been spilled by philosophers of mind over the nature of concepts, often with perhaps startling conclusions. As I observed in Chapter 2, the philosopher Jerry Fodor is famous – or rather infamous – in certain circles for having claimed that concepts are innate; we come into the world pre-equipped with a mental store of concepts, ranging from Pineapple to Porcupine, from Molecule to Atom, and everything in between, even the concept for Doorknobs![2] While we can be fairly confident that babies aren't born with the concept of Door-knobs – and even Fodor has recanted in his later work[3] – it is far from clear what concepts are like.

To my knowledge, no one's ever seen a concept. So we have to infer what they might be like from the language we use, from the way we think and act, and from how we categorise our environment as we experience it. For concepts are central to everything, or nearly everything, that's significant about the mental life of human beings. They populate our conceptual system: our repository of knowledge.

Søren Kierkegaard, the Danish philosopher, made the following observation: 'Concepts, like individuals, have their histories and are just as incapable of withstanding the ravages of time as are individuals. But in and through all this they retain a kind of homesickness for the scenes of their childhood'. Concepts come and go, and are born and die.

Take the concept Phlogiston, which you may be excused from not having come across until now. Phlogiston was thought to be an odourless, colourless substance without weight. It was said to be given off in burning by all flammable materials. As likely as not, you won't have heard of this mysterious substance before. And this is precisely because the theory of combustion assumed by alchemy, which it was part of, had, by the end of the eighteenth century, been overturned, with the arrival of the modern science of chemistry. Your twenty-first century mind was blissfully ignorant of Phlogiston – until now, that is. But having read the preceding sentences you are aware of the non-existence of Phlogiston: you now have a concept for it. And this demonstration reveals a further property of concepts, and their relationship with language: they are automatically called to mind when we read or speak. In the old cliché, when instructed: *Don't think of an elephant*, we confess to having thought of exactly that: an elephant.[4]

Concepts support and sustain our socio-cultural realm. Prime Ministers, monarchs, marriage, the class system and even money are all complex concepts – concepts that continue to evolve. They provide us with the matrix within which we live and breathe, and live out our daily lives. Richard Dawkins has argued that concepts can be thought of, along neo-Darwinian lines, as having lineages. Cultural transmission is facilitated through concepts, or 'memes', to use Dawkins' term – a meme being a mental analogue to the genetic replicator, the gene.[5] A meme is an idea that is replicated in the process of transmission. And replication can, as with genetic material, undergo alterations in the replication process, resulting in often dramatic changes over time.

While concepts are central to language, they are not the same as words: not quite. Recent findings reveal that not only are concepts palpably not the same as words in a language, neither are concepts abstract, rarefied entities. They are grounded in our daily experience as we interact with, and act in, the world. They emerge directly from perceptual states centred on the body. Evidence for this embodied view of human knowledge came, in the first instance, from language. This chapter tells the story of how our concepts body forth.

## The ghost in the machine

In his famous ode, *Intimations of immortality*, William Wordsworth describes his awe at the mystery of the infinite: the earth appears, at least through child-like eyes, as 'apparell'd in celestial light', 'the heavens laugh', with 'joy', with 'bliss', celebrating a 'jubilee'. Childhood, a state of almost pure innocence, provides us with intimations of immortality, and the mystery attendant upon it. The child, full of exuberance, of enthusiasm, is a seer – so Wordsworth contends – still close to the pure mysteries of the Universe which the travails and toil of adulthood draw out of us. He summarises this view:

> Our birth is but a sleep and a forgetting:
> The Soul that rises with us, our life's Star,
> Hath had elsewhere its setting,
> And cometh from afar:
> Not in entire forgetfulness,
> And not in utter nakedness,
> But trailing clouds of glory do we come
> From God, who is our home:
> Heaven lies about us in our infancy!

In somewhat different terms, Louis Pasteur expressed a similar idea:

> I see everywhere in the world the inevitable expression of the concept of infinity ... The idea of God is nothing more than one form of the idea of infinity. So long as the mystery of the infinite weighs on the human mind, so long will temples be raised to the cult of the infinite, whether it be called Brahmah, Allah, Jehovah or Jesus ... The Greeks understood the mysterious power of the hidden side of things. They bequeathed to us one of the most beautiful words in our language – the word 'enthusiasm' – *en theos* – a god within.

The infinite is as impressively humbling as it is paradoxically real. We glimpse the infinite in the ageing of our own reflections in the mirror, of the birth of our children and grandchildren, of the death of our parents, and in time our own. We witness the unchanging pre-eminence of the mountains and distant landscapes, a counterweight to our own fleeting corporeal existence: evidence of mysteries that extend beyond our own flesh and blood. We witness it in the futility of humankind to impose its will on the passage of time, as so poignantly captured by Percy Bysshe Shelly – like Wordsworth, another of the great English Romantic poets. In his sonnet *Ozymandias*, Shelley describes a wandering traveller who comes across a shattered statue lying in a desert. On the broken statue pedestal the following inscription appears:

> My name is Ozymandias, King of Kings:
> Look on my works, ye mighty, and despair!

Shelley continues:

> Nothing beside remains. Round the decay
> Of that colossal wreck, boundless and bare,
> The lone and level sands stretch far away.

The bombast of the long-dead Ozymandias is revealed as hubris, in the face of the sands of time.

The human participation in the infinite is captured by the belief in a non-physical soul. The existence of an immortal soul has been a fundamental axiom of human philosophical thought since prehistory. The immaterial soul is, in Wordsworth's idiom, 'our life's star'.

The seventeenth-century philosophical foundations of psychology reconceptualised the disjunction between a physical body and a soul in terms of a mind–body distinction. The French mathematician and philosopher René Descartes argued, in his *Meditations on First Philosophy*, that the body and mind are different *substances*. Descartes proposed a theory of the separability of mind and body: the thesis of Cartesian dualism. Moreover, he claimed that the unseen substance, the mind, holds dominion over a mechanical apparatus, the body. In the twentieth century the British philosopher of mind, Gilbert Ryle, likened the thesis of an immaterial mind and a corporeal, mechanistic body which it controls as akin to a ghost in the machine.[6]

Cognitive scientists today don't believe in an immaterial substance that controls a mechanistic body. For one thing, an intractable problem for mind–body dualism is to explain how an immaterial substance can effectively communicate with, and thereby control, a material body. Another is how an immaterial mind can be a substance to begin with. Nevertheless, cognitive science emerged from scientific traditions that arose in the context of that belief. The neuroscientist Paul Cisek observes that 'when dualism was rejected, the concept of the non-physical mind was replaced with ... the concept of cognition.' And as such, the distinction between perception – a bodily process – and cognition – a process performed by the brain – retains something of the spirit of the 'ghost in the machine' dogma.

Cognitive science – the interdisciplinary study of the mind – arose in the middle of the twentieth century. Its inspiration came from the prospect – and later emergence – of digital computers. Computers, like human brains, appeared to constitute a mechanism capable of complex reasoning. Cognitive science took the computational processes deployed by computers as an analogy for how the brain computes the mind: for the nature and functioning of cognition. In the mind-as-computer metaphor, perception is akin to input. The information-processing performed by computers is analogous to cognition. And the output produced by a computer corresponds to the action performed by the human organism in response to the computation performed on the perceptual input. In psychology, this is known as the perception–cognition–action (or sense–think–act) model.

Digital computers perform computations by manipulating symbols. A symbol is an object or entity that stands for – which is to say, represents – something else. But there is no meaningful connection between a symbol and the thing it represents – the relationship is arbitrary. In this, symbols used by computers are similar to human language. The word *dog* happens to represent a four-legged, domesticated creature: man's best friend. However, the same creature can be just as well represented by the symbol *chien*, as in French, *kalb* in Arabic or *skyli* in Greek.

In the earliest computers, symbols consisted of scratches on paper or holes in card or tape; these were then fed through early computing machines. In modern digital computers, the symbols take the form of a machine code that the computer can interpret and run to produce outputs. The cognitive scientist Douglas Hofstadter has likened any attempt to decipher machine code to trying to figure out a DNA molecule atom by atom.[7] Hence, software engineers interact with a computer's machine code using a *higher-level* programming language: one that's easier to manipulate. The computer then converts the programming language into the machine language, with which the computer then works.

In analogous fashion, cognitive scientists contend that the computations produced by the brain – the hardware – make use of a brain-specific machine code: the language of thought, aka Mentalese.[8] When we use a natural language, analogous to a higher-order programming language – English, French, Japanese or whatever – this is translated into Mentalese, and thoughts are translated from Mentalese into the natural language used by the individual in order to encode and externalise their thoughts. In the analogy, then, Mentalese corresponds to machine code, and natural languages provide a specific means of encoding and externalising the common code: Mentalese. Mentalese is thus the language in which all human brains carry out their information-processing.

But if computers are truly analogous to human brains, then computers should be able to exhibit intelligence of the kind manifested by humans – or at the very least exhibit the potential for human-like intelligence. The father of the digital computer was Alan Turing, a brilliant British mathematician and logician who played a key role in helping to crack the Nazi enigma code during World War II.

In 1950, Turing published a typically provocative paper.[9] He raised the issue of artificial intelligence, predicting that one day computers would be able to outsmart human brains. Turing set a test – which came to be known as the 'Turing Test' – to provide a standard measure for a machine to be called *intelligent*. Turing argued that if a person interacting with a machine could not tell apart a computer from a human in a conversation, then it could be deemed to be intelligent. Thirty years later, in a now classic thought experiment, the philosopher John Searle demonstrated the impossibility of (contemporary) machines approaching human intelligence. This follows, Searle argued, precisely because they make use of meaningless symbols that are not connected to the world beyond the machine.

In *The Language Myth* I presented Searle's famous Chinese Room thought experiment. It describes a scenario in which a person inside a closed room, without any knowledge of Chinese, can hold a conversation with a Chinese speaker outside it, by following a set of instructions for converting symbols from Chinese into English and back again. The point that Searle makes is that the Chinese Room is an illusion. The English-speaker inside the room doesn't, in fact, *understand* the Chinese characters. He simply combines these by following the instructions with which he is provided.

The larger point is that the Chinese Room is analogous to computational processing in digital computers. While computers can manipulate symbols, they don't actually *understand* the meanings of the symbols. They are blindly following instructions for combining the symbols, in order to produce a particular outcome. While such a machine would pass the Turing Test, it would fail to pass muster as *intelligent* in the sense that a human is intelligent.

One of the things that computers can do extremely well is to perform computations. And this capability has allowed IBM to develop a chess-playing machine: Deep Blue. In 1997, Deep Blue successfully defeated the world's chess champion, the Grand Master Garry Kasparov. But does this mean that Deep Blue, or indeed any computer, is more *intelligent* than a human being? I would say no; it simply means that computers can be designed to be more adept than humans at performing complex computations. But computers perform computations by manipulating meaningless symbols.

Early theories of concepts in cognitive science assumed that concepts were akin to computational symbols – assuming, as they did, the computer-as-mind metaphor. The difficulty for these sorts of theories was this: how do the symbols obtain their meaning? And in what sense do the symbols impart meaning? Put another way, how are symbols grounded in the reality they are meant to express?[10] One way of thinking about this problem is as follows. As perception and cognition were assumed to be very different sorts of things, how do concepts – the stuff of thought – get to represent sensory–motor information – the stuff of perception? How might abstract symbols represent embodied experience: pressure on the skin, taste in the mouth, visual experience, and so on? For instance, the colour blue arises from visual experience. If the concept Blue is represented by a symbol, in Mentalese, which is independent from the experience of blue, how does the concept Blue get locked to the experience blue such that it can represent the colour blue without needing to call up the colour?

And how does a concept such as Doorknob arise? After all, the concept is more than a perceptual experience; a doorknob has a particular function – it allows us to open doors. Jerry Fodor, in his extremely entertaining book *Concepts: Where Cognitive Science Went Wrong*, spends several chapters arguing that concepts such as Doorknob are represented by symbols. But he is completely silent on how such symbols might be acquired from experience of the world. While such concerns are presumably trivial for a philosopher, they are a central concern for the human organism, which must successfully function and, moreover, survive and thrive in the world of experience.

The solution might be that we somehow extract the function of a doorknob, together with our perceptual experience of a door-knob, and 'lock' it to a symbol in our mind – Fodor's position that I critiqued in detail in *The Language Myth*. The symbol would then constitute the concept Doorknob. In this way, concepts for Blue, Doorknob, or whatever are simply place markers for different types of experiences.

However, cognitive scientist Stephen Harnad[11] has observed that such a solution is problematic in at least two ways. First, if a symbol must perform its computation by calling up the sensation (e.g. blueness), or function (facilitating the opening of doors), there is little point in claiming that there are symbols independent from the sensations and functions they represent.

Second, positing symbols for concepts trivialises the difficulty in picking out the objects, events and states of affairs in the world that the symbols refer to. For example, take the concept Justice. It is far from clear that there is a homogenous set of experience types, situations and experiences that in some way correspond to justice. The problem, then, is to figure out how a concept-*qua*-symbol, that has an arbitrary connection with the thing it represents, gets connected to its target experience. How are symbols – the concepts – grounded in the entities they represent?

Human concepts form the basis for inference, interpretations, decision-making and the construction of meaning. While the fields of artificial intelligence and robotics have developed machines that are capable of *learning* about and interacting with their spatial environment, this is a far cry from the astonishingly sophisticated capabilities of the human conceptual system. And part of the reason is that human concepts are grounded in sensory–motor and perceptual experiences. The difficulty for computational symbols – as a means of modelling human concepts – is that they remain forever unconnected to the world.

Gilbert Ryle, in his classic 1949 book *The Concept of Mind,* argued that the dogma of the ghost in the machine is wrong-headed in terms of accounting for the human mind. He observed that there is no separation between perceptual states in the brain and symbol-based concepts: no separation between mind and body. Concepts are directly constituted by the perceptual experiences that we experience. He presented the following striking anecdote to make his point. A visitor came up to Oxford. Upon viewing the colleges and libraries, the visitor exclaimed: 'But where is the University?' The visitor's error was to think that the University was something separate from the buildings and the people that interacted in the buildings. In fact, the University is contingent upon the buildings: the interactions, behaviours and practices that are engaged in, *in* the buildings. There is no principled separation between the buildings and the University.

## The language of the body

In Chapter 3 we saw evidence, from language, that our mental representations are embodied. Language reveals patterns in the mind to us: conceptual metaphors. The mappings which make up conceptual metaphors deploy ideas from domains of sensory–motor experience in order to structure abstract concepts.

But language also provides another kind of evidence that refutes the thesis of concepts as abstract symbols. If concepts are directly grounded in sensory–motor experience, then we would expect the structure of language – its grammar – to reflect this. This follows as we use language to get our ideas across: language is the medium for expressing our concepts and, in the confluence of the two, the mechanism for creating meaning. It stands to reason, therefore, that its organisation – its grammatical structure – should, at least in part, mirror the content it serves to express. If concepts are not directly grounded in embodied experience, then there would be no reason to expect grammar to pattern after embodied experience.

Embodied experience, it seems, is woven into the very fabric of the grammar of a language. Grammar provides, in essence, a system for capturing schematic aspects of sensory–motor and subjective experience. In particular, it provides a mechanism for encoding how the states of affairs we seek to communicate are configured, the attentional resources we are deploying when attending to a particular state of affairs, the spatio-physical perspective from which the state of affairs are experienced and the nature of action and interaction involved. I briefly consider each of these aspects of embodied experience, as manifested by grammar.

In the previous chapter, I concluded that the foundational domains of experience are those of time and space. We inhabit a world of space, and live out our lives in the ongoing flow of time. As we saw in Chapter 4, the stuff that makes up the domain of SPACE is matter, of which two broad types can be distinguished: discrete entities (e.g. objects) and mass entities (e.g. fluids). The stuff that makes up TIME is that of action.[12] As with matter, action can also be broadly subdivided into action that is discrete, or bounded, and that which is unbounded.

These distinctions are captured by a fundamental design feature of the grammatical system of language. The lexical classes noun and verb appear to be common to all, or at least nearly all, of the world's languages.[13] Objects from the domain of SPACE appear to be the prototype for the lexical category noun, while the notion of a dynamic and ongoing process is the prototype that underpins the grammatical category verb.

But these claims need a little more unpacking. On first blush, it may not be clear that nouns are grounded in the domain of space. Consider the following quite diverse set of examples. The relevant nouns are underlined:

> Joyce sent a letter to her lover.
> Her car was making a funny noise.
> Joyce tried to teach Jim the Greek alphabet.
> The only good thing about Jim was his height.
> The explosion in her engine made her late for work.
> Joyce's love for Jim began on a Sunday.

While some nouns are objects (like *letter* and *car*), others concern a relation between two people or things (like *lover*). The noun *noise* expresses a physical sensation, while a noun like *alphabet* refers to a group of interconnected, yet discrete, entities. The noun *height* expresses a scalar concept, while the noun *explosion* concerns an event. The noun *love* describes an emotion while *Sunday* encodes a point in time. Yet, while the rich content associated with the underlined words is quite diverse, what is common to each is that they primarily relate to a portion of a frame. For

instance, while Sunday is a temporal idea, one entity in the 'days
of the week' sequence, it nevertheless refers to a specific portion of
that sequence: Sunday is the seventh day of the week. What makes
something a noun, then, in grammatical terms, is that it designates part of a larger thing. And while this definition of the
generic property associated with all nouns is quite abstract, it is
nevertheless a spatial idea.[14]

Now let's contrast this with verbs. The grammatical property of
any verb relates to the notion of a dynamic process. Consider the
following examples:

> Jim loves wine.
> Jim is drinking wine.

In the first example, the verb *loves* describes a process in which a
state is being designated: the state of loving something. The state
is something that is ongoing, and thus continues through time. In
contrast, the second example describes a process which changes
and thus evolves in a dynamic way through time: *drinking*. By
virtue of drinking, the glass is emptied of its contents. Verbs can
therefore describe dynamic processes (e.g. *to drink*), or states (e.g.
*to love*). But what is common to each is that a 'process' is being
described: something that has an essential temporal contour.[15]
This reveals the following: the grammatical essence of the fundamental word classes of the world's languages – nouns and verbs –
is a direct reflex of corresponding fundamental domains of
human experience: space and time.

Another way in which grammar is informed by perceptual
experience concerns attention – the degree to which an entity is
experienced with greater – or lesser – prominence or salience. In
visual scenes, psychologists have long noted a distinction between
a 'figure' and 'ground' – the figure standing out from the ground,
as exemplified by Figure 5.1, in which an image of a lighthouse
stands out.

The linguist Ronald Langacker has observed that the grammatical subject and object in a sentence encode a distinction in terms
of the attentional resources that grammar applies to the

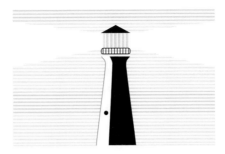

**Figure 5.1.** Figure/ground segregation in visual perception (after Evans and Green 2006)

participants in a sentence.[16] For instance, in a situation in which an agent carries out an action on another entity, the 'agent' – the doer of the action – or the 'patient' – the entity that *suffers* the action – can have greater (or lesser) attention focused upon them. Consider, for instance, the distinction in the following sentences. The first involves 'active voice' – where the agent is in subject position. In the second – which involves 'passive voice' – the patient is in subject position:

| | |
|---|---|
| Jim built the computer from spare parts. | [agent in subject position] |
| The computer was built by Jim from spare parts. | [patient in subject position] |

The difference between the two relates to the relative prominence given to the agent versus patient. In the first sentence, the agent receives greater prominence by virtue of being placed in subject position. But, in the second, the focus is on Jim's object of creation, the computer. And greater attentional prominence is achieved as the first slot in a sentence (akin to the figure) is reserved, in many languages, for the subject of the sentence: the slot which is processed first typically has greatest salience.

Another leading linguist, Leonard Talmy, has pointed out that the grammatical structure of language additionally provides resources to focus attention on different aspects of a complex event. This he describes as the ability to focus or 'window' attention on sub-parts of an event.

Imagine a scenario in which a plant pot falls off a window ledge and down onto the street below, smashing into smithereens on the tarmac. The entire trajectory of the falling plant pot might be described as follows: *The plant pot fell off the windowsill, through the air and onto the tarmac.* Sentences in a language are constructed from grammatical clauses, which can be combined in order to selectively window attention. The trajectory of the falling plant pot could be described by selecting different clauses as follows – I've placed the relevant clauses in brackets, in order to highlight them:

| | |
|---|---|
| The plant pot fell [off the windowsill]. | Initial windowing |
| The plant pot fell [through the air]. | Medial windowing |
| The plant pot fell [onto the street]. | Final windowing |
| The plant pot fell [through the air] and [onto the tarmac]. | Medial and final windowing |

This ability to window attention in language allows us to attend to different aspects of an event sequence, changing the focus of our attention and hence privileging particular aspects of the event sequence over others. Hence, we can foreground certain aspects (the figure) and make others less prominent (the ground).

While attention relates primarily to visual experience, grammar also encodes perceptual reflexes of kinaesthesia – our bodily experience of muscular effort and motion – and somesthesia – our bodily experience of sensations such as pressure and pain. In short, grammatical structure encodes force relations. Consider the following examples:

The ball <u>was rolling</u> along the beach.
The ball <u>kept rolling</u> along the beach.[17]

These sentences highlight our grammatical means of signalling physical force (the underlined expressions). In the first example, the sentence is neutral with respect to force: while something must have caused the ball to roll, this is not mentioned in the sentence. In contrast, the use of *keep* + VERB in the second conveys a scene in which we understand that the ball's natural tendency towards rest is overcome by some external force. This might be the wind, which ensures that the ball remains in motion – or it could be something else. Verbs like *be* and *keep*, in these examples, are known as 'auxiliaries' – they modify the meaning of the main verb, in this case: *roll*. And in so doing, they provide distinct ways of understanding force dynamics across these two sentences.

As a further example of the way in which embodied experience enters into grammar, consider the notion of spatial perspective. Any scene is viewed from a specific perspective: a consequence of where we are located when viewing the scene. Talmy points out that even perspective is encoded in the grammar of a language. To see how, consider the following examples, and determine where the viewer must be located:

> The door slowly opened and the man walked in.
> The man slowly opened the door and walked in.

In the first example, you, the viewer, are located inside the room, while in the second you are located outside the room. How do you know this? After all, both sentences use exactly the same words. The only difference is the word order. But word order, part of the grammar of a language, provides us with a lot of – albeit schematic – information, including, in this case, the perspective from which the scene is being viewed. In the first sentence, the subject of the sentence is *the door*. As a door is not an agent – an entity that can perform an action, unlike, for instance, Jim, who created a computer out of spare parts – this particular subject selects a verb, *to open*, which doesn't require an object. Linguists refer to subjects that can't perform actions, but are rather the subject of them, as the 'theme' of the sentence. In this sentence, *opened* is something that happens to the door, rather than *the door* doing the opening to something else. In contrast, in the second sentence, the subject of the sentence is *the man*. This entity is an agent, and selects a verb with an object, *the door*, which undergoes the action of being opened by the man.

But why should changing the grammatical structure of the sentence in this way affect our interpretation of where the scene is being viewed from? The reason is that grammar can be, and often is, iconic: what comes first in the sentence iconically represents what is viewed first in a scene – word order, here, reflects the sequence of real-world events, at least from the vantage of a specific perspective point. The subject of the sentence corresponds to what is viewed first by the speaker/narrator, and this provides us with the necessary clue to reconstruct the perspective point. In the first sentence, the agent of the action is not mentioned, which implies that the agent is not visible, consistent with a vantage point inside the room. In the second sentence, in contrast, the action of the agent is recorded, implying it is visible, which is consistent with a vantage point outside the room.

## Concepts body forth

Thus far we've seen that grammar directly embeds embodied experiences in its very make-up. Experiences relating to time, space, attention, force dynamics and perspective point give language its scaffolding. Words are then draped across this embodied grammatical framework in order to produce meaning. But what of words themselves, and in particular, the concepts they convey? Might these be embodied too? The computational view of mind doesn't think so. Concepts are abstract, disembodied symbols. But the evidence from language would seem to suggest an alternative – an embodied perspective: concepts are constituted of the very experiences that give rise to them.

Let's consider what the difference is between the two views. Take the example of the experience of dogs. The embodied view assumes, when we perceive and interact with dogs, that this leads to extraction of perceptual and functional attributes of dogs. This information is stored in memory as an approximate replica of a dog: our concept for Dog closely resembles our perception and experience of a dog. When we imagine a dog, this is made possible by re-activating the stored perceptual experience of a dog. This perceptual experience will include information about what a dog

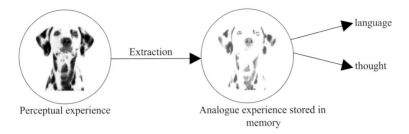

Figure 5.2. Embodied conceptual system

looks and sounds like; what it feels like, for instance, when we pet and otherwise interact with the dog; and how the dog's murmured yowl of contentment makes us feel – satisfaction, pleasure, and so on. All these body-based experiences directly constitute our mental representation for Dog. When we invoke this concept, either by thinking about a dog or by using language, aspects of this stored mental representation become re-activated. But this 'simulated' dog is not quite the same as the dog you saw across the road, on your way to work, or even your pet dog: it is somewhat attenuated in detail. Just as imagining a lover's absent face is not quite as vivid as actually seeing your lover, so the same distinction holds between concepts of things and actually perceiving them. Appropriating the words of William James, embodied concepts are 'devoid of pungency and tang' compared to the experiences they are representations of. This view of concepts is captured in Figure 5.2.

In contrast, in the disembodied theory of concepts, perception is a qualitatively different type of process from conception. When we perceive a dog, the information is re-described into a symbol, which stands for the perceptual experience. In some disembodied theories of concepts, the symbols are represented using natural language: the symbols are thought to be composed of lists of features or attributes. But whatever notation is used, all disembodied theories of concepts assume that the symbol standing for an experience or idea is quite unlike the thing it represents.[18] Figure 5.3 captures the disembodied notion of concepts.

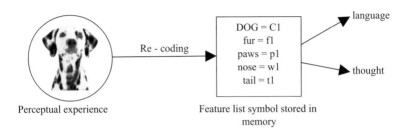

Figure 5.3. Disembodied conceptual system

But recent findings from the psychology lab, and advances in neuroimaging techniques – advances that now allow us to study the brain in action – have begun to settle the question. Given that language draws upon concepts in order to encode and externalise meaning, if concepts are embodied, we should expect to see the effects of embodiment when we use language. However, if embodied mental states play no role in the make-up of concepts, as claimed by the disembodied view, then it is less clear that embodiment should intrude into the use of language. But we now have firm evidence that embodiment intrudes into neurological processing when we use language. And this provides strong support for the view of concepts captured in Figure 5.3.

It is well established that when we perceive actions, of various sorts, these are processed in specific brain regions. For instance, different parts of the outermost layer of the brain, the cortex, are responsible for processing specific types of experience: dedicated areas of the cortex are responsible for interpreting visual, auditory and tactile experience types. Other brain regions, buried below the cortex, process other sorts of experiences. For instance, the amygdala, an evolutionarily older brain structure, is known to process emotion. Recent brain-imaging studies reveal that when subjects are exposed to language of particular types, the corresponding brain regions – regions ostensibly dedicated to processing specific genres of action – are also automatically and immediately activated. For instance, we now know that motor-processing areas of the brain are automatically activated when we use or understand an action word;[19] the amygdala becomes active when we process emotion words;[20] and visual areas of cortex are engaged when we use or understand language relating to visual experience.[21] Moreover, all these brain regions are not otherwise associated with language processing.[22] What this reveals is an embodiment effect: the concepts which language draws upon appear to derive from the self-same brain regions engaged when we perceive the action or experience. In short, perceptual experiences would seem to give rise to corresponding concepts, concepts that language then externalises. According to one leading expert, what this demonstrates is that 'language is a set of cues to the comprehender to construct an experiential – perception plus action – simulation of the described situation'.[23]

The important conclusion from this, and from the direction in which we have been heading in this chapter, is that the traditional distinction between perception and cognition – an artefact of the earlier distinction between body and mind – appears to be too strong. Representations that arise in language use and comprehension are *grounded* in exactly the same types of knowledge that the brain uses when processing our experiences of the world around us. The distinction between perception and cognition, at the very least, is not as clear-cut as some cognitive scientists have claimed. Talmy, one of the pioneering linguists who first saw that language encodes embodied concepts, proposes a unified category, what he calls 'ception'; in this way, Talmy has sought to emphasise the continuity, rather than separation, between perception and conception (or cognition).[24]

## Minds without bodies

What would a mind be like without a body? The hallmark of the human mind, so popular culture contends, is reason: our ability to engage in rational thought. And this stands in contrast to the hallmark of bodily experience: emotion. Mr Spock in *Star Trek* perhaps best exemplifies this folk model: being half-Vulcan, he exhibits a particularly pure distillation of rationality. Emotions, and other bodily distractions, make you weak, so the folk model contends. True strength comes from eliminating emotional weakness, revealing a clarity of thought that transcends petty bodily experience. Yet, while extreme emotion can indeed cloud sound judgement, the neuropsychologist Antonio Damasio has shown that emotion is central to rational thought – without embodied experience we become just as incapable of making sound decisions as when our reason is perturbed by extreme passion.[25] Reason, it turns out, is contingent on having a normally functioning body.

The physical substance that produces the mind is the brain. In evolutionary terms, bodies came first, and brains later. In fact, brainless organisms continue to co-exist and significantly outnumber organisms with brains. The bacteria *E.Coli* that dwell within us are a case in point. And as brained organisms acquired greater complexity, actions caused by brains required more intermediate processing, leading to greater complexity. One consequence of this is that greater complexity has led, in humans, to bigger brains: about three times bigger than we should have for our body size compared with other mammals.[26]

The brain is the organ which forms the centre of the human nervous system. It consists of two halves known as cerebral hemispheres. Each of these hemispheres has an outer layer of grey matter, the cerebral cortex. This outer cortical area is supported by an inner layer of white matter. The two hemispheres are linked by a large bundle of nerve fibres called the corpus callosum. The corpus callosum transfers information between the two hemispheres. The brain monitors and regulates the body's actions and reactions. It continuously receives sensory information, and rapidly analyses this data before responding. Hence, the body and the brain are indissociably linked, with two principal routes of interconnection. The sensory and motor peripheral nerves carry signals from all parts of the body to the brain, and vice versa. The other route, far older in evolutionary terms, is the bloodstream. It conveys chemical signals, including hormones and neurotransmitters. The

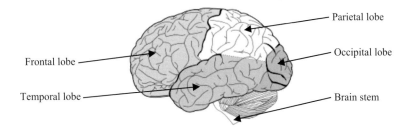

Figure 5.4. The lobes of the human cerebral cortex

consequence of this inseparable link is that the brain and body work together as an ensemble, allowing the brain–body coupling to act and interact with the environment as one.

The oldest part of the brain, for the most part buried below the surface, in sub-cortical regions, is the limbic system. It developed to manage 'fight or flight' chemicals, and is evident in the brains of reptiles and mammals alike. Some of the key structures in the limbic system of the human brain include the amygdala, which I mentioned earlier – important in the processing of fear and reward, as well as mating behaviour; the hippocampus, which is implicated in cognitive maps for navigation; the cingulate gyrus, which regulates our heart rate and blood pressure; and the hypothalamus, which, through hormone production and release, is involved in regulating hunger, thirst, sexual arousal and the wake–sleep cycle.

The most recent part of the brain to have evolved is a layer of neural tissue at the top of the brain. This area is known as the neocortex – *neo* meaning new – and makes up around 90 per cent of the brain's grey matter: the cerebral cortex. The cerebral cortex can be divided into lobes (see Figure 5.4). The characteristic grooved nature of the brain comes from the many folds, known as sulcci, that characterise the brain's cortex. In humans, the frontal lobe in particular has undergone significant expansion. This is the area of neocortex which is associated with the so-called executive functions of the brain such as reasoning, decision-making, planning and abstract thought.

In the course of his work, Damasio came across patients who, whether due to stroke, trauma or a tumour which required surgical resection, all lost, in a tumultuous development, the ability to make rational decisions. And in a parallel development, they lost the ability to feel a particular class of emotions. Damasio demonstrated, through careful observations, clinical tests and use of brain-imaging techniques, that there is a specific region of the brain which processes a class of body-based emotions. This was the area that had been irrevocably damaged in all the patients Damasio studied. And, crucially, these emotions facilitate decision-making in the personal and social sphere. Losing the ability to feel a certain class of emotions compromised their ability to reason effectively, and to lead normal lives.

One of Damasio's patients was a man named Elliot. Elliot had been diagnosed with a brain tumour which attained the size of a small orange. While surgery was successful, in that it saved Elliott's life, the removal and resection of the brain area affected resulted in damage to the ventromedial region in both the left and right prefrontal cortices, as confirmed by brain-imaging scans. Before the operation, Elliot had been a good husband and father, with a successful business career. But afterwards, he appeared to have undergone a personality change. As he recovered from the operation, a different Elliot emerged. While he still possessed the same business and social knowledge as before, Elliot needed prompting to get off to work in the morning. And when at work he became absorbed in the minute of the tasks he was engaged in. He was unable to complete a given task, continually becoming sidetracked. And worse, he was unable to decide between options, rendering decision-making nigh on impossible. When he did manage to decide between options, he often made very poor choices. Unable to function effectively, he lost his job. He then unwisely invested all his money in an ill-advised business scheme which ended in bankruptcy. His wife divorced him, and a second marriage ended in divorce. When Damasio first encountered Elliot he was in his thirties, living on a disability allowance in the custody of a sibling: a far cry from is former life.[27]

Following clinical tests, Damasio concluded that Elliot retained normal intellect: he could reason and think effectively in domains concerning objects, space, numbers and words. His intellect, social knowledge, basic working memory, attentional capacities and language were all intact. Damasio observed that, to interact with him on a casual basis, you wouldn't know anything was amiss. And yet, Elliot was no longer capable of succeeding as an independent human being. He *could still* predict the likely outcome of particular social situations: he retained records of social knowledge. Yet, he *couldn't* effectively make decisions: he might choose badly, or not at all.

Elliot's difficulty in making decisions appeared to relate to the personal and social sphere, particularly in situations involving risk and conflict. Family and friends could pinpoint a *before* and *after* – there appeared to be a distinct change which coincided with the growth of the tumour, and its subsequent removal. Damasio also found that, coincident with his inability to make effective decisions, Elliot lacked an ability to resonate emotionally in exactly those same situations in which he now lacked the ability to make decisions. A striking finding to emerge from Damasio's observations of Elliot was this: while he was aware of the events that had led to the tragedy that had befallen him, and could recount them, he was not pained by them. And perhaps startlingly, Elliot was aware that such events would have previously evoked strong feelings. Elliot's predicament was 'to know but not to feel'.[28]

But what accounts for the parallel loss of sound decision-making abilities – a fundamental aspect of reason – and emotional experience? Elliot, and others with a similar deficit in reasoning, had all suffered damage to the brain area that both processes rational decision-making and, as it turns out, processes secondary emotion – the ventromedial region of the prefrontal cortices.

Primary (or basic) emotions represent a collection of innate responses when certain features in external stimuli, or in our bodies, are perceived. Primary emotions are thus involuntary responses, which are initiated by the limbic system. They result in the enactment of a body state, characteristic of a particular emotion such as fear or anger. The body state enacted consists of a collection of events which affects the overall body state.[29]

For instance, when encountering a potential predator we may experience fear. This is enacted by the adrenal gland releasing adrenaline into the bloodstream. This increases the heart rate, and dilates blood vessels and air passages. In turn, this allows more blood to get to the muscles and more oxygen to the lungs. In dangerous or unexpected situations this can facilitate an increase in physical performance for short bursts of time, facilitating fight-or-flight behaviours. Other aspects of the body's enactment of an emotion can include facial displays, such as baring one's teeth in a display of anger, or a look of fear, expressions that we all instantly recognise.

As the body and brain are indissociably linked, the state enacted by the body is detected by other regions of the brain. This body state is then subject to cognitive processing: motor commands are issued so that we take flight or conceal ourselves, as appropriate, relative to the danger we have detected. To distinguish between the body state being enacted – the 'emotion' – and our conscious awareness of the body state – the pounding heart, our gut contracting, and so on – Damasio refers to the latter as a 'feeling'. Hence, a feeling is the conscious awareness of a particular emotion.

In contrast to primary emotions, which are innate, secondary emotions are acquired. Rather than being an involuntary response to a particular stimulus, they are learned responses to particular people, events and situations, and are based on our individual experience.[30] For instance, due to schooling, education, socialisation and culture, we may acquire particular types of secondary emotional responses to particular individuals and situations. This acquired emotional response emerges, initially, from punishment and reward, our awareness of aesthetic values associated with particular experiences – for example a particular melody, or poem, and so on – as we develop from infancy across the life-span.

Interestingly, Damasio's patients were not immune to feeling primary emotions. Upon hearing an unexpected noise from behind they start with fear, like you or me. Yet, they are unable to feel the range of secondary emotions: love, submission, disappointment, awe, and so on – experiences that you and I take for granted. How, then, can we account for the parallel loss of the ability to reason effectively in the social and personal sphere and the absence of this class of emotional experience?

Damasio realised that secondary emotions are crucial for decision-making. When we are faced with a particular decision in the social sphere – for instance, whether to do business with someone who is the arch-enemy of our best friend – the scenario entails a number of possible outcomes. In this hypothetical situation, one likely outcome might be the loss of our best friend. This imagined outcome triggers one or more secondary emotions: various body states mediated by the limbic system. And the negative body states enacted – guilt, loss and so on – are associated with the possible outcome of the scenario. The real body states enacted by this hypothetical outcome become, then, available to our conscious awareness as a feeling.

Furthermore, the feelings based on these secondary emotions *mark* the hypothetical outcome, providing it with a value. The negative value which marks the outcome may lead to our decision not to proceed with doing business with our best friend's arch-enemy. In short, Damasio suggests that an important function of the ventromedial region of the prefrontal cortices is the following. It marks the situations and scenarios that come to mind when making decisions. Moreover, the value that does the 'marking' is the awareness of a secondary emotion, which is, of course, based on a given body state.

This thesis he calls the Somatic Marker Hypothesis – *soma* being the Greek for body. In a cognitively normal person, a body state arising from a secondary emotion becomes associated, in the brain, with an idea or scenario generated when we make decisions. For instance, the emotional response (body state) that accompanies a particular hypothetical scenario – such as doing business with our best friend's arch-enemy – marks the hypothetical scenario with a negative emotional value. We then use this value, which informs our decision-making process: don't do business with your best friend's arch-enemy, unless you want to lose the friendship of your friend.

In the case of Damasio's unfortunate patients, damage to the ventromedial region impaired their ability to generate secondary emotions and associate them with potential scenarios when making decisions. In short, while they could still generate potential scenarios and outcomes when reasoning, they could no longer mark these outcomes with a quality of goodness, or badness, or pleasure and pain, based on body states. The startling claim associated with this hypothesis is that our body states – whether we feel positive emotions such as optimism, love or awe, or negative emotions such as disappointment, contempt or aggression – can influence, and indeed are central to, our ability to reason in the social and personal sphere.

While decision-making is often regarded as a dispassionate exercise, in which we apply principles of reason, Damasio's conclusion is that without access to a certain class of body-based emotional states, reason fails – or, at least, is seriously impaired. There appears to be a region of the brain which brings together decision-making abilities with a class of emotions. When this region is damaged, patients are no longer able to produce these emotions, consequently impairing their ability to make sound decisions. To be sure, establishing somatic markers – the emotional traces important for reasoning – is not all there is to decision-making. But as Damasio points out, they are essential for restricting the range of possible choices. Without the ability to feel certain types of body-based emotional states, decision-making can become seriously compromised.

## Laying the ghost to rest

Descartes' error was to assume that thought, the substrate of an immaterial soul, has priority over the body, and bodily experience. Much research in cognitive science over the past fifty years or so has compounded this mistake by re-imagining cognition as computations based on abstract symbols, symbols which are not grounded in embodied experience. But the weight of evidence now points to a compellingly different conclusion. When we use language, we are automatically and immediately activating body-based representations. And the symbolic nature of language is itself grounded in embodied states: the schematic meanings directly encoded by the grammar of a language are abstractions derived from embodied states. The human mind is continuous with the human body.

In the final analysis, in accounting for concepts – the bedrock of human thought – we don't need to appeal to magic: the concepts were there to begin with. Rather, concepts, and our conceptual basis for meaning, arise from the nature of the bodies we have, from our emotional states and from our perceptual apparatus. They arise, naturally, as we act and interact in our everyday socio-physical whirl of encounters, with objects, people and the maelstrom of everyday experience. And that should not surprise us.

# Chapter 6     The concept-making engine (or how to build a baby)

In the previous chapter, I presented the case for thinking that concepts arise from embodied experience. But this raises the question: *how*, exactly, do concepts arise in the first place? How do we turn our everyday embodied encounters into concepts? And how does this enable a young infant to begin the slow process towards first comprehending the world, and later developing the sophisticated capacity to *mean* that you and I take for granted? Language, again, illuminates the challenge. The philosopher Mark Johnson,[1] in discussing the concept of containment, describes the start of an ordinary day:

> You wake *out of* a deep sleep and peer *out from* beneath the covers *into* your room. You gradually emerge *out of* your stupor, pull yourself *out from* under the covers, climb *into* your robe, stretch *out* your limbs, and walk *in* a daze *out* of the bedroom and *into* the bathroom. You look *in* the mirror and see your face staring *out* at you. You reach *into* the medicine cabinet, take *out* the toothpaste, squeeze *out* some toothpaste, put the toothbrush *into* your mouth, brush your teeth *in* a hurry, and rinse *out* your mouth.

The recurrent use of the expressions *in* and *out* in this passage – which I've highlighted in italics – reveals something quite striking. A great number of everyday objects and experiences are categorised as specific instances of the schematic concept container: not only obvious containers such as bathroom cabinets and toothpaste tubes, but also less obvious *containers* such as bed-covers, clothing and rooms, and even states such as sleep, stupor and daze.

This reveals that spatial information appears to form the bedrock of many of our everyday concepts. While it is perhaps obvious that we should conceptualise a bathroom cabinet as a container, it is less clear that more abstract concepts like being in a state of sleep can also be thought of, at least in part, as a container. But this is exactly what our everyday language suggests. In Chapter 3, I showed how conceptual metaphor enables abstract concepts to be structured in terms of more concrete sensory–motor experiences. And in this way the human conceptual system is enriched, facilitating, in part, the full panoply of concepts upon which language depends, and which we take for granted in our daily lives and encounters.

But in this chapter I want to ask, and answer, a slightly different question. Where do our early concepts come from? How do babies and young infants, individuals yet without the symbolic power of language, construct their earliest concepts from their initial interactions with their world of experience? And what do these early concepts look like?

## How to build a baby

Children start building a repertoire of simple concepts almost from birth: very young infants are interpreters of the world from the get-go. The developmental psychologist Jean Mandler has shown that even newborn babies – infants who cannot yet act upon the world – are nevertheless perceiving and construing it.[2] And their conceptualisation of objects around them is 'already on the march, perhaps even earlier than 3 months of age.'[3]

A child's earliest representations take the form of 'schemas': relatively sketchy concepts that derive from a child's experience of perceiving the world in motion. A baby, in its first month or so of life, has limited visual acuity: objects are fuzzy and fleeting, the details blurred. And so, what a child perceives is the nature of the motion that a given object undergoes. While some of the child's key landmarks, like caregivers, pets and so on, undergo volitional motion – parents move about in the child's perceptual space voluntarily – others, such as a mobile on a crib, must be physically manipulated to creep around in a slow pendulum of motion. And this, as we shall see, gives rise to a baby's first inkling of the distinction between biological and non-biological motion: the type of motion that distinguishes the streak of the startled pet cat on hearing baby's wail from the jerky, mechanical motion of the mobile on baby's crib.

So how do small children form their rudimentary concepts? It turns out that infants, not yet capable of language, nevertheless make use of the perceptual cues available to them – for instance, the difference between the types of motion exhibited by a toy versus a parent. And this allows them to begin to build a store of meanings or simple concepts. These early concepts are descriptions of what is taking place in the quotidian scenes that a small child witnesses and is party to – a baby is dressed and undressed, has its nappy changed and is fed. Caregivers interact with the child – the child is touched, held, kissed and spoken to by faces that come and go, peering into its squinting eyes.

Early concepts include things like Self-motion and Containment. The concept of a Container, for instance, involves understanding more than simple perceptual details of the geometric make-up of a box. It also involves knowing that a container has an inside and an outside. But more than this, it involves understanding the force-dynamic properties that containers afford.

When I, an adult, carry a cup of coffee, the coffee self-evidently moves with the cup. The coffee cup – to me – is more than a mere assemblage of geometric perceptual relations. It is something that has a particular function, entailed by its geometry, to be sure. But it constrains and controls the whereabouts of the coffee, allowing me to bring it to my lips to take a sip. What this reveals is that for something to go beyond the merely perceptual, to be a concept, we must understand the functional consequences of the entity, as we interact with it in everyday encounters – and while babies self-evidently have little experience of coffee cups, it's nevertheless this sort of information they perceive and ascribe to containers: their milk bottle, toy boxes and a host of other containers they come to perceive and interact with.

**Figure 6.1.** A bottle or a bulb? (adapted from Tyler and Evans 2003)

This idea – of the functional consequence of containment – has been strikingly illustrated by the Belgian linguist Claude Vandeloise. Consider the image in Figure 6.1. Vandeloise observed that this image, in principle, could represent either the relationship between a bottle and a cap or a light-bulb hanging from the ceiling:

But while we can say: *The bulb is in the socket,* to describe this image, it sounds decidedly odd to say: ?*The bottle is in the cap* (linguists use a preceding question mark to indicate that a sentence is semantically odd, as in the case of this sentence). So, why does one sentence sound fine, while the other is plain weird?

The relevant factor here is force dynamics: '[W]hile the socket exerts a force on the bulb and determines its position, the opposite occurs with the cap and the bottle'.[4] Not only is the position and the successful function of the bulb dependent on being *in* – which is to say, partially contained by – the socket; the socket also prevents the bulb from succumbing to the force of gravity and falling to the ground. In contrast, the successful functioning of the bottle is not contingent on being *in* the cap: the bottle holds the fluid irrespective of whether it is *in* the cap or not.

This demonstrates that our understanding of containment concerns more than simply a geometric relationship between one entity – the container – and the thing contained. More than this, we understand that spatial relationships have consequences: consequences central to the way we interact with containers and the entities they contain. A container constrains, in various ways, the objects it contains. For instance, both a prison cell and a jeweller's safe are examples of containers *par excellence*. Not only do they restrict the location of the entities they contain, but they do so in specific ways: a prison cell deprives an inmate of his or her freedom, while a jeweller's safe prevents the potential theft of the valuable asset inside.

What very young infants appear to do, then, is understand the significance, and, hence, meaning, of the sensory–motor displays they can initially only observe, and later interact with. And in so doing, they perceive humanly relevant consequences – meaning – `in the spatial displays to which they are exposed[5].

So how does a baby's mind get built? How do young infants come by their earliest concepts? Young children appear to re-describe their earliest sensorimotor experiences – experiences of things moving by and past them, of being touched, held, carried, having their nappies changed – from their earliest days of life. Mandler refers to these early concepts, like the notion of containment, as 'image-schemas'. A child's first concepts are schematic, in the sense that a baby is able to abstract away from specific figural details and begin to understand the function that similar objects enable. For instance, a milk bottle and a box are very different: not just in terms of the materials they are made from, but also their dimensions, shape and the sorts of things they habitually contain. But what is common to both is that they locate entities, fixing them in space: the entities contained – baby's milk, toys, or whatever – are supported, transported and so on, by virtue of being contained by a bottle or a box.

In addition to being a schematic notion, an image-schema is imagistic – not in the sense of being a visual image, but rather, early concepts involve perceiving the common functional properties of related objects – both a bottle and a box fix their contents in space. And these functional properties are recorded, in the baby's conceptual system, as something meaningful. In this sense, then, the notion of 'image' refers to the sensory–motor properties common to all entities that might be construed as containers. In short, Mandler's claim is that a child's earliest concepts are both highly schematic *and* imagistic: they arise from a baby re-describing common aspects of spatial displays into a rudimentary theory of the object's function.

A child's first concepts – image-schemas – allow the child to begin to develop a rudimentary conceptual system. Moreover, these early concepts slowly become accessible to conscious thought. They structure and give meaning to the spatial displays the child perceives in everyday encounters and interactions. With the Container image-schema, a child is able to begin, slowly, to identify instances of containers. From as early as two and a half months after birth, human infants already understand that for something to fit into a container there must be an opening, and that the entity contained moves with the container.[6] Later in the child's cognitive development, image-schemas provide the underlying meanings upon which more complex concepts are built. And in time, they undergird the concepts onto which language is mapped, beginning from around a child's first birthday.[7]

## The anatomy of an image-schema

The notion of an image-schema was developed by the philosopher Mark Johnson in his now classic book, *The Body in the Mind*. Johnson proposed that the fundamental way in which embodied experience manifests itself in our conceptual systems is in terms of image-schemas. As these are central to the development of the human conceptual system, I now want to explore some of their defining characteristics.[8]

For one thing, image-schemas are pre-conceptual in origin: they arise prior to the existence of other concepts; hence they

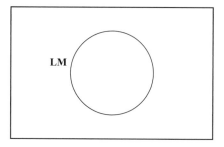

**Figure 6.2.** Bounded Landmark image-schema

are, or are among, our earliest concepts – infants don't need any concepts at all to develop image-schemas. Image-schemas include rudimentary concepts such as Contact, Container and Balance. These sorts of concepts are meaningful because they derive from and are linked to our earliest sensory–motor interactions: the baby sees a tall tower of blocks wobble and fall over. In time, as it begins to crawl, and tries to stand, it gradually learns how to maintain an upright stance, often falling over in the process. And so, a child's emerging concept of Balance arises from its direct experience of the world: a child's world is structured, and directly mediated, by the human body. What this means is that image-schemas are concepts, but of a special kind: they are foundational for the emerging conceptual system. Nevertheless, they are a far cry from the rich ideas we come to represent, later, in our minds; but of course, babies have to start somewhere.

So, let's look at an image-schema in more detail. We might represent our rudimentary containment concept – what I'll call the Bounded Landmark image-schema – as in Figure 6.2. This image-schema consists of the structural elements interior, bound-ary and exterior.[9] The 'landmark' (LM), represented by the circle, consists of two structural elements: the interior – the area within the boundary – and the boundary itself. The exterior is the area outside the landmark, contained within the square. The container is represented as the landmark because the boundary and the interior together possess sufficient structural properties – e.g. closure and continuity – to make it stand out from the area

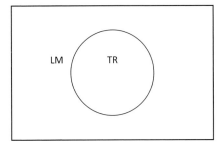

**Figure 6.3.** Container image-schema

outside the boundary – the exterior – which doesn't count as part of the space inside the boundary.

But the Bounded Landmark schema is not a container – not quite. For that, it must work in conjunction with an entity that can move around in space, a 'trajector' (TR). Together, the landmark and trajector give rise to the more complex Container image-schema (see Figure 6.3). What makes something a container, then, is that it can contain and actively support another entity. As with baby's bottle of milk, milk moves wherever the bottle goes: the location of the milk is contingent on the bottle which contains it.

Although Figure 6.3 now captures the basic Container schema – the trajector is enclosed by the bounded landmark – there are a number of further image-schemas that it gives rise to. And these become evident through language. When infants begin to acquire language, image-schemas provide the conceptual basis for word meanings. Spatial words like *in, into, out, out of* and *out from* all relate to the Container schema: an abstract image-schematic concept that underlies all these much more specific spatial meanings.[10]

For instance, one variant of the Container schema underpins our spatial use of the English expression *out of*, as in: *Jim went out of the room*. The moving entity, the trajector, is Jim. And the landmark is the room. This is captured in Figure 6.4. Here, Jim undergoes motion so that he comes to be located on the exterior portion – *outside* – the room.

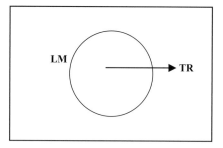

**Figure 6.4.** Image-schema for *go out of*

The image-schema in Figure 6.4 is both more specific and more detailed than the image-schema in Figure 6.2: it involves motion as well as containment. This shows that image-schemas can possess varying degrees of schematicity, where more specific image-schemas arise from more fundamental or schematic ones. In this case, the image-schema for a Path of Motion is integrated with the basic Container image-schema. And their intersection gives rise to the Go Out Of schema.

Another feature of image-schemas is that they derive from our interaction with the world around us. For instance, the image-schema for Force arises from the way in which we act upon other entities – the young infant attempting to lift an object that's too heavy – or our experiences of being acted upon – as when a door closes unexpectedly, knocking the child over. Johnson explains:

> [F]orce is always experienced through interaction. We become aware of force as it affects us or some object in our perceptual field. When you enter an unfamiliar dark room and bump into the edge of the table, you are experiencing the interactional character of force. When you eat too much the ingested food presses outwards on your taughtly stretched stomach. There is no schema for force that does not involve interaction or potential interaction.[11]

There may be as many as seven different types of rudimentary Force schemas that emerge relatively early in life. I have diagrammed these below.[12] In each of the figures, the small dark

Figure 6.5. Compulsion image-schema

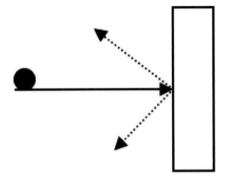

Figure 6.6. Blockage image-schema

circle represents the source of the force, while the square represents an obstruction of some kind. An unbroken arrow represents the force vector – the course taken by the force – while a broken arrow represents a potential force vector.

The first is the Compulsion image-schema (Figure 6.5). This emerges from the experience of being moved by an external force. Think of a small child being pushed along helplessly in a large, dense crowd of older children on its first day at nursery school, or being blown along in a very strong wind, going home after school. These are the sorts of experiences from which this image-schema is constructed. In Figure 6.5, the dense crowd (the black circle), forces the hapless child (the square) to follow the path indicated by the dashed arrow.

The second force-related image-schema is Blockage (Figure 6.6). This derives from encounters in which obstacles resist force: for example, when a running child can't stop in time, and collides with a table. In Figure 6.6, the table (the oblong) represents an impassable force that the young child (the dark circle) bounces off, as indicated by the dashed arrows.

**Figure 6.7.** Counter-force image-schema

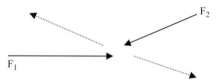

**Figure 6.8.** Diversion image-schema

The third is the Counter-force image-schema (Figure 6.7). This arises from the experience of two entities meeting with equal force. Imagine a child bumping into another on the playground: F1 and F2 represent the two counterforces.

Next up, we have the Diversion schema (Figure 6.8). When one entity in motion meets another; this can often lead to diversion. A young child, paddling in the sea with its parents, might experience the gentle pull of the current. As it wades through the breakers, it feels the current's tug, pulling it away from the course it attempts to make back to the beach. In this sort of experience, which I recollect vividly from my own childhood, the child is gradually pushed further along the shoreline than it intended. Again, F1 and F2 represent the two counterforces.

Figure 6.9 diagrams the Removal of Restraint schema. This concerns situations in which an obstruction to force is removed, allowing the energy to be suddenly released. For instance, imagine a young child leaning on a door: the door suddenly opens, and the child falls inwards into the adjacent room. In this diagram, the child leaning on the door (dark circle) suddenly finds that its opening leads to it being unceremoniously dumped on its bottom. This trajectory is indicated by the dashed arrow.

The sixth image-schema is Enablement (Figure 6.10). Johnson proposes that this arises from our sense of potential energy, or lack of it, as we perform a particular task. While most people who are fit

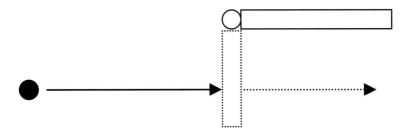

**Figure 6.9.** Removal of Restraint image-schema

**Figure 6.10.** Enablement image-schema

**Figure 6.11.** Attraction image-schema

and well feel able to pick up a bag of grocery shopping, for example, few people feel able to lift up a car. While this image-schema doesn't involve an actual force vector, it does involve a potential force vector (as indicated by the dashed arrow). A child slowly learns what its physical capabilities are through the experience of trying to lift objects that are too heavy. And so, it is this property that marks Enablement as a distinct image-schema in our minds.

Finally, the Attraction schema (Figure 6.11) emerges from experiences in which one entity is drawn towards another due to the force exerted upon it. Some of a pre-school child's earliest experiences involve observing household chores, such as Mum or Dad vacuuming the floor. A vacuum cleaner is designed to *attract* debris. And of course, young children experiment with gravity from a very young age, repeatedly dropping food, plastic spoons and whatever else lies in reach from their high-chair.

As image-schemas derive from interaction with the world, they are inherently meaningful, in the sense that embodied experiences

have predictable consequences. To return to the coffee cup
example: if you move the cup slowly up and down, or from side
to side, you expect the coffee to move with it. This is a consequence of containment: the cup exerts force-dynamic control over
the coffee. This kind of knowledge, which, admittedly, we take for
granted, is acquired as a consequence of our interaction with our
physical environment. For example, walking across a room holding a cup of coffee without spilling it actually involves highly
sophisticated motor control that we also acquire from experience.
This experience gives rise to knowledge structures that enable us
to make predictions: if we tip the coffee cup upside-down, the
coffee will pour out.

What this also reveals is that image-schemas are analogue
representations. I'm using the term 'analogue' here to capture
the idea that image-schemas take a form, in the conceptual
system, that mirrors the sensory–motor experience being represented. Because image-schemas derive from experiences of acting
and interacting in the world, they are represented as summaries of
perceptual states in our minds, and in the emerging conceptual
systems of small children. An image-schema, although schematic,
nevertheless captures the types of experiences of which it is a
representation: in this sense it is like, and so an analogue, of the
range of experiences it stands for.

But what makes an image-schema conceptual, rather than
purely perceptual in nature, is that it allows us to make predictions: we understand the humanly relevant consequences that
arise from upending our coffee cup. And as such, babies aside,
we don't actually need to experiment with upending containers to
know that this will only lead to a great big mess.

This property – that of being analogue in nature – is a defining
feature of human concepts more generally. As we saw in the
previous chapter, concepts are multimodal. And as image-
schemas derive from experiences across different modalities –
different types of sensory experiences – they are not restricted to
a particular type of sense-perception. For instance, blind people
have access to image-schemas for Containers, Paths and so on

precisely because the kinds of experiences that give rise to these sorts of concepts rely on a range of experiences, in addition to vision. These include hearing, touch, and our experience of movement and balance.

Image-schemas can also be internally complex. Often, perhaps typically, they are composed of a number of elements that can be analysed separately. For example, the Container schema, as we have seen, is a concept that consists of interior, boundary and exterior elements. It also involves an entity that can be placed or can move inside the container. The Container image-schema is accordingly a complex configuration, one that involves integrating various aspects of experience.

Another example of a complex image-schema is the Source–Path–Goal (aka Path) schema. Because a path is a means of moving from one location to another, it consists of a starting point or source, a destination or goal and a series of contiguous locations in between, which relate the source and goal. Like all complex image-schemas, the Path schema amounts to a holistic experience: it has internal structure, but it emerges to us as a coherent whole.

One consequence of its internal complexity is that we can identify different aspects of a Path schema. We saw this in the previous chapter, where I discussed the way in which different portions of the trajectory of a plant pot falling onto the street from a windowsill can be conveyed in language. And this follows because the internal elements of a holistic image-schema can be deconstructed into its component parts:

| | |
|---|---|
| The plant pot fell [off the windowsill]. | Initial windowing |
| The plant pot fell [through the air]. | Medial windowing |
| The plant pot fell [onto the tarmac]. | Final windowing |
| The plant pot fell [through the air] and [onto the tarmac]. | Medial and final windowing |

One temptation, in reflecting on image-schemas, is to think that they might be much like mental images. For instance, if you close your eyes and imagine the face of your mother or father, child, partner or lover, what you have is a mental image. Image-schemas are quite different. Mental images are detailed, and result from an effortful and partly conscious process that involves visual memory. Image-schemas are schematic, and therefore more abstract in nature. They emerge from ongoing embodied experience. This means that you can't close your eyes and *think up* an image-schema in the same way that you can *think up* the sight of someone's face, or the feeling of a particular object in your hand. But we know we must have an image-schema for Containment, as otherwise we'd be at a loss to understand the everyday spatial uses of words such as *in, out, into, out of, through*, and a host of others.

In the final analysis, image-schemas provide an important conceptual plank for more abstract thought.[13] They afford the young infant the conceptual building blocks for complex concepts. And in so doing, they provide more abstract concepts and conceptual domains with a rudimentary structure. The reason we can talk about being *in* states like love or trouble is because abstract concepts like Love are, in part, structured, and therefore understood, by virtue of the fundamental concept Container. In this way, image-schematic concepts facilitate the rise of conceptual metaphors. In our adult lives we can say *John is in love*, or *The government is in a deep crisis*. And in so doing, we import inferential structure from our early acquired knowledge of containers and containment – that they can be difficult to get out of – to help us understand more abstract ideas such as emotional states, or complex governmental scenarios, involving national finances and politics.

## The rationalist's retort

One response to all this is to cry: humbug! None of this means that concepts are constructed from birth onwards. After all, we could simply be born with the distinction between biological versus non-biological motion. And more than that, it could be the case that *all* concepts – or at least, the primitive concepts required to construct them – are innate, from Biological Motion, to the mysterious, odourless substance Phlogiston, to Doorknobs.

A particularly lurid version of this position is that defended by philosopher Jerry Fodor.[14] As we saw in the previous chapter, Fodor thinks that almost everything is innate. Fodor claims:

> Everybody's a rationalist in the long run ... Everybody accepts that primitive concepts are psychologically simple; everybody accepts that simple concepts are unlearned. What distinguishes Descartes' kind of Rationalism from say Locke's – in so far as they differ in their views about concept attainment – is an issue over how big the primitive basis actually is.[15]

Fodor is a card-carrying member of the rationalist doctrine, and he is also its high priest: he is sceptical of the human capacity for learning, and tries to pack as much as possible into our genetic make-up. Surely we don't actually learn concepts, he argues: we are born with them. Fodor believes that there must be a fairly substantial set of primitive concepts etched into the micro-circuitry of the human brain at birth. He thinks this because, without a conceptual starting point, we couldn't learn concepts to begin with. He asks: how can you learn the meaning of a concept without having prior concepts in the first place, that help you acquire the concept to be learned? And Fodor's mischief is to claim that even an arch-empiricist like Locke has to assume a rudimentary stock of concepts with which we are all born.

Fodor's idea is that we are all born with a universal language of thought: Mentalese, an idea we met in the previous chapter.[16] Fodor contends that Mentalese is our internal, private language and it is this that makes thought possible.[17] Mentalese is made up of innate concepts, he claims, that can be combined.[18]

One reason for supposing that there is such a thing as Mentalese, as I observed in *The Language Myth*, is this: we are able to think, and to draw inferences, even in the absence of spoken language – hence the language of thought must be distinct from a natural spoken language like English. Indeed, individuals who suffer brain trauma to the language areas of the brain and suffer a catastrophic loss of language can nevertheless still think and carry on functioning in an otherwise normal way: they can do arithmetic, reason, maintain friendships and can even tie their own shoe-laces. Thought, and otherwise normal functioning in the world, continues, even in the absence of language.

Being an internal 'language', Mentalese would have the equivalent of words: its symbols. But clearly, the symbols of Mentalese would have to be qualitatively different: being a language of thought, they wouldn't have sounds associated with them. And the symbols would be associated with meanings: the states, experiences and objects in the world that they represent, such as Containment, Biological Motion and even Bedknobs and Broomsticks. Moreover, the symbols would be combined using rules of mental syntax, allowing us to form complex ideas.

But what's the rationale for thinking that the mind really does come pre-installed with a ready-made set of concepts that, almost from the get-go, provides each of us with our language of thought? According to Fodor, this follows because '[t]he only psychological models of psychological processes that seem even remotely plausible represent such processes as computational'.[19] As he has famously put it, the computational mind is 'the only game in town'. And being the only game in town, it follows that thought is facilitated by a language of thought common to all human minds: a universal Mentalese.

One reason we can discount Fodor's faith in an innate stock of ready-made concepts is because the notion of the mind he assumes is wrong. As we saw in the previous chapter, concepts are not abstract symbols that provide the mind with its computational base. In fact, concepts are directly grounded in embodied states and experiences: the world is meaningful for us because of our embodied interaction with it – we have intelligent bodies that allow us to make sense of the world around us, in and through our interactions. And our embodied intelligence gives rise to bodied minds.

But a more serious problem with assuming an innate language of thought – Mentalese – is that it radically underestimates the learning capabilities of human infants. It turns out that to assume that a child's earliest concepts 'lack internal structure is not only unnecessary but also actually incorrect'.[20] Some biases clearly have to be built into the human infant's mind for it to be able to form rudimentary image-schemas. But it is quite another matter to posit that there are 'innate concepts of, say, animacy, and inanimacy, not to mention dogs and chairs'.[21]

In short, genetic space is limited. And it has way more important tasks to attend to – for instance, constructing a nervous system – than building in knowledge about dogs and chairs, 'especially since a person can live a long and successful life without encountering either of these things.'[22] It seems that key ideas, like animacy, which distinguish concepts such as Dog versus Chair can't be innate. And in the final analysis, and as I observed in Chapter 2, this sort of approach, on my assessment, is akin to the alchemy practised by Dr John Dee. It appeals to the mystical, to magic even: let there be concepts!

## Born to see structure in the world

So, what then are the inherent biases that allow us to segregate the world of perception into different sorts of stuff? What is it that enables a child to begin the process of forming concepts? The answer entails a brief tour of what is actually innate, in terms of perceptual processing, before we can return to the issue of how, exactly, perceptual experience is re-described into image-schemas.

It transpires that while image-schemas, and indeed other more complex concepts, are not innate, we nevertheless have a host of innate mechanisms that do, in fact, allow an infant to parse the slipstream of sights, sounds and physical interactions that make up the bustle of its early life. And so, it is from the child's early perceptual experiences that meaningful experiences – concepts – begin to develop.

Perhaps unsurprisingly, given the importance of the visual modality for primates in general, and humans in particular, much of the work on various aspects of spatial perception has tradition-ally focused on visual cues. So, here's a brief tour of the role of visual perception in the experience and construction of spatial 'percepts' – our sensory–motor constructions of the external world, derived from perceptual stimuli.

Before objects can be identified, visual details must be pro-cessed and integrated by the visual system. Visual scenes exhibit low-level variation. This comes from a number of sources. For instance, adjacent regions of light and dark areas of a surface allow us to discriminate light intensity; differentially oriented strands on an object's surface enable us to discriminate surface patterns; and direction of light and motion provide further cues. Visual texture, then, such as perceiving the distinction between curly versus straight hair, or a tiger's stripes versus a leopard's spots, arise from our ability to perceive contrast in light versus dark areas, colour, and other textural differences.

In addition, psychologist Béla Julesz[23] discovered that humans are hard-wired to recognise textural primitives, which he calls 'textons'. These are fundamental components of visual texture. Examples of textons include straight lines, line segments, curva-tures, widths, lengths, intersections of lines and so on. And precisely because we already expect to see textons in the percep-tual displays we experience, we have a head-start in our ability to discriminate the world around us. We can perceive curves, straight lines and so on, because our perceptual apparatus is expecting to find these sorts of geometric shapes as we gaze out into the world.

Moreover, in addition to textons, the visual psychologist Irving Biederman[24] proposes that our brains come ready-equipped to perceive basic object shapes, what he calls 'geometric icons', or 'geons' for short. Geons are simple volumes such as cubes, spheres, cylinders and wedges (see Figure 6.12). There may be as many as thirty-six primitive geons which can be combined in a range of ways, allowing us to recognise more complex objects. For instance, low-level perceptual experience – 'low-level', in this sense, means prior to a fully formed percept percolating up to

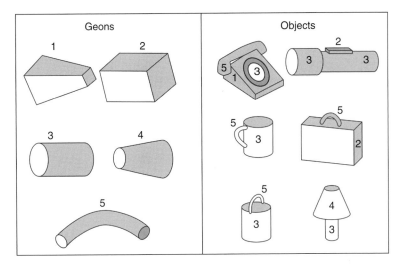

**Figure 6.12.** Geons and object recognition (after Biederman 1987; reproduced with permission).

conscious awareness – enables us to recognise a complex object, such as a desk lamp, by first perceiving the simpler geons which make it up; we notice that the lamp or coffee mug can be separated into the distinct geons which compose them. This idea is also captured in Figure 6.12.

While a baby comes ready-equipped to perceive aspects of visual texture (textons), and object shapes (geons), we are also born with higher-level biases that allow us to *see* the way objects are grouped. One such bias is our ability to perceive a figure that saliently stands out from its ground: recall that I discussed this ability to perceive figure/ground segregation in Chapter 4. Figure–ground organisation appears to be an evolutionary response to our physical environment. Our visual system has evolved in order to be able to perceive three-dimensional objects as distinct from the surrounding terrain in which they're embedded. It is, accordingly, a hard-wired response to this predictable feature of the world.

A second type of a high-level perceptual bias relates to 'gestalt grouping principles'. Gestalt psychology was a movement which

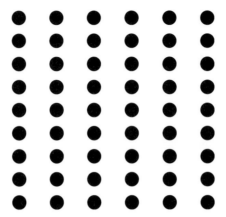

**Figure 6.13.** Column of dots

emerged in the first decades of the twentieth century. 'Gestalt' is the German term for 'form', 'shape' or 'whole configuration'. The Gestalt psychologists – Max Wertheimer, Kurt Koffka and Wolfgang Köhler – proposed a number of innate grouping principles that enable us to perceive forms. I present some of these below.[25] These principles give overall coherence to our low-level perceptual awareness of textons and geons, among other things.

For instance, the Gestalt principle of proximity (or nearness) guides how we perceive elements in a scene which are closer together: elements which are closer are perceived as belonging together as a group. This is strikingly illustrated in Figure 6.13. The consequence of the greater proximity or nearness of the dots on the vertical axis is that we strikingly perceive the dots as being organised into columns rather than rows.

If the scene is altered so that the dots are closer together on the horizontal axis, then we perceive a series of rows, as illustrated in Figure 6.14. This shows that our vivid sense of perceiving rows versus columns is not something objectively there in the world; our minds are predisposed to *group* elements in a scene that are closer together; we make sense of the world in this way because our brains take proximity as a way of recognising a meaningful distinction in information contained in the visual displays we see.

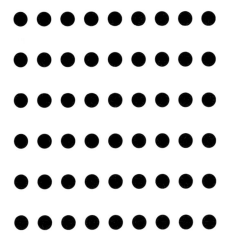

**Figure 6.14.** Rows of dots

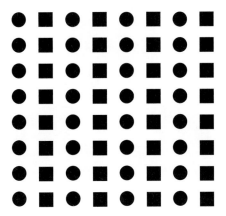

**Figure 6.15.** Columns of shapes

Another example is the principle of similarity: entities which share visual characteristics such as size, shape or colour are perceived as belonging together in a group. For example, in Figure 6.15, we strikingly perceive columns of shapes rather than rows. In fact, the shapes are equidistant on both the horizontal and vertical axes. But due to our innate predisposition to group objects based, here, on similarity, similar shapes – squares or circles – are perceived as forming distinct columns.

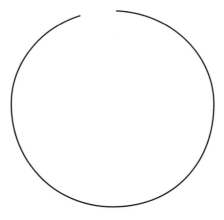

**Figure 6.16.** An incomplete figure subject to perceptual closure

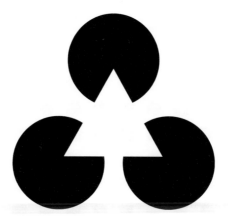

**Figure 6.17.** Subjective contour: A white triangle

A particularly interesting grouping principle is that of closure: incomplete figures are often *completed*, or *closed*, even when part of the visual information is missing. For instance, in Figure 6.16 we cannot but help perceive a circle, even though the *circle* is incomplete. This is achieved by extrapolating from information which is present to create the *missing* part of the circle.

Another, similar perceptual *trick* is illustrated in Figure 6.17: a white triangle is perceived as being overlaid on three black circles,

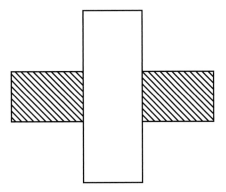

**Figure 6.18.** Two rectangles

even though the image could simply represent three incomplete circles. This gives rise to the perception of subjective contours. It resembles closure, in so far as there is the appearance of edges: but notice, what we perceive as *edges* are in fact parts of the blank area of the visual field. Yet we *do* strikingly perceive the missing edges of the triangle: it is as if we can actually *see* them.

A final example relates to the principle of good continuation, which arises from our innate preference for continuous figures. I illustrate this phenomenon in Figure 6.18. Here, we perceive two unbroken rectangles, one passing behind another, even though this is not what we actually see. In fact, the shaded rectangle is obscured by the first, so we have no direct evidence that the shaded area represents one continuous rectangle rather than two separate ones.

Innate biases also extend to our perception of motion, essential for the survival of our species as well as numerous others. Motion detection appears to have evolutionary priority over shape detection.[26] The evolution of the eye emerged in the first place in order to detect motion. In fact, only eyes relatively high up the evolutionary scale produce stimulus in the absence of motion. And moreover, the evolutionary development of vision and the detection of motion are evident in the human eye, as the visual scientist Richard Gregory explains:

> [T]he edge of our retinas are sensitive only to movement. You can
> see this by getting someone to wave an object around at the side of
> your visual field where only the edge of the retina is stimulated.
> Movement is seen, but it is impossible to identify the object, and
> there is no colour. When movement stops the object becomes
> invisible. This is as close as we can come to experiencing primitive
> vision. The extreme edge of the retina is even more primitive:
> when it is stimulated by movement we experience nothing; but a
> reflex is initiated, rotating the eye to bring the moving object into
> central vision.[27]

Our visual system involves eyes which can move in the head, as
when we keep our heads stationary and move our eyes from side
to side, or up and down. Consequently, we have two distinct ways
of detecting motion. The first involves the eyeball remaining
stationary. In this situation – for instance, when a car speeds
past – an image of the moving car runs sequentially across adjacent photoreceptors on the retina – the cells at the back of our
eyes that detect objects in motion. The perception of motion
arises, in this case, as different photoreceptors are understood by
the brain as relating to different locations in space – they form a
'topographic map', where adjacent photoreceptors correspond to
adjacent locations of the car, at different points in time.

The second method involves movement of the eyes in the
eyeball socket when we follow an object in motion. In this case,
it's not that the speeding car is running across different photoreceptors. Instead, information from the eye muscles, which
stretch in response to the movement of the eye, is understood
by the brain as relating to motion of the tracked object.

Another way in which we perceive motion arises from our
everyday motion through space: the natural consequence is that
the location from which we view our environment changes. This
leads to an ongoing change in the light stimulus we perceive. This,
which is projected onto the retina, gives rise to the phenomenon
of 'optic flow'.[28] Optic flow is the perceptual experience of a radial
pattern which arises from the observer's direction of self-motion
through the passing landscape. As we travel through the world,

and as we approach objects, they appear to move towards us, flowing past as we move beyond them. Moreover, different objects, at different points in the visual field, appear to move towards and past us at different rates. Imagine sitting on a train and travelling through the countryside. Distant objects such as clouds or mountains appear to move so slowly that they are stationary. Objects closer to us, like trees, appear to move more quickly. And objects close by, like electric cable poles at the side of the track, appear to whiz by in a blur. This motion, the optic flow pattern, provides us with important cues as to distance.

Moreover, the optic flow also varies as a consequence of the angle from which we gaze out of the window, and the direction the train is travelling in. For instance, if you're driving along a high-speed motorway, as you gaze through the windscreen, objects which are dead-ahead – and so centred in your visual field – will appear to remain stationary. In contrast, objects which are more peripheral in the visual field, such as passing trees, houses or animals grazing in a field, will appear to move more rapidly. But, because the edges of centred objects won't be in foveal vision, their edges will also have optic flow associated with them. And these patterns provide us with important information about both distance and direction of travel; optic flow is essential, not just for our ability to drive a car safely, but for any form of navigation in space.

In addition, we also have innate biases that allow us to distinguish between different types of motion: for instance, the distinction between the motion of, say, humans, and the motion of non-animate objects such as a wind-up mechanical toy.[29] Based purely on movement cues, we can quickly distinguish biological from non-biological motion. Humans, it turns out, are even adept at distinguishing between different types of biological motion based solely on movement cues – for example, running versus jogging versus walking versus jumping, and so on. We are skilled at recognising the characteristic gait of different types of motion, which we construct from their distinctive sequences of pendulum-like motions.

Evidence for this ability comes from the work of the psychologist Gunnar Johansson.[30] He videotaped actors, in complete darkness, who had points of light fixed at ten main body joints. This provided the only illumination, eliminating, in the process, all non-movement cues, such as the body contours of the actors. Human participants were then asked to identify biological motion and the motor activities engaged in by the actors. Johansson found that when the actors remained perfectly still, even with the points of light glowing, the observers failed to recognise the actors as having a human form. But remarkably, as soon as the actors began moving, the watching observers instantly recognised them as human. Moreover, subjects were even able to precisely identify the type of motion – walking, jogging, jumping and so on – and this based purely on the light display.

## The concept-making engine

These sorts of perceptual biases, biases we are all born with, allow us to see a world full of structure: we recognise objects as distinct from the landscape they are part of. And we recognise animals as distinct from inanimate entities, and caregivers and other humans as markedly distinct from the pets – cats and dogs – that inhabit our daily world. We arrive into the world pre-equipped with an ability to perceive structure in our surroundings; at birth, or soon afterwards, we are able to harvest information derived from perceptual experience of the world in order to provide our perceptual experience with structure.

But, on their own, these innate perceptual biases are not sufficient to begin to build a conceptual system, to give rise to concepts. In addition, we come pre-equipped with a very general learning ability, one that allows us to analyse perceptual representations and to transpose them into rudimentary concepts. This concept-making engine works by parsing the structured perceptual cues we experience.[31] In the process, human infants begin to form a rudimentary theory about the nature of the entity in question. By abstracting away from points of difference across different entities – for instance, the different shapes, sizes and materials associated with containers in a child's everyday world – all that remains are points of similarity. Allied to this, the commonality associated with containers is their functional relevance: containers are meaningful for us because they allow entities to be located and transported. And this information leads to a schematic representation concerning the nature of a type of entity. Thus armed with a rudimentary image-schema, the young infant is also able to make predictions about the nature of the experiences it perceives, and to begin to form expectations as a consequence.

So, let's look in a little bit more detail at how an image-schema arises from spatial experience. Take the concept of Animal, for instance. How then does the human mind, our concept-making engine, produce this idea? Infants see many examples of entities undergoing animate motion everyday, from siblings, to caregivers, to the pet cat. While the child, at least in its first month of life, isn't getting very good information about what the entities moving around them look like, it can nevertheless discriminate objects moving in space from the background of their world of experience. This is due, of course, to their ability to perform figure/ground segregation.[32] But by three months – the youngest age studied – children are able to discriminate biological motion, both people and other mammals, from non-biological motion.[33] By two months – again the earliest age studied – children recognise entities that interact with them in a reciprocal way: young infants smile at caregivers, but quickly learn not to smile at inanimate entities.[34] And between four and six months – again the earliest studied – infants are able to perceive the difference between an entity coming towards them of its own volition versus an object that moves towards them when pushed by something else.[35] What this reveals is an early awareness of a distinction between the animate versus inanimate – a deep understanding that is more than simply the ability to recognise visual aspects of a scene. By their early months of life, children seem to have an understanding of animals versus non-animals.

The concept for Animal most likely consists of combining more fundamental image-schemas: Path, Motion, Self-initiated Motion and probably others. And in so doing, a young infant is able to begin to understand that Animals are of a different type of entity from, say, a clockwork toy that cannot move without being wound up by a parent or sibling. Early concepts for Animal seem to be constructed from visual as well as other sorts of cues, well before the baby can directly interact with and manipulate the object. And all of this arises precisely because the baby perceives a world full of structure: it associates humanly relevant consequences with particular types of perceptual structure. A container supports and serves to locate an entity: babies exhibit surprise, from a young age, when a box fails to contain dolls placed in it. Even very young infants have an understanding of the function and value of containers. In short, they have, by early in life, an image-schema for Container.

We don't, therefore, need to assume that concepts must be built in. We have perceptual structuring principles that we are born with. And we come equipped with a concept-making engine that allows us to interpret these perceptual cues as meaningful, and to begin to construct abstract representations of these meaningful things. Human infants automatically abstract meaning from the cacophony of the perceptual swirl that they are born into.

## Primary scenes of experience

Many of our earliest experiences involve a host of relatively simple phenomenological feelings. A baby cuddled by its mother while being breast-fed experiences warmth; but a consequence of being warm is that the baby experiences a special bond with its mother: intimacy. And as the young child moves from being a passive observer of its environment, and begins to roll over and, in time, crawl, it begins to interact with its everyday world of experience. A young infant, beginning to take its first steps in life, learns how to coordinate its actions. In placing wooden blocks on top of others, it begins to perceive a relation between the relatively simple phenomenological experience of height and quantity: a direct consequence of a higher tower of blocks is that there are more of them.

In our adult lives we take this correlation between height – or vertical elevation – and quantity for granted. When I visit my local pub, I know that the greater the height of beer in my glass, the greater the quantity – and the happier I am! The taller pint glass contains more beer than the smaller half-pint measure. I hardly need think about it. But our understanding of these sorts of relationships, of warmth and intimacy and vertical elevation and quantity, arise early in the life.

Corresponding pairs of phenomenologically simple sets of experiences such as these have been dubbed 'primary scenes' by the linguist Joseph Grady[36]. So here's the idea. When a baby experiences warmth, cradled against its mother, a ubiquitous and re-occurring consequence is that the baby feels intimacy. Intimacy is a relatively abstract idea, of course. It isn't the same as the experience of shared body heat, not quite. For an adult, with rich life experience, intimacy is often a complicated, and sometimes even contested, notion. But, in our earliest experiences of the world, for the baby, our rudimentary experiences of intimacy arise from physical interaction with others, and especially the feeling of physical warmth. And over time, a rudimentary concept of Intimacy arises, grounded in our earliest experiences of being kept warm by a caregiver.

Grady's claim is that a great number of our early abstract concepts, concepts such as Intimacy, Quantity and so on, arise in precisely this way. They derive from primary experiential scenes, where the young infant feels a response to a phenomenologically simple experience type: the act of being warmed by a mother correlates with the baby's feeling of intimacy, of being comforted and loved.

A primary scene, then, involves a physical experience, and a subjective response to it: the act of providing warmth, and the baby's feeling of comfort or intimacy. And over time, and with experience, the child's concept of Intimacy is enriched, as it experiences a wider range of human affection. But in the beginning, abstract concepts appear to arise from sensory–motor experiences associated with primary scenes – the more concrete, sensory experience of warmth is associated with the more subjective experience of feeling intimacy.

But what's the evidence for the existence of primary scenes: correlations between a phenomenologically simple sensory–motor experience and a corresponding subjective response, as when Warmth correlates with Intimacy? Again, language provides us with a revealing vantage point. When describing two lovers who have fallen out, we say: *Those two are being really cold towards each other*. But here the word *cold* doesn't literally mean physically cold. In an example like this, we take the word *cold* to refer to emotional intimacy. Here *cold* is being used, metaphorically, to describe emotional *distance*.

In Chapter 3, I discussed what I termed 'primary' conceptual metaphors. It transpires that our earliest conceptual metaphors – those that are foundational for a welter of more abstract concepts – derive from primary scenes of experience.

I can describe one of my university students as *top of the class*. And of course, no one gets confused: no one thinks that I might mean that the student in question is somehow suspended on the ceiling. On the contrary, because we all have, in our heads, the primary conceptual metaphor, QUANTITY IS VERTICAL ELEVATION, we can use language relating to the concept of Vertical Elevation, here *top* – to designate Quantity – here the student who achieved the best numerical average on an assignment. And we do this all the time: *The price of meat has gone up*; *The stock-market is down*, and so on. Similarly, because we all have the primary metaphor INTIMACY IS WARMTH, we seemingly effortlessly understand ascriptions of being *cold* as relating to aspects of emotional *distance*.

Grady's colleague, Christopher Johnson, investigated the emergence of primary conceptual metaphors arising from primary scenes of experience in children's early acquisition of language.

In one study, Johnson investigated children's acquisition of the word *see*.[37] When a child sees that something is the case – the cat darted from the room when the child grabbed its tail in shrieked excitement – the child, inescapably, knows it to be the case that the cat has fled, as attested by its disappointed 'Ohhh!' This correlation, between seeing and knowing, gives rise to the primary conceptual metaphor: KNOWING IS SEEING. While I can bemoan the fact that we have few political leaders with vision, no one in their right mind would take me to mean that I am bemoaning the fact that too many politicians wear spectacles. A consequence of our early primary scene, in which seeing inevitably correlates with knowing, is that the primary metaphor – KNOWING IS SEEING – arises.

Johnson found that when young children begin acquiring the verb *see*, they initially appear to conflate the meanings arising from the primary scene. Initial usages of *see* encompassed both the 'visual perception' meaning, and the 'knowing' meaning. But later, as children begin to gain a better understanding of how the verb is used by their caregivers, they slowly begin to discriminate, reserving *see* for those situations involving just visual perception. What this points to is this: infants appear to map their early language acquisition onto primary scenes of experience. In the primary scene, seeing and knowing are tightly conflated. As a consequence, a child's earliest usage of the English word *see* involves both components: *seeing* and *knowing*. But only later, as the child develops a more mature linguistic system, does it begin to deconflate the two ideas, reserving *see* for visual perception.

This provides an important line of evidence that, at an early stage in a child's conceptual development, abstract concepts such as Knowing derive from an image-schematic notion such as visual Seeing. More abstract concepts arise, naturally, from the sensory–motor components of our everyday, humanly relevant scenes of experience. We are born to perceive the world. And even more than that, we are fated to make sense of it. We are embodied creatures, and our earliest concepts exhibit natural meaning, arising from our intelligent bodies.

# Chapter 7    The act of creation

In his classic work on creativity, Arthur Koestler recounts the following:

> Chamfort tells a story of a Marquis at the court of Louis XIV who, on entering his wife's boudoir and finding her in the arms of a Bishop, walked calmly to the window and went through the motions of blessing the people in the street. 'What are you doing?' cried the anguished wife. 'Monseigneur is performing my functions,' replied the Marquis, 'so I am performing his'.[1]

In this story, we might expect the Marquis, upon finding his wife in the arms of another, to react in quite a different way. We might expect anger, jealousy, rage, violence even. But, as Koestler describes, we get something unexpected:

> ... the tension mounts as the story progresses, but it never reaches its expected climax. The ascending curve is brought to an abrupt end by the Marquis' unexpected reaction, which debunks our dramatic expectations; it comes like a bolt out of the blue, which, so to speak, decapitates the logical development of the situation. The narrative acted as a channel directing the flow of emotion; when the channel is punctured the emotion gushes out like a liquid through a burst pipe; the tension is suddenly relieved and exploded in laughter.[2]

In his 1964 book, the name of which gives this chapter its title, Koestler explores the process that gives rise to imagination and creativity. The story of the Marquis involves two incompatible frames of reference: those of the celibate priest and of lovers. Yet, in the story, the two frames become interconnected; they become linked despite providing otherwise incommensurable, and even conflicting, contexts. The humour arises precisely because the

154

otherwise clashing frames intersect and inform one another. Koestler argues that this illustrates the process at the heart of the creative act. Creativity arises when an idea intersects in this way with two frames of experience. This process he refers to as 'bisociation': two distinct frames become linked or integrated in order to create novel meaning.

The commonplace view of creativity is that it is performed by an elite, rather than everyman: it arises from a superior intellect. The literary brilliance of Shakespeare, for instance, or the intellectual feats of Einstein are borne from minds that are somehow removed from the quotidian, arising among the peerless few, hewn from other-worldly material. Einstein was exceptional in a way that you or I could never be: his thought processes worked in a different way from yours or mine, so received wisdom holds. Einstein could creatively produce novel insights beyond the ken of the everyday mind.

But cognitive scientist Margaret Boden[3] has forcefully refuted such a view. Creativity – the bisociaton described by Koestler – she argues, arises from the commonplace mental operations that are part and parcel of the everyday mind. It is not that Shakespeare or Einstein or any of the other stand-out geniuses in the history of ideas have different sorts of minds. Nor are they doing radically different sorts of things when they think. The basic creative thought processes are the same. The difference lies in how they make use of the self-same creative processes that we all possess: using the ordinary to produce the extraordinary. The creative act is something common to us all: the human mind *is* the creative mind.

To illustrate, consider the following:

> Q. What do you get if you cross a kangaroo with an elephant?
> A. Holes all over Australia!

While not necessarily the world's most original joke – as evidenced, perhaps, by your groan as your read the punch-line – this particular use of language reveals something fundamental about everyday meaning-making: the act of creation. Our ability to make sense of the joke, to *get* the punch-line, comes not from language: the meaning is not there in the words themselves. Rather, understanding comes from the creative manipulation of two different bodies of knowledge: kangaroos and elephants. Moreover, the everyday, creative mind must bisociate, or integrate, aspects of these two types of knowledge. Language provides a glimpse of the underlying, dynamic cognitive operation that produces meaning: a process that integrates underlying knowledge structures in the act of creation. This process has been dubbed 'conceptual blending', the subject of this chapter.[4]

In the case of the joke, you can only *get it* by conjuring up an organism with the size of an elephant and the self-locomotional ability of a kangaroo: one that happens to live in Australia. Such an organism doesn't in fact exist. Moreover, the punch-line doesn't explicitly tell you to come up with such a creature. You created it as you read the joke. Indeed, creating this organism is the only way you can make sense of the joke.

Blending is not just the conceptual operation we make use of to produce meaning and creative thought. It is central to almost every facet of life. Once a conceptual blend has been created, making use of the bodies of knowledge, such as conceptual metaphors and image-schemas discussed in previous chapters, we can come to live inside it: blends are not only useful, they form the backdrop to our lives. And they evolve in the process.

It is estimated, that today, there are around 2.5 billion people in the world with regular access to a computer. But getting a computer to do what you want is less than straightforward. The earliest personal computers made use of a disk operating system (DOS), which required the computer user to memorise arcane codes which had to be typed in at the cursor in order to get the computer to do anything useful. Today, contemporary computers employ a desktop graphical interface system in its place. In this visual metaphor, the computer screen is treated as if it were the user's desktop, upon which objects such as documents and folders are placed. A document can be opened into a paper copy in a 'window'. And small applications, known as desktop accessories, can also be placed on the desktop and opened, such as a calculator or notepad.

But the desktop is an imaginative feat: a blend. It involves the integration or blending of a real-world desktop with a series of computer commands. And in the computer desktop blend there are elements from real-world offices that don't usually appear on desktops – these are elaborations that are unique to, and arise from, the creative act itself. In the Microsoft version of the blend, the computer desktop features a 'recycle bin' for disposing of unwanted files. In most people's experience of offices, wastepaper bins are not normally found on top of someone's desk. Perhaps stranger still, in the Apple version of the blend, the 'trash can' also serves as the means whereby disks can be ejected: the user places the icon for the CD or DVD in the trash can so that the disk can be retrieved.

For many of us, especially inveterate computer users, it might take a moment's reflection to realise just how odd it is, at least from the perspective of a conventional office, to place an item a user wishes to retrieve into the trash can. But the blend works, and works exceptionally well. It does so because it provides us with a means of making sense of how to get our PC, Chromebook or Mac computer to do what we want it to do. The computer desktop blend takes parts of our experiences of working in real offices and transposes them into a form that works for issuing computer commands. It provides us with a means of understanding how we can communicate with the computer, and in so doing reduces the complexity involved in computer use to human scale: a scale that makes, after a little practice, intuitive sense.

For seasoned computer users, the desktop computer blend seems completely natural. Many users may not have even noticed that it's a metaphor at all. Yet the blend is in fact not very old. It was first developed at the Xerox Palo Alto Research Centre, in the United States, in 1970. Its first commercial exploitation was in the Commodore 64 computer in 1983, with a trash can already featuring on the computer desktop. It was popularised by Apple Macintosh in 1984, and has subsequently been deployed by operating systems including various versions of Microsoft Windows, Linux, and a variety of Unix-like systems. Moreover, the desktop blend has been refined and has evolved. In a recent version of the Microsoft Windows desktop interface, various gadgets can appear on the desktop including a clock, a calendar and a barometer, replete with information relating to place, temperature and atmospheric conditions. And of course, with the advent of touch-based computing, the desktop blend is now under attack from the rise of apps.

Another ubiquitous example of our extraordinary creativity facilitated by blending is talking animals. Talking animals are a staple of film and fiction, from Dr Doolittle to Walt Disney. The talking donkey in the animated movie *Shrek* is a mix of irreverence and black humour, which parodies the entire fairy-tale genre. But the humour comes from the fact that Donkey, famously voiced by Eddie Murphy, is a fast-talking, wise-cracking African American donkey. At the beginning of the film, once Donkey has been sprinkled with fairy dust and rises into the air, a soldier exclaims: 'He can talk!' Donkey replies:

> That's right, fool! Now I'm a flying talking donkey! You might have seen a house fly, maybe even a super fly, but I bet you ain't never seen a donkey fly!

While we all know that animals can't actually talk, inside the Shrek film-world, we operate in the blend. In the blend, Donkey *can* talk, and we laugh and cry with him.

A final example comes from religious practice. The Eucharist, also known as Holy Communion, is practised by millions of Christian worshippers throughout the world. It is re-enacted in accordance with instructions given by Jesus at the Last Supper as recorded in several of the gospels of the New Testament. It involves the drinking of wine and breaking and eating of bread. While there are different interpretations of the significance of the Eucharist, many denominations, and especially the Catholic Church, treat the Eucharist as a sacrament: when the bread and wine are consecrated in the Eucharist, they cease to be bread and wine; they become, quite literally, the body and blood of Christ. And by consuming the bread and wine, the worshipper achieves divine grace: eating and drinking of the sacred is accompanied by Christ's soul and divinity.

But the Eucharist is a blend. The enactment involves imaginatively integrating aspects of the sacred (Jesus Christ) and the profane (the worshipper), and by integrating Christ's body and blood with bread and red wine. Only in the blend is divine grace attained. The blend provides the medium whereby the practice becomes sacrament. For the believer, by eating the sanctified bread and drinking the wine, he or she literally becomes, if only momentarily, one with the spirit of Christ.

## A cognitive iceberg

Somewhere between 75 and 90 per cent of an iceberg lies below the water line. Similarly, language provides clues as to the cognitive iceberg that underlies meaning. One of the leading proponents of blending – the contemporary account of creativity – is cognitive scientist Gilles Fauconnier. He describes the situation as follows:

> Language, as we use it, is but the tip of the iceberg of cognitive construction. As discourse unfolds, much is going on behind the scenes: New domains appear, links are forged, abstract meanings operate, internal structure emerges and spreads, viewpoint and focus keep shifting. Everyday talk and commonsense reasoning are supported by invisible, highly abstract, mental creations which ... [language] ... helps to guide, but does not by itself define.

To illustrate this cognitive iceberg, imagine a discussion between an American and a European. The topic of conversation is politics, and specifically the moral values of American versus European politicians as reflected in what is important to American and European voters respectively.

Many Europeans are puzzled by the seemingly paradoxical belief system held by some American voters, which simultaneously upholds with almost religious zeal the right to bear arms on the one hand, and, on the other, the seemingly fundamentalist commitment to the pro-life, anti-abortion lobby by many prominent American politicians. In contrast, many Americans are troubled by the perception of an often hedonistic lifestyle of some (typically male) European politicians, with high-profile cases illustrating a loose interpretation of what it means to be faithful to one's spouse. One recent example which confirms, for some Americans, this stereotype are the antics of French President François Hollande. Not only did Hollande replace the mother of his four children, Segolène Royal, with the journalist Valèrie Trierweiler, who became France's 'First Girlfriend' – Hollande and Trierweiler never married – he later allegedly had an affair with a French actress, while still with Trierweiler. Hollande was reported to have repeatedly sneaked out of the Elysèe Palace – the residence of the President of France – on the back of his bodyguard's moped, for clandestine trysts with his new paramour. But despite Hollande ditching Trierweiler, once his escapades were revealed by the press, the French electorate barely batted an eyelid.

In such a conversation, to illustrate the divergent attitudes between American and French electorates, the following remark might be uttered:

> If Bill Clinton had been President of France, then he would not have been harmed by his affair with Monica Lewinsky.

What, then, does such an expression reveal about the meaning-making mechanisms that operate behind the scenes?

First things first, however. What does this utterance convey? The utterance represents a thought experiment of sorts: what linguists refer to as a 'counterfactual'. The linguistic *if... then...* construction provides an instruction: imagine a scenario X that runs counter to fact, for instance: winning the lottery. Given such a hypothetical scenario, then scenario Y unfolds, for instance:

buying a Rolls Royce. In the utterance above, we are asked to imagine that Bill Clinton is now not the President or former President of the United States. He has been transformed into the President of France – scenario X.

Moreover, in this counterfactual scenario he has an affair with Monica Lewinsky – who presumably now works as an intern in the Elysèe Palace. And Clinton is subsequently found out. But in contrast with what we know to have happened in the United States – a special prosecutor investigated the allegation of Clinton's affair, Clinton was ultimately impeached by the House of Representatives, and he suffered great political and reputational harm – the situation is different in the resulting counterfactual scenario. In the 'Clinton-as-President-of-France' scenario, Clinton suffers no harm (scenario Y). Moreover, once the X and Y counterfactual scenarios have been established, they are used in order to perform inferential work as we evaluate the political differences between the United States and France. The counterfactual scenarios that we set up allow us to examine exactly how far apart attitudes are in the two countries.

When we think and speak, we engage in an ongoing act of creation. Gilles Fauconnier argues that this is achieved by setting up what he calls 'mental spaces'.[5] Mental spaces are small, localised packets of information which we use in order to partition and keep track of our thoughts in ongoing discourse. Moreover, mental spaces are built by words and phrases. For instance, the 'if X then Y' linguistic construction sets up a foundation and expansion sequence of counterfactual mental spaces. And as the discussion relates to Clinton as hypothetical French President, we recruit relevant information. This includes a role for French President, rather than other French political roles – the French political system also includes a Prime Minister, for instance, but that role is not recruited. We also add a role for mistress of French President, and for French electorate.

But the counterfactual spaces must be counterfactual to something. Fauconnier argues that in conversation, mental space creation proceeds from a 'base space': a mental space which

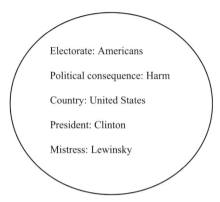

**Figure 7.1.** Mental spaces relating to 'United States'

anchors the mental space construction process. In the case of a counterfactual scenario this provides information which is taken to reflect reality. Moreover, language prompts us to add content to the mental space. The proper noun *Bill Clinton* sets up an entity in the base 'USA' space, while mention of Lewinsky sets up an entity that corresponds to Lewinsky in the base space, with the roles 'American President' for Clinton, and 'mistress of Clinton' for Lewinsky. Other relevant information for the base space, drawn from the domain of American politics, may also be recruited to the base space. Figure 7.1 depicts this base space. The circle represents the mental space, with a summary of its content inserted inside.

As intimated, a counterfactual (X) space arises from the base space. In this space, Clinton is now the French president. The counterfactual space is expanded, giving rise to a further (Y) counterfactual space: Clinton-as-President-of-France has an affair with Monica Lewinsky. But in this Y space, he suffers no political harm. Moreover, counterparts are established between the base space and the counterfactual X and Y spaces. Counterparts can be established, for instance, by matching a role (e.g. President) or a value that fills the role (e.g. Bill Clinton). In the present scenario, the values 'Clinton' and 'Lewinsky' are respectively established as counterparts across mental spaces, becoming connected with the roles 'French President', and 'Mistress of French President' respectively. It is by

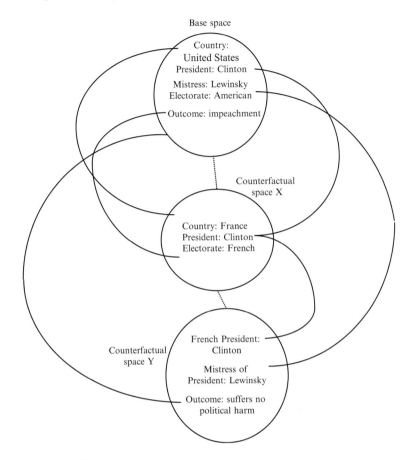

**Figure 7.2.** Network of mental spaces

virtue of being connected that a counterpart in one space can refer to a counterpart in another, as we shall see shortly. Figure 7.2 captures the mental space network for this. Connectors between counterparts are represented by a solid line in Figure 7.2.

The counterfactual spaces must exist if we are to make sense of the remark above. The remark prompts us to construct a scenario that is counter to fact: Clinton is President of France; he has an affair with Monica Lewinsky, but he does not suffer political harm. Of course, Clinton could not, in reality, have been President of France: he's not French, he wasn't born in France, he doesn't speak French and, as far as I know, he has no particular desire to be President of France. However, the remark prompts for space-building, allowing us to construct a counterfactual scenario.

Finally, as the mental spaces remain connected to one another in our minds, as represented by the dashed lines which link them in Figure 7.2, we can shift the viewpoint from which we view the content contained in each of the spaces in the network. For instance, once the counterfactual spaces have been built, we can shift the viewpoint back to the base space. From this viewpoint, the counterfactual spaces point to a deep disanalogy between the United States and France: in the United States, Clinton has an affair with Monika Lewinsky, is found out and is consequently impeached. In France, Clinton also has an affair and is found out, but suffers no political harm. Thus, the network of mental spaces allows us to compare and contrast how the same event – an extramarital relationship by the elected head of state, and his attempt to conceal it – would be interpreted, and its consequences, in two different political contexts. While in the US Americans, and particularly American law-makers, take a dim view, the French are apparently far more sanguine about such matters; in fact, and on the contrary, in France, the magazine that reported President Hollande's clandestine affair is sued for breaching the President's right to personal privacy. What this all reveals – at least from the perspective of the mental spaces laboratory that we've constructed in our minds – is just how far apart the two countries are in terms of their views of the relative significance of infidelity on the part of their presidents.

One significant advantage of assuming that meaning construction involves the creation of mental spaces relates to the problem of reference. Distinct mental spaces contain counterparts and connectors, which, while not identical, are related to one another. Indeed, a previously intractable problem for philosophers of language has been how to account for identity and reference in language use. For instance, consider the following utterance:

> Last night I had a dream that I was David Beckham. I scored the winning goal in the FIFA World Cup final for England. And then I sent myself fan mail.

Traditional accounts have difficulty in explaining how it is that an expression like *myself* can refer both to David Beckham *and* the fan (of David Beckham). But by assuming meaning involves mental spaces construction, we have an elegant way of accounting for natural language examples such as this. The mental spaces perspective assumes that semantic space is divided into discrete packets of information when we think and speak; and there are distinct, albeit related, counterparts populating the distinct mental spaces into which we partition thought.

To understand this discourse, there must be a 'base' space, where we have an ardent David Beckham and England football fan. A base space of this sort is presumed by the space-building expression: *last night I had a dream*. But the football fan does have a dream, which builds a new 'dream' space connected to the base space. The dream space is, of course, like the Clinton-as-President-of-France space, a counterfactual. The fan in the base space, and David Beckham, in the dream space, are set up as counterparts: they share identity – across the mental spaces – because of the peculiar logic of the dream; in the dream the fan *is* David Beckham.

They clearly don't share identity in the real world, as represented by the base space, where there are distinct entities for both. But in the dream space, the fan and David Beckham are one and the same. And because they share identity, the fan – from the base space – can send David Beckham fan mail, with *myself* referring, simultaneously, to David Beckham and the ardent football fan. This is possible, and fully interpretable, precisely because we are holding two distinct mental spaces in our heads with counterparts linked by an identity connector. This is diagrammed in Figure 7.3.

## The act of creation

In his early research, Fauconnier developed a theory of Mental Spaces.[6] As we have just seen, the essential insight of this work was that thinking and speaking involve partitioning by mental

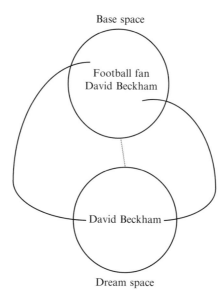

**Figure 7.3.** Dreaming of David Beckham

spaces; and mental spaces contain counterparts linked by connectors. In subsequent research, an even more striking insight followed. Working with language scientist Mark Turner, Fauconnier pointed out that there is a qualitative difference between the nature of base mental spaces and mental spaces which capture counterfactual scenarios such as Clinton-as-President-of-France, or a football fan dreaming he or she has become David Beckham.[7] In contrast to the former, mental spaces of the latter sort appear to be acts of extreme creativity.

In essence, imaginative feats of this sort involve combining parts of existing knowledge in new ways, giving rise to the integration of different kinds of information contained in mental spaces that portray dreams, counterfactuals and the like. Mental spaces that arise in this way, from blending parts of existing knowledge, go beyond the input upon which they are based, producing new knowledge, new insights and imaginative breakthroughs. They constitute the crucible of creativity. But far from coming out of thin air, they arise in a principled way.

Conceptual blending involves a network of mental spaces, as I described in the previous section. The spaces that provide the content grounded in experience are referred to as 'input spaces'. In contrast, the mental space that gives rise to novel or emergent meaning is termed the 'blend'. And, as described in the previous section, counterparts are identified. In the case of blending, counterparts are identified across more than one base space: the input spaces. And it's these input spaces which are integrated in the blend in order to produce novel content. Fauconnier and Turner argue that counterparts are established by virtue of a 'generic space'. This is a space that is generic to both the input spaces: it allows entities in the input spaces to be identified *as* counterparts. Together, the generic space, the two (or more) input spaces and the blend form an 'integration network': they produce novel meaning, and thereby facilitate the act of creation.

To illustrate how this process works, let's reconsider the kangaroo and elephant joke that we first met at the outset of the chapter. We all carry in our heads a lot of information regarding elephants, for instance. Even if you have never actually encountered one, not even in a zoo, you'll still know quite a bit about elephants. This comes from reading books, cultural knowledge, nature programmes on TV, and so on. You are likely to know that elephants inhabit regions of Africa and India, and that they are the largest land-dwelling mammals. You might also know, through cultural folklore, that they are reputed to have extraordinarily good memories. You will certainly know that they have grey skin, trunks and tusks, that they are social creatures that live in family groupings and that they are under threat from poachers who hunt them for their ivory.

You will also know quite a bit about kangaroos. You'll know that they are residents of Australia, and that they get about by hopping. You may also know that their young are referred to as joeys, and that female kangaroos have pouches where they rear their young. Moreover, each of these coherent bodies of knowledge relating to elephants and kangaroos occupies distinct regions of conceptual space, somewhere in our minds.

Conceptual blending works by selecting specific elements from each of these bodies of knowledge. Not everything we may know about kangaroos and elephants is relevant for understanding the punch-line. In the joke, the punch-line provides the outcome, the result: holes all over Australia. The relevant information appears to be body size, mode of locomotion, and geographical location. Hence, this type of information for each organism is available in input spaces. But in order to know how to integrate the information to form a blend, we must know which elements in the two input spaces are counterparts.

To do this, we construct the generic space (see Figure 7.4) which allows us to identify counterparts. The generic space relates to generic properties of both inputs: animal, geographical location, physiology and size and mode of locomotion. It provides a tool for recognising which elements across the input spaces match one another.

Once counterparts have been identified, we selectively project some – although not all – of these to a new region of conceptual space: the blend. The relevant information we extract for 'elephant' has to do with its large size. For 'kangaroo' we extract knowledge concerning its manner of motion, and its geographical location. These elements then undergo an operation known as 'compression': while elephant and kangaroo relate to two distinct organisms in the input spaces, in the blended space they are compressed – features from each of the two organisms are integrated into a single organism. And in so doing, we create a new organism that has the size of an elephant, gets around by hopping and lives in Australia. And this act of mental creation allows us to make sense of the joke. These are the key elements of information that must be blended together in order to create the fantastical creature we require to understand the punch-line.

Figure 7.4 illustrates the following. The punch-line prompts for the formation of an integration network relating to the mode of locomotion, size and location of kangaroos and elephants. Two input spaces arise. They are input spaces in the sense that they provide the content which is integrated in the blend. The

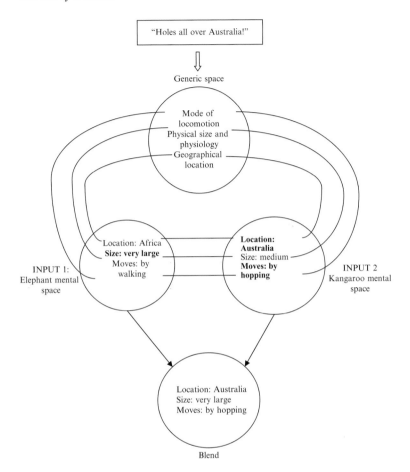

Figure 7.4. Integration network for elephant/kangaroo joke

generic space establishes counterparts across the input spaces, by highlighting which elements should be connected. Counterparts are represented by the solid horizontal lines that connect elements from the two input spaces. The blend arises from selective projection to the blended space of the elements in boldface in the input spaces.

In describing how this blend arises, I've been addressing one of the component processes of blending: 'composition'. Blending joins together – or composes – aspects of the input spaces in the

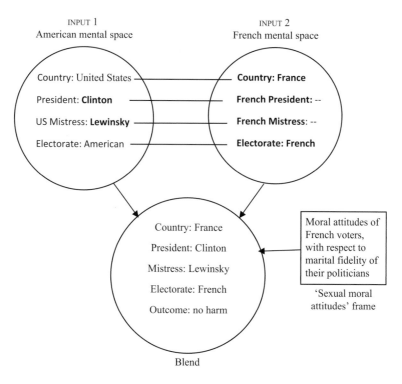

**Figure 7.5.** Clinton-as-President-of-France blend

blended space. However, a blend arises from a further two component processes. The second provides the blend with additional information in order to round it out, and thus complete the composition process: this is known as 'completion'.

To illustrate, let's reconsider the Clinton-as-President-of-France example from the previous section. This integration network, perhaps self-evidently being a counterfactual, arises from the blending process. Scrutinised through the lens of blending, the counterfactual X/Y scenario arises from two input spaces (see Figure 7.5).

Figure 7.5 illustrates the following. There are two input spaces: one relating to Clinton as American President, and one with corresponding roles in the French presidential system. Counterparts are identified using a generic space (not diagrammed) along the lines described for the kangaroo and elephant integration network. The counterparts are signalled by the horizontal lines holding between the two input spaces. Importantly, blending arises from the compression of the values from the US input space – the identities 'Clinton' and 'Lewinsky' – with the roles from the France input space. That is, only the elements in boldface from the two input spaces are projected to the blend. And in the process, they are compressed into unique entities. In the blend, Clinton is President of France, and Lewinsky is the mistress of the French President.

But in order to derive the central inference of the blend, that Clinton suffers no harm as French President in having an affair, this is not enough. In addition, information on the moral stance held by the French towards the sexual indiscretions of their political leaders must also be recruited. This comes not from the France input space, but is added directly to the blend. This is captured in Figure 7.5 as the 'sexual moral attitudes' frame. This frame provides information relating to moral attitudes held by, or ascribed to, the French. It is recruited during the blending process in order to infer how the French would respond to Clinton-as-President-of-France having an affair with Monica Lewinsky in The Elysèe Palace. The recruitment facilitates the inference that Clinton, now French President, suffers no political harm from being found out in his affair with Lewinsky. This then enables the blend to be completed.

Finally, we live in the blend, modifying it in the process. This is called 'running the blend'. For instance, in 1997, at the height of the scandal surrounding Bill Clinton and his alleged affair with Monica Lewinsky, reports emerged of a blue Gap dress belonging to Lewinsky. The dress was alleged to bear presidential semen stains, the result of Lewinsky administering oral sex. Later DNA tests by the FBI confirmed that the stains matched the President's DNA 'with a high degree of probability'. The blue dress became a symbol not only of Clinton's affair, but also of his lying under oath, denying that he had had an affair with Lewinsky. In short, the blue dress became a symbol of Clinton's lack of a moral compass. For many Americans, especially Republicans, the blue

Figure 7.6. 'We're all wearing the blue dress now. Impeach.' (Source: *The Daily Kos,* reprinted with permission)[8]

dress was more than simply a stained dress submitted as evidence in an impeachment trial of the forty-second President of the United States. It represented the moral abyss that Bill Clinton, a Democrat, inhabited.

Several years later, after Republican President George W. Bush had taken the US to war in Iraq on the basis of *evidence* that Saddam Hussein had stockpiled weapons of mass destruction, the spectre of the blue dress re-emerged. Car bumper stickers and badges featuring the phrase 'We're all wearing the blue dress now' began to appear, especially among Democrat supporters. And one activist even launched a campaign putting up posters above American highways. The image in Figure 7.6 appeared on an I-80 overpass in Berkeley, California in July 2007.

In the original blend, the blue Gap dress symbolised Clinton as a perceived liar, and therefore untrustworthy. Following the invasion of Iraq by Clinton's successor, based on at best question-able claims that Saddam Hussein possessed weapons of mass destruction, the blend evolved. The blue dress came to symbolise misrepresentation by a political leader more generally. In the slogan 'We're all wearing the blue dress now', not only does the blue dress symbolise a lie, it is being borne by the American electorate. The American electorate has been lied to, and the country has been taken to war where American lives are being sacrificed for this lie. According to the caption in Figure 7.6, George W. Bush should be impeached for having committed perjury. As it turned out, there were no weapons of mass destruction in Iraq: President Bush took the United States to war predicated on his insistence that there were such weapons, *and* that he had the evidence.

The extension of blends is commonplace. Indeed, it can often be used for humorous effects. Consider the following excerpt from the TV series *House*, starring Hugh Laurie. Here, the curmudgeonly Dr House is discussing his friend Wilson with Dr Cuddy:

DR HOUSE:   I'm a night owl, Wilson's an early bird. We're different
            species.
DR CUDDY:   Then move him into his own cage.
DR HOUSE:   Who'll clean the droppings from mine?

In the blend, the metaphorical and literal meanings of *night owl* and *early bird* are integrated. What begins as a discussion on different sleeping habits of two men evolves, in which they are conceptualised in terms of different types of bird.

While the formation of a blend involves composition, elaboration and, ultimately, running the blend, the hallmark of blending is compression. This, in essence, is the consequence of the three processes I've been discussing. The act of everyday creation, when we think and talk, results in 'emergent structure', structure that is not apparent in the original inputs. In the example of Clinton-as-President-of-France, the blend results from our ability to compress different types of information – in order to fuse it – into a single coherent conceptual entity. With the Clinton blend, we fused the value Bill Clinton with the role President of France. This specific compression resulted in a new entity that was the sum of the parts: Clinton, the individual, as President of France.

Consider a recent striking example. An article in *The Sunday Times* newspaper, with the headline 'Fish shrink to avoid the plate', reported that the average size of fish caught has been falling over recent decades. In the 1950s, the average size of fish caught at Key West in Florida was 44lbs; in the 1980s this had reduced to 20lbs, while in 2007 it was a mere 5lbs. The article explained the situation as follows:

> Overfishing the world's oceans is making fish shrink as well as reducing their numbers, a leading marine scientist has warned.[9]

Of course, fish are not intentionally shrinking. Rather, evolutionary pressures are coming to bear as a consequence of overfishing. The bigger fish are more prized by fishermen, and hence, being caught, they no longer have the opportunity to reproduce. The result is that smaller fish have greater opportunities, producing offspring which are more likely to be smaller. But the causal event sequence that drives this change is complex. In the blend, the evolutionary cause-and-effect event sequence is compressed into a simpler cause–effect relation: the fish themselves are deliberately shrinking in order to avoid being caught.

## Reducing complexity to human scale

A conceptual blend is an imaginative feat that often allows us to grasp an idea in a new way. The way this is achieved, and the overarching goal of everyday creativity – of blending – is to reduce complexity to human scale.[10] And in so doing, this provides us with global insight.

Recall the computer desktop metaphor. Attempting to provide computer commands to get the machine to do what is required is arduous. But conceptualising computer commands in terms of working in an office environment reduces the inherent complexity to manageable proportions. This greatly facilitates our ability to interact with our desktop and laptop computers. And even when certain features clash with our ordinary office environment, such

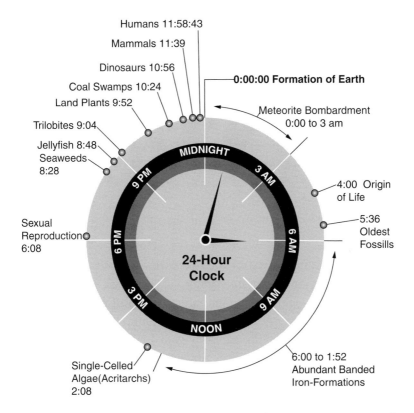

Figure 7.7. Evolution in a day (Source: University of Wisconsin, Department of Geoscience)[12]

as recycle bins being located on the desktop, we live and function within the blend. Blending allows us to reduce great complexity to the scale of human experience. And in so doing, we can better grasp it.

To illustrate, imagine the following scenario. You're attending a lecture on evolution, and the professor says: 'Imagine that the history of the planet Earth is condensed into a 24-hour day. Life began around 4am, dinosaurs emerged at 10.56pm, and humans arrived on the scene at 11.58pm, just before midnight.' Figure 7.7 illustrates just such a representation.[11]

Representing the vast tracts of evolutionary time as a single day reduces complexity to a scale that we can comprehend. This is

**Figure 7.8.** The evolution of man (© David Gifford/Science Photo Library)

achieved by compressing diffuse structure – over 4.6 billion years of evolution – into a more compact, and thus a less complex, structure. This achieves human scale, because the 24-hour day is perhaps the most salient temporal unit for humans. This conceptual blend thereby achieves global insight by facilitating comprehension of evolutionary time, since we otherwise have no understanding of the vast timescales involved.

Another example is provided in Figure 7.8. This shows an image that is typical of those often deployed to represent human evolution. But it compresses huge timescales, over 6 million years, into a simple sequence.

Take another example. Climate change is a hugely complex scientific problem.[13] It's one that's being tackled by climate scientists, computer modellers, economists, geographers and a multitude of other scientists. Since the turn of the century, an increasing awareness of the potential perils of climate change among the general public, especially in the United States, has increasingly led to calls for action by individuals and communities to help save the planet. This began to happen as climate change scepticism in the United States, fostered under the Bush administration, began to wane. In part, this was due to pressure from an increasing scientific consensus regarding the man-made causes of climate change. Also important in bringing the perils to public attention were awareness-raising campaigns, especially Al Gore's famous slideshow presentation on climate change, captured in David Guggenheim's 2006 documentary film *An Inconvenient Truth.*

In 2006, Fred Krupp, President of the US-based Environmental Defense,[14] initiated a hard-hitting television advertising campaign in the United States promoting what was termed a *low-carbon diet.*[15] In addition to an ad campaign, the campaign featured a booklet with the same title. The purpose of the campaign was explicitly to reduce the complexity of the fight against climate change, thereby empowering individuals to be able to do something about it. As Krupp pointed out in an article accompanying his ad campaign:

> It's no wonder the scale of climate change can feel overwhelming. An ice sheet the size of Rhode Island melts into the sea off Antarctica. A blizzard of disease carrying insects reaches high-elevation cities for the first time. Whole islands in the Pacific are ready to disappear beneath the waves. But, while there is much to be done, an important part of the solution to global warming may be right in your kitchen.[16]

The purpose of the ad campaign was to encourage healthy use and rationing of natural resources. This was to be achieved by individuals consuming less energy, especially in the kitchen, one household at a time. Just as a food diet involves reducing one's (calorie) intake, a low-carbon diet involves a reduction in consumption of household energy by taking a number of practical steps, ranging from installing more energy-efficient kitchen appliances, to using energy-saving bulbs, to amending one's consumption of energy, to recycling packaging and waste products. The net result would be to reduce the carbon footprint, one individual and one household at a time.

The power of extolling a low-carbon diet, according to activists, is that it reduces the complexity of the challenges surrounding global warming to human scale. As one activist expressed it:

> People see global warming as such a large problem, and they go, 'Well, what can I do about it?'"Miller said. 'But if you're on the diet, you can say, 'Here are all these little things we can do.'[17]

A *low-carbon diet* is a blend. It is an imaginative feat that integrates factors relating to global warming with household energy consumption and individual behaviour, resulting in a reduction in consumption of energy. And the ad campaign aimed to convey the blend, and to ask people to buy into it.

In this integration network, *low-carbon diet* relates to individual activity – especially in and around the household – in order to reduce carbon emissions. It consists of an input space relating to carbon emissions management, and a household energy husbandry input. It also consists of a third input, a Dieting frame – which provides the blended space with its primary organisational structure. The blend is the venue, following composition and pattern completion, for the network's creativity to emerge: the reduction of energy consumption in and around a single household causes a reduction in carbon emissions.

Of course, reducing household energy consumption doesn't *directly* reduce carbon emissions: it's the production of electricity in power stations, for instance by burning fossil fuels, that produces carbon dioxide. A household, in contrast, consumes rather than produces electricity. Nevertheless, the blend provides a mechanism for integrating highly diffuse cause–effect chains relating to carbon dioxide production and hence carbon emissions, and household energy management, in order to reduce the complexity involved in climate change, and specifically the ways of tackling this problem, to human scale.

In the blend, mitigating the effects of climate change is boiled down to saving energy in an individual household. The rhetorical point of the integration network is to convince the energy user of the need to adjust individual behaviour: energy savings in the home cause a reduction in carbon emissions. The consequence is that living inside the *low-carbon diet* blend specifically relates to a means of mitigating carbon emissions (*low-carbon*), centred on an individual-level reduction in consumption (*diet*). And that specifically relates to reducing energy consumption in the individual household. In short, the blend provides individual energy consumers with a way to counter climate change: it reduces the complexity of global warming to human scale. The individual infers that change(s) in household energy consumption (the cause) will result in a reduction in carbon emissions, thereby helping to save the planet (the effect).

## The power of blending

While blending works behind the scenes, forming the cognitive iceberg beneath the surface of language, language is, often, directly implicated in the blending process. For instance, the linguistic compound *low-carbon diet* is an example of such a 'lexical blend'. It projects the phrase *low-carbon* from input 1 in Figure 7.9 with the word *diet* from the completion frame. The result is that the

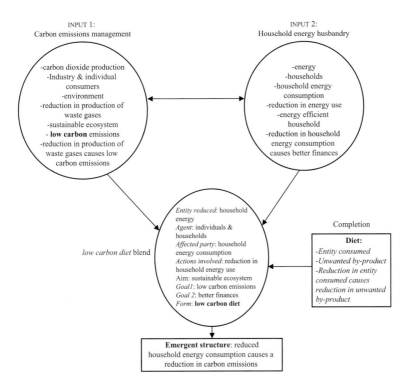

**Figure 7.9.** *Low-carbon diet* integration network

novel coinage *low-carbon diet* provides a lexical anchor, so to speak, for activating the low-carbon diet blend, and indeed the entire integration network to which the blend remains connected. One way in which blending is both innovative and powerful, therefore, arises from the blending mechanisms which contribute to the formation of new linguistic phrases; and these linguistic phrases are symbols for the underlying idea.

So, let's now consider another example of lexical blending, which reveals the way in which blending can be deliberately deployed for political and ideological ends. In so doing, this case study provides a means of illustrating the real-world power of human creativity, and the blending process that sub-serves it.

In early 2004, some British tabloid newspapers began manipulating language for specific political ends. This resulted in scaremongering over European Union (EU) enlargement. On May 1st 2004, new member countries were set to join the EU that included sizeable Roma (Gypsy) communities. These former eastern-bloc countries included the Czech Republic, Slovakia, Hungary, Poland and Slovenia. Citizens of the new member states would be eligible to move to and settle in the United Kingdom, to get jobs without the need for work permits or visas. And, should they be unable to secure work, they would be entitled to claim unemployment and other benefits from the welfare state after having resided in the United Kingdom for just three months. The tabloid press, in a series of articles, argued that the impoverished Roma from eastern Europe would 'flood in' to the United Kingdom in order to claim unemployment benefit. In January 2004, *The Sun*, the UK's biggest-selling daily newspaper, claimed that the influx would be 'tens of thousands', while the *Daily Express*, another tabloid daily, suggested that '1.6 million gypsies are ready to flood in'. The *Daily Express* featured a map with the heading 'The Great Invasion of 2004: Where the Gypsies are coming from'. The map evoked World War II imagery, as popularised in the well-known British sitcom *Dad's Army*.

*Dad's Army* is a cultural institution in the United Kingdom among a particular age group. It depicts the mishaps that befall several members of a group of the Home Guard during World

War II. The Home Guard, in wartime Britain, were made up of elderly dads and granddads, who served as part-time soldiers. Their function was to provide a last line of defence for the home front in case of Nazi invasion. The map, like the opening credits to *Dads' Army*, featured arrows racing across Europe aimed at the United Kingdom, with a solitary Union Flag-coloured arrow attempting to repulse the *invasion* of the, presumably, evil foreign hordes.

The figure of 1.6 million Roma as proclaimed by the *Daily Express* represented something of an exaggeration. In fact, 1.6 million was the combined population of ethnic Roma living in Poland, Hungary, the Czech Republic and Slovakia, according to the Independent Race and Refugee News Network (IRR News Network). In a comment piece on the IRR News Network, Arun Kundnani branded the figure of 1.6 million 'a ridiculous estimate of how many might settle in Britain'.[18]

One of the ways in which the press sensationalised the issue was to dwell on what became known as *welfare shopping*: the arrival of Roma migrants who, it was claimed, would be motivated to come to the United Kingdom purely to 'leech' on the social welfare system rather than being serious about finding a job. For instance, *The Sunday Times*, which like *The Sun* is owned by News UK (a Rupert Murdoch company), got in on the act and ran a piece which compared the benefits available to an unemployed family with two children in the Czech Republic with the relatively far superior sums available in the United Kingdom. In the Czech Republic the welfare available was, in 2004, only around £100 per month.

*Welfare shopping*, the expression, was itself an extremely ingenious coinage. It both captured the allegedly malicious motivation of the Gypsy *invaders*, at least from the perspective of the tabloid press, while simultaneously condemning them. And its success depended on conceptual blending. The integration network for *welfare shopping* didn't just include information relating to economic migrants and their perceived potential misuse of the welfare system. It is also involved projection of the words *welfare* and *shopping*. These two words are not normally associated, as they belong to different spheres. However, in the blend they become compressed into a single unit. A new expression is formed: *welfare shopping*. It specifically relates to the phenomenon of economic migrants whose real motivation, it was alleged, is not to find work; rather, their intention was to move to the United Kingdom in order to claim the welfare payments which the unemployed are routinely entitled to in the United Kingdom. The expression, therefore, both identified and negatively branded a particular phenomenon.

What is more, when the British tabloid press began running stories about welfare shopping, no actual *welfare shopping* had yet occurred. The relatively poorer former eastern-bloc countries had not yet joined the EU. Moreover, it wasn't even clear that there was any evidence that anyone intended to move to the United Kingdom expressly to take advantage of the welfare system.

What prompted the tabloid campaign was the realisation that among the existing EU countries, the United Kingdom was almost alone in not having amended its laws on length of residence for citizens to be eligible for unemployment benefit – one consequence of membership of the EU is that citizens from any member state enjoy the same privileges as nationals.

What the tabloid newspapers wanted was this. They argued that the British government should change the law. Rather than a three-month residency period being required to qualify for welfare payments, they wanted a longer period. Indeed, this is what other well-off EU member states had done. This would deter *welfare shopping*. Or so the tabloid press argued.

The combination of *welfare* and *shopping* entailed the formation of an integration network in order for the newly coined expression to make sense. So how does the integration network come about? As before, there are two input mental spaces which arise in order to make sense of the tabloid newspaper reports. The first is a mental space for 'economic migrants'. This includes the following elements: economic migrants, particularly ethnic Roma, who move to other wealthier EU countries in order to seek a job, for financial gain. The second input space involves the 'UK welfare state'. This includes elements relating to the following: the unemployed, who have no job, and therefore receive welfare payments.

But according to the *welfare shopping* blend, it is not just that the gypsies were going to come to the United Kingdom expressly to claim unemployment benefits. Far worse than this, they were potentially going to be moving from country to country within the EU, sampling the various welfare benefits on offer and taking the best deal. Not only was this practice deemed despicable, the tabloids would have it that this was totally un-British. Moreover, recalling wartime imagery, this practice should be repulsed, just as the Brits nobly repulsed Hitler, initially standing alone, in the last Great Invasion.

As is perhaps already clear, the notion of moving from place to place in order to find the best deal doesn't come from either of the two input spaces. Rather, it comes from our knowledge associated with shopping. After all, what we know about shopping is that it involves shoppers, who move from store to store in order to locate the best deal. Shoppers have no particular allegiance to specific shops. Their motivation is primarily the lowest price and hence the best deal. And it is this knowledge which provides the blend with its organisational structure. As we've seen with the discussion of the Clinton-as-President-of-France and *low-carbon diet* blends, it's often the case that a blend draws on other knowledge sources in order to provide it with key organisational information, and so complete it.

The *welfare shopping* blend draws on the following elements of knowledge. From the economic migrant input space we get the gypsies: our economic migrants. As they are not seeking jobs, this feature isn't projected to the blend. Rather, they are seeking welfare payments. This piece of knowledge comes from the 'welfare state' input space. However, they are seeking the best welfare payments, which they achieve by moving from country to country. These elements come from our knowledge of the shopping frame, which is added directly to the blend in order to complete it. The *welfare shopping* integration network is depicted in Figure 7.10. The knowledge relating to 'shopping' is depicted as a square box, which provides the blend with its core organisational structure. It is this structure that allows us to make sense

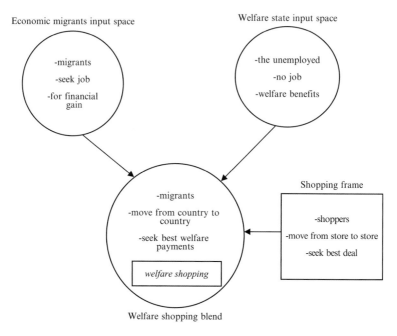

**Figure 7.10.** Integration network for *welfare shopping*

of the information drawn from the two input spaces that is combined in the blend.

A salient feature of this integration network is the projection of the words *welfare* and *shopping*. The word *welfare* comes from the 'welfare state' input, while *shopping* comes from our knowledge relating to 'shopping'. Importantly, the expression, once formed, provided the tabloid newspapers, and indeed others – their readers, as well as politicians, political commentators and so on – with a linguistic anchor that referred to a complex web of ideas. In other words, the expression *welfare shopping* remains connected to the blend that gives rise to it, which in turn remains connected to the input spaces. The expression *welfare shopping*, by virtue of arising in the blend, provided the tabloid press with a means of portraying a particular group – financially impoverished ethnic Roma in former eastern-bloc countries – as a threat to the United Kingdom's financial resources. Moreover, their use of this term, and the blend that it is embedded within, represented an attempt to influence the opinion of their readers, and in turn that of politicians. They sought to portray something that had not happened as a real threat. They did so by making use of conceptual blending, and the linguistic expression which arose due to blending – *welfare shopping* – in order to attempt to change the law.

## The mystery of creativity

In her seminal work on creativity, Margaret Boden observes the following:

> Creativity surrounds us on all sides: from composers to chemists, cartoonists to choreographers. But creativity is a puzzle, a paradox, some say a mystery. Inventors, scientists, and artists rarely know how their original ideas arise. They mention intuition, but cannot say how it works. Most psychologists cannot tell us much about it, either. What's more, many people assume that there will never be a scientific theory of creativity – for how could science possibly explain fundamental novelties? As if all this were not daunting enough, the apparent unpredictability of creativity seems (to many people) to outlaw any systematic explanation, whether scientific or historical.[19]

In this chapter I've been sketching the outlines of a theory of creativity: conceptual blending. Originally developed by Fauconnier and Turner, many other researchers have now contributed to the study of blending.[20] Far from being intractable to scientific study, the underpinnings of the act of creation are beginning to come into view. And language provides the lens which allows us to study this cognitive iceberg.

Conceptual blending is a mechanism that is central to the way we think. It provides a means of integrating and compressing often very complex knowledge, typically in the process of ongoing meaning construction. But this account is not without problems, and unanswered questions remain. After all, the nature of meaning construction and creativity is exquisitely complex. While

Blending Theory has attempted to provide a single well-articulated and coherent account of meaning construction, one potential drawback is that the range of phenomena claimed to exhibit conceptual blending may not, in fact, arise from a single mechanism. For instance, conceptual blending, a single unified mechanism, is held to be responsible for phenomena as diverse as solving riddles, performing mathematic calculations, the creation of novel word and word compound coinages, grammatical constructions and neurological (or perceptual) binding – as we saw in Chapter 4, perceptual binding is the process occurring in the brain that allows us to perceive distinct sensory experiences as forming a unified percept; sensations processed in different brain regions for taste, touch, weight, visual experience and so on undergo binding to form a unified percept, such as an apple or a blue cup. Fauconnier and Turner have argued that conceptual blending may be responsible for perceptual binding operations in the brain of this kind.[21]

While all these phenomena involve integration of some kind, it is far from clear that a single mechanism can adequately account for the full range of knowledge types and neurological mechanisms involved. Indeed, research in cognitive neuroscience suggests that perceptual binding is a consequence of timing mechanisms in the brain, rather than integration or blending per se. Nevertheless, there is a truly deep insight at the heart of the blending paradigm: human creativity results from integration, an everyday operation, and integration can be studied in a principled way.

While it does now appear possible to begin to sketch a science of creativity, the downside is that the account presented in this chapter barely begins to scratch the surface, and much remains to be done. For one thing, we require a science, at the very least, for each of the constituent processes that make up blending – composition, completion and running the blend. Each of these are likely to be driven by distinct and diverging principles. We also need to study the way in which blending applies in different modalities. For instance, language and music are different representational systems, which make use of a variety of different compositional mechanisms – only some of which may be overlapping. And this is a consequence of the divergent nature of their representational format.[22] Indeed, we now know that language itself, for instance, is in part contingent on the modality in which it is expressed.

By way of example, for many of us, when we think of language we think of the spoken word. However, there are around 130 recognised sign languages used in the world today.[23] Like spoken language, sign language makes use of a grammar system and a vocabulary. Until recently, however, and based on the study of spoken language, linguists had thought that all languages must exhibit what is known as Duality of Patterning. This so-called 'design feature' of language requires that a language is made up of a fixed repertoire of meaningless symbols which can be combined into meaningful units. For instance, the sounds [t], [ɪ] and [p] can be combined to form the words 'pit' or 'tip' in English. However, it has been discovered that there is an emerging 'village' sign language used by a community in southern Israel that hasn't yet developed full-blown Duality of Patterning. While the Al-Sayyid Bedouin sign language exhibits a means of combining units into the equivalent of words and sentences, it doesn't yet fully make use of a fixed set of meaningless symbols to do so.[24] And this is a consequence of the medium it makes use of, as well as the fact that it emerged only a few generations ago. Unlike spoken language, sign language makes use of the manual–gestural medium. In Al-Sayyid Bedouin sign language, language-users have flexibility in making use of hand shape, motion of hands and so on in producing words. Among at least some of its users, there is not yet the equivalent of a fixed repertoire of sounds such as in a language like English. This reveals something quite startling. The mechanisms that constitute language may not be universal, but may be contingent on the medium in which it is expressed, or possibly the stage of development the language has attained – or indeed both. This will have consequences for the study of the integrative mechanisms that apply in the distinct modalities in which language can occur.

In addition, distinct types of reasoning may involve distinct integration types. For instance, mathematical thought may be a distinct type of process vis-à-vis the ability to construct a persuasive and logical argument as in rhetorical practice, for instance. While both types of thought processes may involve integration of some type, it is not clear to me that there is, or could be, a single unified mechanism that would account for both – unless we reduce such mechanisms to the most schematic kind, and hence reduce the study of conceptual integration to the banal.

One of the most speculative claims made by Fauconnier and Turner for conceptual blending is that this is the single mechanism that gave rise to human creativity, which supposedly exploded onto the scene around 50,000 years ago during the period that archaeologists refer to as the Upper Palaeolithic.[25] First of all, it is not clear that there was a single great explosion of creativity. The archaeological evidence is somewhat more ambiguous, and different human groups exhibited creative behaviours – such as cave painting, body decoration, manufacture of jewellery, and so on – at somewhat different periods, as I'll discuss later, in Chapter 11.[26] Moreover, cooperative behaviour that has a deep-seated pro-social basis in cognitively modern humans may have driven at least some of the cognitive adaptations, culminating in symbolic abilities of which language is a paradigm example. And these may have facilitated creativity. Indeed, some researchers argue that it is the emergence of symbolic behaviour, such as language, that may have allowed the creative potential of the human mind to emerge in the first place.[27]

Finally, a science of blending must grapple with the respective contribution of knowledge of different types in the process of creative thought. For instance, meaning arises from integrating different types of knowledge. Language provides a level of knowledge which is integrated with non-linguistic concepts in meaning construction. In short, the importance of the discovery of blending is that we have the programmatic promise of a science of creativity. But the challenge is to now divide the problem into manageable chunks and investigate the processes at play in distinct symbolic systems and modalities, and in the integration of distinct types of knowledge.

## Meaning in mind revisited

This chapter brings to a conclusion this part of the book. I've been considering meaning in mind – the conceptual bases of knowledge, and the cognitive underpinnings of our unprecedented capacity for meaning-making. I've considered conceptual metaphor as a foundational principle, available to the human mind, for constructing knowledge representation. I've also considered the role of subjective knowledge, such as time, which, while elaborated by conceptual metaphor, is a consequence of fundamental design features of the human mind. We've looked at the embodied nature of concepts, as well as how these arise from birth onwards, a combination of innate organisational and learning mechanisms, in conjunction with socio-physical experience of the world. And finally, in this chapter I've looked at how this range of knowledge can be integrated in acts of creative thought. Our next task, to fill out our account of meaning-making, is to examine what language brings to the table, and how it makes use of the mind's knowledge systems in producing meaning. This is the challenge I now take up.

# III

# Meaning in language

To imagine a language is to imagine a form of life.
Ludwig Wittgenstein, *Philosophical investigations*

# Chapter 8    Webs of words

The American poet Emily Dickinson, commenting on the power of words, once said: 'I know nothing in the world that has as much power as a word. Sometimes I write one, and I look at it, until it begins to shine'. And, in one of popular fiction's most memorable explorations into the nature of words, Humpty Dumpty examines their ultimate, shape-shifting malleability. In *Through the Looking Glass*, Humpty asks Alice how old she is. This leads to a discussion of the nature of word meaning:

> Humpty: 'There's glory for you!'
>
> 'I don't know what you mean by "glory,"' Alice said.
>
> Humpty Dumpty smiled contemptuously. 'Of course you don't – till I tell you. I meant "there's a nice knock-down argument for you!"'
>
> 'But "glory" doesn't mean "a nice knock-down argument,"' Alice objected.
>
> 'When *I* use a word,' Humpty Dumpty said in rather a scornful tone, 'it means just what I choose it to mean – neither more nor less.'
>
> 'The question is,' said Alice, 'whether you CAN make words mean so many different things.'
>
> 'The question is,' said Humpty Dumpty, 'which is to be master – that's all.'
>
> Alice was too much puzzled to say anything, so after a minute Humpty Dumpty began again. 'They've a temper, some of them – particularly verbs, they're the proudest – adjectives you can do anything with, but not verbs – however, *I* can manage the whole lot of them! Impenetrability! That's what *I* say!'
>
> 'Would you tell me, please,' said Alice 'what that means?'
>
> 'Now you talk like a reasonable child,' said Humpty Dumpty, looking very much pleased. 'I meant by "impenetrability" that we've had enough of that subject, and it would be just as well if

you'd mention what you mean to do next, as I suppose you don't
mean to stop here all the rest of your life.'

'That's a great deal to make one word mean,' Alice said in a
thoughtful tone.

But is Humpty Dumpty right: can words mean anything we want?
The traditional view of language and the mind is a clear no.
We have a mental dictionary, so received wisdom maintains. This
mental dictionary, or 'lexicon', contains all the words we know.
And each word has a prescribed sense – what it conveys – and a
prescribed set of referents – things in the world it can refer to.
For instance, when I use the word *doorknob*, I have a mental
representation both of what this word means, as well as the sorts
of entities in the world to which it can apply.

Conventional wisdom maintains that even when words appear
to have different meanings, this is because we have different
entries in our mental lexicon. Take, for instance, the English
word *bank*. This can refer either to a bank of a river, or a financial
institution. The different meanings seem to relate to separate
dictionary entries in our minds.

As it turns out, in the case of *bank*, there is good evidence that
this view is probably correct. The Anglo-Saxon word for *bank*
meant side of a river. But later, English borrowed the term *banque*
from French, which had in turn borrowed it from Italian, with
the financial institution meaning. The two English terms, *bank* as
in river versus *bank* as in financial institution, are pronounced,
and spelled, in the same way. But in fact, they are different words
with very different histories: they just happen to look and sound
alike, due to chance.

But, cases like *bank* aside, the norm is both for words to
have multiple related meanings, and for those meanings to be
extremely flexible. And while words cannot mean just anything – otherwise we'd end up talking past each other, without
having a clue as to what a word like *glory* actually means, as in
Alice's case – words nevertheless are malleable; their meaning
is always interpreted and realised in a specific communicative
context.

Let me show you: imagine you're in a queue waiting to be served at a fast food counter. When it's your turn, the server says: *What's up?* Now, while this greeting could be interpreted as a question about how you're feeling today, everyone would be bemused, at the very least, if you started to monologue about how miserable you are, and what a bad day you've been having. In fact, this *greeting* indicates – and is understood to mean by all relatively sane people – that the server is available to take your order. While words, and other linguistic expressions, are potentially open-ended, they are always constrained by the way they are used, their contexts of use – where they are used – and the other words which surround them in an utterance.

In the previous part of the book, I focused on aspects of representations in our conceptual system, including the processes that facilitate meaning-making. But language self-evidently plays a prominent role in the creation of meaning. In this chapter, we begin to turn our attention to language, focusing specifically on words. I'll take you on a whistle-stop tour of words: what their semantic representations consist of, and why it is they can often have such eye-popping flexibility in what we use them to convey.

## Words are changelings

Despite the traditional 'dictionary' view – that words are static, dictionary-like entries in the mind – the reality is strikingly different. Words reveal, often, quite startling variation in what they mean. As one expert has aptly put it: 'Word meanings cannot be pinned down, as if they were dead insects. Instead, they flutter around elusively like live butterflies'.[1]

To get a sense of the changeling-like behaviour of words, think about what *fast* means in each of the following sentences and expressions:

That car is going fast.
That parked BMW is a fast car.
That doddery old man is a fast driver.

Overtaking is only permitted in the fast lane of the motorway.
fast food
a fast girl
fast asleep

In these examples, *fast* actually conveys quite different things.
In the first example – the car going fast – *fast* relates to rapid
locomotion. In the second, it doesn't: the car is parked after all,
and hence stationary. Here, *fast* concerns the potential for speed.
In the third example, *fast* doesn't concern the movements of the
old man: the old man is not a *fast* driver, in the sense that he turns
the steering wheel rapidly. After all, he's infirm and *doddery*.
Here, *fast* relates to exceeding the designated speed limit, which
involves our background knowledge about the conventions and
legal restrictions for using a motor vehicle on the public highway.
And in the next example, a *fast* lane doesn't mean, self-evidently,
that the lane itself is travelling fast. We seemingly effortlessly
understand, here, that *fast* pertains to the venue for rapid speed,
rather than that a particular motorway lane has morphed into
an animate entity, jumped up, and sped off in hot pursuit of
Usain Bolt. Moreover, in an idiomatic expression such as *fast
food*, while *fast* relates to rapidity in some sense, it involves food
prepared quickly, often in order to be taken away. But more than
that, it relates to a particular genre of food, such as hamburgers.
And as we continue down the list, *fast* increasingly moves away
from directly concerning rapid motion. A *fast girl*, for instance,
is someone who sleeps around, and perhaps one to whom suspect
morals are attributed. And finally, *fast asleep*, which might
describe someone who falls asleep rapidly, is normally taken
to mean more than this: someone who is *fast* asleep is also sound
asleep.

These examples strikingly reveal the variation in meaning
across a single word, a phenomenon we first met in Chapter 1,
where we considered the multiple meanings of *kill*. But even
words that, on the face of it, mean the same thing always have
to be interpreted in context. Consider the following uses of *want*:
*I want a pizza, I want a beer, I want love*. The type of *want* in each

case is quite different. Wanting a pizza versus a beer involves a different type of desire, involving different bodily needs, such as food versus thirst, and the socio-cultural contexts that are associated with eating pizza versus drinking a beer. Wanting love arises from a different type of neuro-biological need, involving things like attention, affection, intimacy, physical contact, and so on.

An implication of wanting something is that we don't have it. Moreover, this implication shows up in some uses of *want*, when it can more clearly describe absence in addition to the desire for something. When I say: *He died for want of love*, *want* here clearly relates to a particular kind of absence which causes a particular outcome, namely death.

These examples illustrate two things. First, a word like *fast* exhibits perhaps, on the face of it, surprising malleability. And second, even a word such as *want*, a word that ostensibly has a single, fairly circumscribed meaning, is interpreted in different ways depending upon the words it's coupled with. To correctly interpret each of these specific instances of *want*, we must understand the kind of desires and socio-cultural associations that are evoked by pizza, beer, and love, including the nature of the desire invoked by each, and how these desires are satisfied,

So, if word meaning is not an all-or-nothing affair, if it involves semantic variation, what exactly *is* word meaning? A word encompasses three distinct sorts of knowledge, knowledge that we must all have stored somewhere in our minds if we are to correctly use and understand each of the many thousands of words we hear and use on a daily basis.

Take the verb *open* – recall that Humpty claimed verbs are proud and difficult to control:

He opened his mouth.
She opened the curtains.
He opened the letter.
The surgeon opened the wound.
The sapper opened the dam.
The customer opened a bank account.

A striking feature of these various instances of *open* is the range and complexity of the background knowledge upon which we must draw in order to understand what each usage means. Opening a mouth involves use of musculature to create an aperture for eating or speaking. But opening curtains doesn't, strictly, create an aperture at all; it involves the removal of a screen, to allow light to enter a room. And opening a letter involves a quite different type of opening again. Opening a wound entails understanding the range of instruments a surgeon might use and the purposes for doing so. In contrast, a sapper *opening* a dam involves the use of explosives to blow up the dam, as in a military intervention. Finally, the kind of opening involved in starting a bank account is altogether more abstract; in point of fact, there is no physical act of creating an aperture. But we probably wouldn't want to say that this type of *open* is unrelated to the more concrete kinds: *open* is not like the word *bank*, with two unrelated meanings that come to be associated with the same form by accident. The use of *open*, to create a new bank account, feels, intuitively, as somehow being related to the more physical types of opening events.

This reveals that one aspect of knowing what *open* means involves a potentially vast and complex body of encyclopaedic knowledge that we carry around with us in our heads. After all, we must know that opening can involve particular kinds of apertures, or genres of apertures, created by particular means and for particular purposes. We also know that open, as a consequence, involves creation of something, often for the first time, and need not involve a physical aperture, as captured by the bank account example. To successfully use the word, the word's meaning must be rather more, then, than a dictionary-like definition in our heads. It involves a plethora of embodied knowledge, relating to the scenes and experiences which we encounter in our daily lives. It also involves scenes that we may have no direct experience of – such as, presumably, blowing up dams as part of a military campaign – which are acquired through cultural learning and transmission.

In addition to this rich encyclopaedic knowledge, a word's meaning must also encompass the usual set of real-world referents to which a word can apply. For instance, while I can talk about opening a letter or a briefcase, a bra, by way of example, is not something that we ordinarily apply the verb *open* to – a bra is normally *undone* or *unfastened*, rather than *opened*. So part of what we know, when we use a word, concerns the sorts of entities that the word *open* normally applies to.

A third type of knowledge for words encompasses the other words and grammatical constructions with which a word normally co-occurs. With advances in corpus linguistics – the study of large bodies of naturally occurring spoken and written language – it has become increasingly clear that part of what we know about word meaning includes their usual usage patterns.[2] Let me show you what I mean, based on my discussion of this phenomenon in *The Language Myth*: take the words *explain* and *afraid*. The following sentences, featuring these very words, sound odd to native speakers of English (recall that a question mark preceding a sentence indicates that it sounds weird):

?The doctor explained him the news.
?She saw the afraid soldier.

The reason is that while *explain* and *afraid* could appear in these sentences, these just aren't the normal positions in a sentence where native speakers tend to use these words. So, compare these same sentences, now involving *tell* (rather than *explain*) and *scared* (rather than *afraid*):

The doctor told him the news.
She saw the scared soldier.

*Tell* and *scared* have broadly similar meanings to *explain* and *afraid*. But now, we see, the sentences are just fine. In contrast, *afraid* can be used successfully in relative clauses, introduced by *who*:

She saw the soldier who was afraid.
(cf. ?She saw the afraid soldier)

And *explain* tends to be used prior to direct objects, *the news*, rather than indirect objects, *him*:

> She explained the news to him
> (cf. ?She explained him the news)

It's not that *explain* and *afraid* cannot be used in these contexts: the semantically odd sentences are perfectly understandable. Corpus linguistics reveals it's just that they tend not to be. What this shows is this: not only do we have knowledge of what words mean and which real-world referents they usually apply to; we also have grammatical information about words, too. Part of our knowledge of words includes knowing which sorts of grammatical constructions they occur in. *Explain*, for instance, occurs before a direct object (*the news*), while *tell* can occur before an indirect object (*him*). We carry around a mental corpus in our heads, which allows us to use words based on the patterns in which we typically hear them used in our everyday encounters with our fellow language-users.[3]

## Webs of words

While each English word has, on average, around 2.5 distinct meanings, some words can have considerably more.[4] One of the most intensively studied words is the English preposition *over*. Consider some of its many different meanings:

| | |
|---|---|
| The picture is over the sofa. | 'above' |
| St. Paul's is over the river from Southwark. | 'on the other side' |
| Your article is over the page limit. | 'exceeds' |
| The movie is over. | 'completion' |
| The government handed power over to an interim authority. | 'transfer' |
| The relationship had altered over the years. | 'temporal' |
| The clouds are over the sun. | 'covering' |
| Jim looked over the document quite carefully. | 'examining' |
| The committee agonised over the decision. | 'focus of attention' |
| Joyce found over forty kinds of shells on the beach. | 'more than' |

| | |
|---|---|
| The heavy rains caused the river to flow over its banks. | 'excess' |
| She has a strange power over me. | 'control' |
| I would prefer tea over coffee. | 'preference' |
| After the false start, they started the race over. | 'repetition' |

What is remarkable is that this little word, *over*, should have so many distinct meanings, indicated on the right. And unless you were to stop and think about it, you might not notice that we are dealing with different meanings. But we are. In each of these examples, the meaning is not being derived from the linguistic context – this contrasts with examples such as *want* and *fast*, where the linguistic context seems to be inducing the semantic variation in the word's use. In the *over* examples, we come face to face with an instance, very common in language, where a single word-form has a range of distinct, albeit related, conventional meanings.

For instance, take the 'above' meaning for *over*: *The picture is over the sofa*, versus the 'covering' meaning: *The clouds are over the sun*. The 'covering' meaning is stored in our mental word web for *over*, as a separate meaning from the 'above' variant. It has to be. After all, with this 'covering' meaning, the clouds are below the sun, at least from our earth-bound perspective. It is by dint of the clouds being below the sun that the sun is thereby occluded from view. But in contrast, in the 'above' meaning, the lamp is above rather than below the table. And with the latter, there is no sense that *over* is designating a covering relation.

So the question is, how do words in general, and a specific word such as *over*, come to have so many distinct meanings? We know from historical evidence that the 'above' meaning was among the earliest to be used with *over*. It transpires that all the distinct meanings for *over* that we see today developed, ultimately, from this 'above' meaning. To begin to get at this, take for instance a relatively simple scene such as a horse jumping over a fence, as diagrammed in Figure 8.1.

In the sentence *The horse jumped over the fence*, the point at which the horse is *over* in the sense of 'above' the fence is

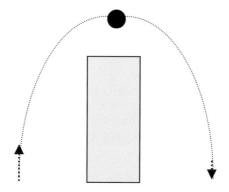

**Figure 8.1.** The trajectory for: *The horse jumped over the fence*

indicated by the black circle. But a consequence of what we know about the kind of jumping engaged in by horses is that they continue on their trajectory, under the force of gravity; they come to be located on the ground on the other side of the fence. And so, by virtue of the horse beginning its jump on one side of the fence and completing it on the other, this gives rise to what I will call a semantic 'parameter': 'on the other side'. This parameter is an atom of meaning that arises in everyday scenes like the one in Figure 8.1. The idea is that any scene we witness, or experience, is multifaceted. In Figure 8.1, the word *over* can be taken to refer to the point at which the horse is directly above the fence (the black circle). But the parameter – 'on the other side' – can become detached from the scenes that gave rise to it. And it turns out, over time, this parameter has been reanalysed by English-speakers as a new distinct meaning.

A sentence such as *The ball landed over the wall* is intermediate between the 'above' meaning of *over* and the 'on the other side of' meaning. For a ball to land over, in the sense of on the other side, of the wall, it must have followed a trajectory similar to that captured in Figure 8.1. But in a sentence such as the following: *Southwark is over the Thames*, this cannot mean that Southwark, a London borough, is somehow suspended above the River Thames. Nor can it mean that Southwark has somehow undergone a motion trajectory, akin to jumping horses. Our admittedly

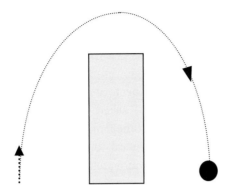

**Figure 8.2.** End-point focus in a motion trajectory

more mundane interpretation is that Southwark is located on the other side of the Thames, on the South Bank of the river, at least from the perspective of the person making the utterance. In short, an example such as this provides direct evidence that we have a distinct 'on the other side of' meaning associated with *over* in our minds.

The parameter 'on the other side' has become detached from the motion contexts that have given rise to it. In the minds of contemporary English users, it stands alone as a distinct meaning of *over*, one that can be used without implying a motion trajectory.

A further consequence of the motion trajectory diagrammed above is that being located on the other side implies the end-point of the trajectory. This is captured in Figure 8.2, where the end-point of the jump is indicated, again, by a black circle.

The end-point of the trajectory can also come to be reanalysed as a distinct semantic parameter. The end-point of the jump signals the completion of the jumping process. And in this way, a 'completion' parameter emerges: after all, when the end-point of a process is reached, the process – in this case, a motion trajectory – is complete. Evidence that *over* also has a distinct 'completion' meaning comes from sentences of the following sort: *The movie is over.* In this example, *over* conveys completion, rather than a more concrete, vertical relationship.

In previous research, my colleague Andrea Tyler and I demonstrated that a number of distinct meanings for *over* have derived from reanalysis of this everyday scene of experience.[5] New semantic parameters emerge, implicated by this very scene of experience: the motion trajectory diagrammed in Figure 8.1.

One question Tyler and I asked was this: why should these new derived meanings become conventionally associated with *over*, rather than a different word-form? The answer is that these new meanings for *over* are motivated both by how we experience 'over' relationships and by language use. The 'above' meaning is a salient feature of the dynamic scene – the position indicated by the black circle in Figure 8.1 – and it is conventionally encoded by the word *over*. The new, derived meaning, therefore, naturally comes to be attached to *over*, rather than a different word.

But the complex motion trajectory in Figure 8.1 gives rise to more than two new meanings: 'on the other side' and 'completion'. It is also the basis for the 'exceeds' meaning: *Your alcohol blood level is over the legal limit*; the 'temporal' meaning: *The relationship had altered over the years*; and the 'transfer' meaning: *The government handed over power*. What this shows is that re-occurring, humanly relevant scenes from our everyday action and interaction with the socio-physical world of experience are complex. They implicate a number of different semantic parameters. And these can come to be associated with a word-form, allowing a word to extend its semantic reach – Table 8.1 presents a summary of the different meanings that have arisen from the scene diagrammed in Figure 8.1.

But it turns out that the relationships between the various conventional meanings associated with *over* are not an unstructured mush: they exhibit surprisingly complex organisation. While some of the meanings are more salient in the minds of English-speakers, others are more peripherally associated with *over*. This is a consequence, in part, of frequency: the 'above' meaning is by far the most frequent meaning associated with *over* in our everyday language use. In part, this is because of the way in which the meanings of *over* have evolved. Historical evidence tells us that, in general

Table 8.1 *Cluster of meanings deriving from motion trajectory over an obstacle*

| Nature of meaning | Meaning | Example |
|---|---|---|
| Original meaning | 'above' | The picture is over the sofa. |
| Scene involving a motion trajectory over an obstacle | 'on the other side of' | St. Paul's is over the river from Southwark. |
| | 'exceeds' | Your article is over the page limit. |
| | 'completion' | The movie is over. |
| | 'transfer' | The government handed power over. |
| | 'temporal' | The relationship changed over the years. |

terms, more concrete meanings were around prior to more abstract ones: the 'temporal' meaning of *over* – *The relationship evolved over the years* – is more abstract than the 'above' meaning, and emerged later. These different lines of evidence, frequency and how recently a meaning emerged makes it possible to construct what the word web for *over* might look like in our minds.

The distinct meanings for *over* developed over time and by degrees.[6] And each is progressively less well connected to the original 'above' meaning for *over*. Tyler and I modelled this finding using a radiating lattice structure[7] – a 'semantic network' – which allowed us to represent the conceptual core and periphery of a word's related meanings: we did this in terms of physical proximity and distance (Figure 8.3). It also allowed us to capture the details of the relationships between distinct senses for *over*.

Figure 8.3 reveals the following. The range of meanings for *over* all derive, ultimately, from the 'above' meaning. And the various meanings are grouped into clusters. This clustering in our minds directly reflects the nature of embodied experience – how we experience scenes of experience – and usage-based effects – the role of our everyday use of language in driving

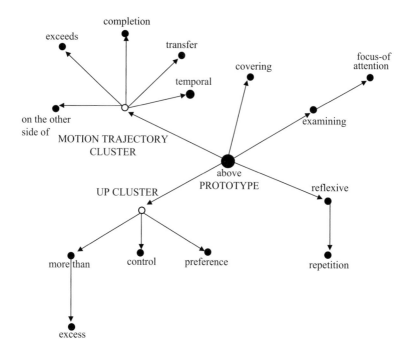

**Figure 8.3.** The semantic network for *over* (adapted from Tyler and Evans 2003: 80)

meaning extension. Each cluster of meanings derives from a salient scene of experience, which gives rise to new, distinct atoms of meaning – semantic parameters – that come to be convention-ally associated with *over* as new meanings. In Figure 8.3, distinct clusters are symbolised by the small unshaded circles. The distinct meanings themselves are represented by the small black circles, while the arrows indicate a likely sequence in the emergence of derived meanings. Finally, the use of the term 'prototype' acknowledges that this radiating lattice structure captures some-thing important about the way words are organised in the human mind: a word amounts to a category of distinct meanings, which are more or less central to the category.

Our mental category for *over* corresponds to the way in which our minds form categories: any kind of category. We categorise objects from other aspects of our lives in a similar way. As I explained in

Chapter 6, in our everyday lives we extract information, via sense-perception, about the world around us. And we use this information to group entities in our minds based on shared attributes, and relations between those attributes. For instance, entities that have wings are grouped into the category 'bird'.

But while many members of this category have feathers and can fly, some, such as ostriches, can't fly, and others, like penguins, can neither fly nor do they have feathers. As a consequence, our mental category for Bird tends to be organised around a prototype: a member of the category that best exemplifies the most salient attributes associated with the category. While I might think of a robin or a sparrow as a prototypical bird, and you might consider a jay or something else as prototypical – depending on where we live, and hence the sorts of birds that for you and me are most prevalent – neither of us would consider a penguin to be anything more than a marginal member of what we take a bird to be. In this way, members of the category Bird are structured, in our minds, as being more or less typical, depending on how conceptually close they are to the prototype.[8] So here's the point: in just the same way, words like *over* can be thought of as categories, with more or less typical meanings.[9]

But is there additional evidence that words really are structured in this way, as semantic networks in our minds? There is: it comes from psycholinguistic experiments – experiments which try and tap into what people know, and how they are drawing upon this knowledge when they use or understand language.[10] For instance, when native speakers of English are asked to sort sentences involving *over,* printed on cards, into piles, the piles invariably correspond to the distinct meanings I've depicted in the semantic network in Figure 8.3. And when language-users are asked to rank the meanings based on how prototypical they are, again, the 'above' meaning is consistently ranked as more central – more prototypical – in the word web than other meanings for *over.*[11]

In general, English-speakers consistently rate more concrete meanings, like the on-the-other-side-of meaning, as being more central, and hence more prototypical, than more abstract meanings, like the 'temporal' meaning (e.g. *The relationship endured over the years*). This also reflects the way in which word webs grow in our minds, as a word develops and extends its range of meanings. New word meanings derive, in large part, from embodied experience: recurring scenes that we experience in our everyday lives give rise to new semantic parameters. And so, it stands to reason that it is the concrete elements of these scenes that give rise to new word meanings in the first instance, with their more abstract parameters emerging later.

But a final caveat is in order. I've been implying that a word's semantic network has a relatively stable core, from which new meanings emerge – in the case of *over* that's certainly true. But webs of words can, over time, give rise to a reconfiguration of their semantic core: their prototype. And this can happen for a variety of reasons.

One such example is the English preposition *before*. At an early point in its historical development, *before* had an 'in front of' meaning. But this meaning is largely now only preserved in linguistic fossils such as the mid-eighteenth-century nursery rhyme, *Sing a song of sixpence*:

> Sing a song of sixpence,
> A pocket full of rye.
> Four and twenty blackbirds,
> Baked in a pie.
> When the pie was opened,
> The birds began to sing;
> Wasn't that a dainty dish,
> To set **before** the king?

The highlighted instance of *before* conveys an 'in front of' reading. Yet for our twenty-first-century minds, this particular meaning is all but extinct, restricted to very specific linguistic contexts requiring supporting verbs such as 'set', as in *set before*. But in other contexts the 'in front of' reading of *before* is nigh on impossible. Consider the following example: *John stood before me*. Informal experiments with native speakers reveal that the first interpretation that comes to mind is the 'first in temporal sequence' meaning: 'John rose to standing position prior to me'; the 'John is in front of me' interpretation, seems, nowadays, to require more effort. But the historical evidence demonstrates that the earliest meaning associated with *before* was the spatial meaning, rather than the temporal one which has come to usurp it.

One reason for this reconfiguration is that words form a system, with interlocking relations. And if the semantic territory across words becomes too close, this can lead, over time, to a semantic recalibration: a word can shift its inherent semantic make-up. As *in front of*, a complex preposition, has evolved, it has gradually taken over the semantic territory once occupied by *before*. This has led to a shift, in the minds of English-speakers, in the word web of *before*. For contemporary speakers, the temporal meaning now lies at its epicentre.

Curiously, the same shift has not occurred with *behind*: *behind* still has a spatial meaning at the heart of its semantic network – *John stood behind me*, which can only mean John is posterior in space, rather than in time. In part, this is because the preposition *in back of*, which corresponds to *in front of*, has not taken hold, at least not to the extent exhibited by 'in front of'. For instance, while *in back of* exists in American English, it doesn't exist at all in British English.

In other situations, words continue to happily co-exist, but they do so by forming an interlocking system where different words share out which parts of semantic space they relate to. A case in point involves the prepositions *above, over, under* and *below*. The prototypical meanings for each of these concern specific regions of space along the vertical axis.

*Above* describes a spatial relation where one entity is higher than another, but not in relative proximity: *The flock of birds are somewhere above the city*. In contrast, *over* encodes a higher-than relation which implies contact or, at the very least, close proximity to the city: we can say, for instance, *The flock of birds are over the city*, where the use of *over* suggests close proximity. But in contrast with *above*, it is decidedly odd to use *over* in the same sentence with *somewhere*. And this is because the use of *somewhere* implies that the birds are obscured from view and hence less proximal: ?*The flock of birds are somewhere over the city.*

This point is quite subtle, so I'll pursue this a bit more. Compare the difference between *The tablecloth is over the table* and *The tablecloth is above the table.* In the former, the tablecloth is draped over the table, so that it is in contact with the table surface. In contrast, in the latter, the typical interpretation would be that the tablecloth is somehow suspended so that it's not in contact with the table. It would be legitimate to use *above* in this way when the tablecloth is, for instance, folded and stored on a shelf above the table.

And just as *over* and *above* contrast in terms of the 'higher-than' region along the vertical plane, *under* and *below* behave in an analogous way in the 'lower-than' region. Compare being *undersea* versus being *below the sea. Undersea* means to be below the water's surface: immersed in the ocean. In contrast, the use of *below*, in this context, can usually only refer to a location beneath the seabed, such as when laying oil pipes.

Figure 8.4 summarises the distinction made by these four words in cutting up vertical space. The thick bold line represents the ground, while the dashed lines divide up vertical space in terms of relative proximity higher and lower than the ground respectively.

In the final analysis, we carry around with us webs of meaning for each word we know. Each word web, in our minds, is structured in terms of more central and more peripheral meanings, with more peripheral meanings chained in a network of related meanings. These webs of words have developed over historical time, a consequence of the sorts of scenes of experience we encounter and the humanly relevant consequences of these scenes. It is these consequences – what I am calling parameters – which allow our words to gradually take on new meanings, extending their semantic range. In this way, our minds develop an ever expanding, albeit motivated, set of linguistic symbols. And these allow us to communicate our experiences of our social–physical world.

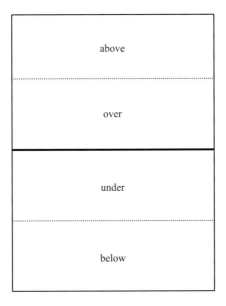

**Figure 8.4.** English prepositions of vertical space

## Does conceptual metaphor change word meanings?

I want to now consider an issue that has, from time to time, cropped up in the research literature. Some researchers, most notably George Lakoff among these, have claimed that conceptual metaphor plays *the* critical role in creating new word meanings. According to Lakoff, many of the distinct meanings for *over* derive from the application of conceptual metaphor.

For instance, Lakoff claims that *over*'s 'control' meaning (e.g. *She has a strange power over me*) is motivated by the independently existing CONTROL IS UP metaphor.[12] On this view, the reason that *over* has acquired a 'control' meaning is because we have the conceptual metaphor CONTROL IS UP: this drives a meaning extension, such that *over* gets a new 'control' meaning.

But let's look at what the conceptual metaphor account of word change commits us to: it predicts that words jump from one meaning to a fully formed new one – semantic extension in word meanings should be discontinuous. But in fact, this is not how words, or other grammatical constructions for that matter, derive new meanings. A new word meaning emerges gradually, beginning with minor shifts in the semantic territory that it covers. Over time, these semantic flavours may stabilise, leading to a new, conventional meaning: one we associate with a particular word or construction, and carry around in our semantic memory.

For example, the original meaning of the *(be) going to* construction is related to motion: *John is going to town*. But today, this construction also has a future meaning: *It's going to rain*. It has been claimed that the conceptual metaphor TIME IS OBJECTS IN MOTION (ALONG A PATH) – the Moving Time mapping I discussed in Chapter 4 – has led to the development of this new future meaning for the *(be) going to* construction.[13]

However, the *(be) going to* construction also exhibits semantic flavours that are intermediate between the motion and future meanings:

| | |
|---|---|
| I'm going to eat. | 'intention' |
| John is going to do his best to make Mary happy. | 'intention' and 'prediction' |

In the first example, the speaker is expressing an intention to go and eat. But a consequence of this is that the speaker must move to an appropriate location to facilitate the act of eating. Hence, there is a remnant of the original motion meaning apparent here. And, in any case, motion towards some goal implies an intention to reach that goal for some purpose. In short, intentionality is an inference that arises from the act of moving from A to B: it is a semantic parameter that arises from motion scenarios, just as we saw earlier with similar cases for *over*.

In the second example, motion is no longer apparent. But what we do have is the parameter: 'intention', plus the additional parameter: 'prediction'. John intends to try and make Mary happy. And thus, the utterance predicts that John will attempt to make Mary happy. In short, a consequence of intending to do something is that the intention is thereby predicted. Prediction,

**Figure 8.5.** Semantic evolution of the 'future' meaning of *(be) going to.*

which appears to be a pre-requisite for a future meaning, is a consequence of intentionality. Intentionality, in turn, is a consequence of motion. What we have, then, is a chaining effect in semantic evolution, whereby distinct semantic parameters emerge. And these pave the way for a full-blown 'future' meaning for *(be) going to*, as illustrated in Figure 8.5.

Importantly, the evolution of the 'future' meaning was indirect. The 'intention' and 'prediction' parameters appeared first. They emerged prior to the full-blown 'future' use of *(be) going to*. But this finding is not what Conceptual Metaphor Theory predicts: we should see a discontinuous jump from one domain, MOTION THROUGH SPACE, to another, TIME. But in actual fact, there are incremental shifts in meaning that ultimately result in a new 'future' meaning. We can capture this staged development of the 'future' meaning in the U-shaped curve of the diagram in Figure 8.6. The reality contrasts with the position assumed by Conceptual Metaphor Theory, which predicts a direct jump from the 'motion' meaning to the 'future' meaning, as represented by the dashed line running from stage I to stage IV.

So, how might we account for a 'control' meaning for *over*, given that I've now excluded conceptual metaphor as the driving force for meaning extension? It is more likely that *over* developed

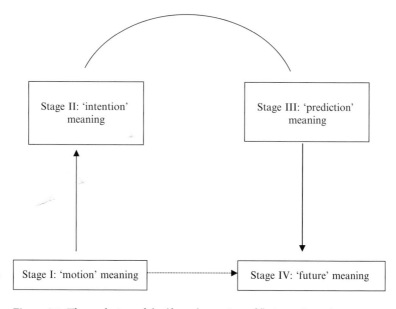

Figure 8.6. The evolution of the 'future' meaning of 'being going to'

its 'control' meaning from recurring scenes where one individual, higher than another, exerts control over another. This is a
functional consequence of many sorts of physical encounters,
especially those involving physical combat such as wrestling,
boxing, judo and other martial arts. A consequence of one person
being 'over' their combatant is that, in such scenes of experience, a
semantic parameter of 'control' naturally emerges. And over time,
*over* can gradually take on what starts as a situated inference, until
eventually a new, fully formed 'control' meaning emerges.

## The illusion of semantic unity

One consequence of words amounting to categories of distinct,
albeit related, meanings is that this can give rise to the illusion of
semantic unity. For the sake of variety, let's consider a different
word: the English noun *time*. This word encompasses a range of
quite distinct conventional meanings:[14]

| | |
|---|---|
| The time for action has arrived. | 'moment' |
| Time flies when you're having fun. | 'temporal compression' |
| Time drags when you have nothing to do. | 'protracted duration' |
| The relationship lasted a long time. | 'duration' |
| His time [=death] had come. | 'event' |
| Time flows on forever. | 'matrix' |

In the first example, *time* refers to a discrete temporal point or moment, without reference to its duration. This we might dub the 'moment' meaning. Next up, *time* refers to the phenomenologically real experience whereby the duration, while objectively constant as measured, for instance, against a clock, 'feels' as if it is shorter than it actually is. This amounts to the phenomenon of 'temporal compression' that I discussed in Chapter 4. In the next example, *time* refers to the experience of time lasting longer than usual – the duration 'feels' as if it is more than it actually is. This is the phenomenon of 'protracted duration', also discussed in Chapter 4. In the next sentence, *time* has a 'duration' meaning. And in the next, *time* has an 'event' meaning. In English, *time* can be used productively to refer to events of different sorts, for instance, childbirth: *The young woman's time had come*, or even the end of a particular activity, for instance the end of the licensed period for selling and purchasing alcohol in a pub – e.g., *The publican rang the bell to signal time* – or the end of a football match – e.g. *The referee blew time*. In the final sentence, *time* refers to *the* event in which all else occurs. This I dub the 'matrix' meaning, as here *time* refers to a manifold or matrix within which we conceive of all existence unfolding.

But a consequence of having a single word-form – *time* – for a range of distinct, albeit related concepts, is the illusion of semantic unity. In English, we often think about time as if it is some sort of homogenous entity. But all too often, misunderstandings can arise precisely because English-speakers are using the same word to refer to different things. Consider this exchange on Yahoo Answers, where web users can ask questions and receive responses from fellow web users (names have been changed):

TOM:        'would one say that the word 'time' as in our daily lives,
            calanders [*sic.*] how we use it in our languages, how we act,
            just the word alone 'time 'is used more often? [*sic.*] we use it
            that word to navigate ones survival?'

ARTIST:     'Here is a good example of how time effects [*sic.*] us. if you
            want to be successful then 'be on time'.'

TOM:        'great answer. just a question basically of how many usages it
            has in our daily lives and i would say its in our hearts minds
            and soul constantly..and i think its time i do the dishes
            LOL thanks'

In his initial post, Tom attempts to clarify what he is asking
about when he uses the word *time*. Tom is asking about
the frequency with which a particular usage of *time* occurs.
But his clarification only serves to enlarge the domain, to cover
a wide array of different temporal ideas. Time 'as in our daily
lives' might refer to duration, or to the passage of time, as in
the sense of time as a matrix. Or indeed, it might relate to
time in its clock-time sense, as when we say 'What time is it?'
The use of the term *calanders* [*sic.*] might relate to event-
reckoning systems, or again to duration, or indeed to the
matrix meaning for time, all of which are distinct. And finally,
enlarging the use of *time* out to relate to 'how we use it in our
languages' covers a whole host of different meanings for time.
In the end, we are not really clear what the question is asking.
Is it about the different meanings of the word *time*, or
something else?

But what is evident is this: the fact that in English *time* has so
many different meanings leads the questioner to think that there
is something inalienably central to the various uses of the word.
And hence he, like many of us, assumes that there is something
homogenous about the category to which the word *time* refers.
The response by Artist points to two distinct concepts: time as a
temporal point – a moment – and time as referring to a measurement system, as in clock-time, and specifically the idiom *on time*,
which refers to 'being punctual', a conventional meaning associated with this phrase.

While English has one word – *time* – for a range of quite distinct experience types, other languages don't have a single word that covers all of this semantic territory. For instance, recent research on the Amazonian language Amondawa reveals that there is no equivalent of the English word *time* in that language.[15] Another example is the Inuit languages – the languages spoken by native Americans, particularly in northern parts of Canada. Moreover, even languages that are genetically related to English utilise distinct words to describe the semantic territory covered by the single lexical form, *time*, in English.

French is a good example of this. For instance, the French word *heure* ('hour') is used to describe the moment meaning of English *time*:

C'est l'heure de manger
'It's time to eat'
(Literally: 'It's the hour to eat')

But some of the other meanings of the English *time* are covered by the form *temps* ('time'). The consequence is that while for English-speakers, time is a unified category, in French it isn't. And for some languages it may not even constitute a category to begin with, as in the case of the Amondawa or the Inuit languages. In essence, because of the way the English word *time* has developed, with a set of distinct, albeit related, meanings occupying a single semantic network in the minds of English-speakers, we inevitably come to think of the word as relating to a coherent and unified category. This leads English-speakers to perceive semantic unity. But this, ultimately, is an artefact of English, rather than being an objective feature of Time, whatever Time ultimately is.

## The encyclopaedic nature of meaning

At the outset of J.R.R. Tolkien's *The Hobbit*, Gandalf the wizard comes to see Bilbo, the eponymous Hobbit. Gandalf attempts to persuade the rather excitement-adverse Bilbo to come on an adventure. Bilbo, upon seeing Gandalf, greets him:

> 'Good Morning!' said Bilbo, and he meant it. The sun was shining, and the grass was very green. But Gandalf looked at him from under long bushy eyebrows that stuck out further than the brim of his shady hat.
>
> 'What do you mean?' he said. 'Do you wish me a good morning, or mean that it is a good morning whether I want it or not; or that you feel good this morning; or that it is a morning to be good on?'
>
> 'All of them at once,' said Bilbo. 'And a very fine morning for a pipe of tobacco out of doors, into the bargain.'

And finally, in attempting to curtail the conversation, Bilbo concludes:

> 'Good morning!' he said at last. 'We don't want any adventures here, thank you! You might try over The Hill or across The Water.' By this he meant that the conversation was at an end.
>
> 'What a lot of things you do use Good morning for!' said Gandalf. 'Now you mean that you want to get rid of me, and that it won't be good till I move off.'

One of the hallmarks of language is that it is encyclopaedic in nature. Not only do we carry around with us, in our minds, webs of meaning for individual words; in addition, each node in each of our mental word webs is linked to a vast repository of encyclopaedic knowledge. We got a glimpse of this when I discussed the verb *open* earlier.

The exchange between Gandalf and Bilbo, and the use of *Good morning*, illustrates this property of language and further demonstrates the strikingly malleable nature of linguistic expressions. As Gandalf observes, *Good morning* can be put to a remarkably wide array of communicative functions. We have rich encyclopaedic knowledge for the range of situations that words, and other expressions, can be used in, and the functions they can perform in those situations. In this section, I explore exactly what it means to say that word meaning is encyclopaedic in nature. I ask, what must our encyclopaedic knowledge look like, in our minds, for words to be so protean in nature?

Take for instance, the different interpretations associated with, on the face of it, the relatively unremarkable word *book*:

| | |
|---|---|
| That's a heavy book. | 'tome' |
| That antiquarian book is illegible. | 'text' |
| That's a boring book. | 'level of interest' |
| That's a long book. | 'duration' |

In each of these sentences, *book* takes a slightly different meaning. In part, this is a consequence of the different linguistic contexts in which the word is embedded. The word *book* can variously refer to the physical tome, as when we describe the book as heavy; it can refer to the text within the tome; or it may relate to how interesting we find the book's content; or to how long it takes to read the book.

But we wouldn't want to say, in each of these distinct interpretations, that *book* has a different underlying meaning. In each case, the underlying meaning relates to the physical artefact that a reader interacts with by reading the text printed on the book's pages. In this way, these different interpretations for *book* don't relate to distinct conventional meanings for *book*. So, here, we are not dealing with distinct meanings in *book*'s word web. Instead, these are context-dependent interpretations, arising from a single underlying meaning. And as such, this linguistic behaviour differs from a word such as *over,* in my earlier discussion, where there are clearly a range of quite distinct, conventional meanings forming part of our word web for *over*. So, how do we account for the different interpretations of *book*?

The answer necessitates uncovering the nature of the non-linguistic information to which the word *book* provides access. This knowledge can be usefully thought of in terms of a mental encyclopaedia.[16] A word like *book* comes with a vast, structured body of knowledge – everything we might know about books. This includes our knowledge of how we interact with books. For instance, we know what a book looks and feels like, and the nature of its physical organisation. Books are physical artefacts of

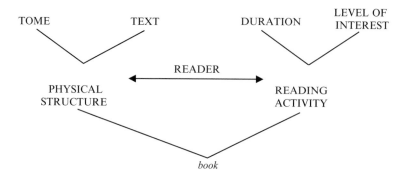

**Figure 8.7.** Encyclopaedic knowledge for *book*

a particular kind: they consist of pages bound together, with print on the pages, and the pages sequenced in a particular order. We also know that books can be electronic, which we interact with via electronic devices: eReaders simulate the physical properties of books, such as the way in which pages are 'turned' on a Kindle or a Nook device, for instance. We also know that books can be interacted with in a range of quite different ways: the blind interact with Braille-based books by touch. We also have knowledge regarding audio books, and so on. I have diagrammed some of this encyclopaedic knowledge in Figure 8.7.

Figure 8.7 captures some of the types of knowledge we must have, for *book*, in our minds. For instance, we know that books often constitute physical entities. We also know that readers interact with books through the process of reading. These two distinct sorts of knowledge – knowledge relating to an artefact, on one hand, and the process of reading, on the other – are captured in Figure 8.7 by the two types of knowledge in our heads: PHYSICAL STRUCTURE and READING ACTIVITY respectively. The word *book*, at the bottom of the diagram, provides mental access to these knowledge structures. And while I am using language to denote this knowledge, the terms PHYSICAL STRUCTURE and READING ACTIVITY are mnemonics: they represent the rich and detailed bodies of analogue (which is to say, non-linguistic) knowledge that we have for these notions.

Moreover, both these bodies of knowledge are related by virtue of our knowledge of what a READER is and does – the entity that interacts with the physical artefact by handling the tome and reading the printed text. This knowledge is captured, in Figure 8.7, by the double-headed arrow that connects our knowledge of the READER to the PHYSICAL STRUCTURE and READING ACTIVITY knowledge structures. Moreover, each of these knowledge units, again, consists of a large, detailed, but structured body of knowledge. I attempt to evoke this, again using mnemonics, to stand for the detailed, multimodal knowledge we undoubtedly possess: these are TOME, TEXT, LEVEL OF INTEREST and DURATION.

The knowledge unit PHYSICAL STRUCTURE concerns the physical artefact. This, presumably, includes the detailed knowledge we must have concerning the material aspects of what books are, including their dimensions – books are normally entities that we can hold in our hands – their weight, their binding – paper or cloth – and so on. This aspect of our knowledge about books is captured by the TOME mnemonic. In addition, books consist of text which is interacted with through the process of reading: the TEXT knowledge structure.

Our knowledge of the READING ACTIVITY relates to the process involved in interacting with books, especially the nature of the interaction with the text itself. One consequence of this is that reading takes up a period of time: the DURATION knowledge unit. Depending on the amount of text involved, reading can take lesser or greater amounts of time. Another consequence is the level of interest that a given book holds for the reader: our knowledge of LEVEL OF INTEREST. While one reader might judge a particular book to be interesting, another might find it to be boring – all a matter of taste.

Now, with an understanding of some of the encyclopaedic knowledge that the word *book* can potentially access, let's see how this accounts for the different interpretations of *book* in the earlier sentences. In essence, each of the sentences activates a different component of the encyclopaedic knowledge network for *book* in our minds. For instance, the interpretations in the first two sentences require activation of our knowledge of a book as a PHYSICAL STRUCTURE. But each involves differential activation of sub-parts of this knowledge. In the first sentence, what gets activated is the TOME knowledge structure, while in the second it is the TEXT component that is activated.

In contrast, the interpretations for *book* in the final two sentences arise from activation of the READING ACTIVITY knowledge unit. In the third sentence, for instance, it is the DURATION component that is activated. And in the final sentence, the LEVEL OF INTEREST component is activated.

We must have encyclopaedic knowledge, of the sort represented in Figure 8.7, to be able to correctly interpret the different usages of *book* in each of these sentences. What this further reveals is that our knowledge of words incorporates a large meaning potential, allowing us to use words in a range of ways, even when it is ostensibly the same word that we are drawing upon. Words exhibit malleability, not just because we have word webs in our minds. But also, each word meaning is connected to a large encyclopaedic inventory of knowledge. This allows us to create and innovate, in the way we use language, and consequently in terms of the raft of meanings we can employ words to convey.

## The private life of words

I began this chapter with Alice and Humpty Dumpty. And in a chapter all about words, it's fitting we should also end it with Lewis Carroll's brilliant wordplay. As a student and later a tutor at Oxford, Carroll was exposed to the theories of the most influential philologist in late Victorian England, Friedrich Max Müller.[17] The prevalent nineteenth-century view of language was that words are organic: they change and mutate in and through language use. His celebrated linguistic jokes sought to uncover what he viewed as the private life of words: for Carroll, words are alive, and exist

independently of their speakers – words have multiple shades and
hues. Humpty Dumpty is Carroll's language analyst-in-chief, who
interprets words in his own idiosyncratic way.

During their conversation, Alice asks Humpty about the meaning of the Jabberwocky poem:

> 'You seem very clever at explaining words, Sir,' said Alice. 'Would
> you kindly tell me the meaning of the poem called 'Jabberwocky'?'
>
> 'Let's hear it,' said Humpty Dumpty. 'I can explain all the
> poems that were ever invented – and a good many that haven't
> been invented just yet.'

This sounded very hopeful, so Alice repeated the first verse:

> *'Twas brillig, and the slithy toves*
> *Did gyre and gimble in the wabe;*
> *All mimsy were the borogoves,*
> *And the mome raths outgrabe.*

> 'That's enough to begin with,' Humpty Dumpty interrupted:
> 'there are plenty of hard words there. '*Brillig*' means four o'clock
> in the afternoon – the time when you begin *broiling* things for
> dinner.'
>
> 'That'll do very well,' said Alice: and '*slithy*'?'
>
> 'Well, '*slithy*' means 'lithe and slimy.' 'Lithe' is the same as
> 'active.' You see it's like a portmanteau – there are two meanings
> packed up into one word.'
>
> 'I see it now,' Alice remarked thoughtfully: 'and what are
> '*toves*'?'
>
> 'Well, '*toves*' are something like badgers – they're something
> like lizards – and they're something like corkscrews.'
>
> 'They must be very curious looking creatures.'
>
> 'They are that,' said Humpty Dumpty: 'also they make their
> nests under sun-dials – also they live on cheese.'
>
> 'And what's the '*gyre*' and to '*gimble*'?'
>
> 'To '*gyre*' is to go round and round like a gyroscope. To '*gimble*'
> is to make holes like a gimblet.'
>
> 'And '*the wabe*' is the grass-plot round a sun-dial, I suppose?'
> said Alice, surprised at her own ingenuity.

'Of course it is. It's called '*wabe*,' you know, because it goes a long way before it, and a long way behind it – '

'And a long way beyond it on each side,' Alice added.

'Exactly so. Well, then, '*mimsy*' is 'flimsy and miserable' (there's another portmanteau for you). And a '*borogove*' is a thin shabby-looking bird with its feathers sticking out all round – something like a live mop.'

'And then '*mome raths*'?' said Alice. 'I'm afraid I'm giving you a great deal of trouble.'

'Well, a '*rath*' is a sort of green pig: but '*mome*' I'm not certain about. I think it's short for 'from home' – meaning that they'd lost their way, you know.'

'And what does '*outgrabe*' mean?'

'Well, '*outgrabing*' is something between bellowing and whistling, with a kind of sneeze in the middle: however, you'll hear it done, maybe – down in the wood yonder – and when you've once heard it you'll be *quite* content.'

In the two *Alice in Wonderland* books, Carroll provides 'a distinctive response to anxieties about meaning and agency, arriving at humorous solutions which elude rational scholarship'.[18] Words are not fixed points in time: they change and evolve, and the same word can mean quite different things on different occasions of use. But words always have to be interpreted: we use language to communicate, and sometimes to amaze. And so it is that while words have a private life, they are *never* fully independent of their language-users, as Humpty's virtuoso interpretation reveals. We have an innate capacity for meaning-making that allows us inside the secret life of words, as Humpty shows. It is this meaning-making capacity that, in part, endows words with their shape-shifting powers to begin with. And this is the subject to which we now turn.

# Chapter 9    Meaning in the mix

In the novel, *As I Lay Dying*, William Faulkner narrates the thoughts of his protagonists using a stream-of-consciousness technique. One character, Vardaman, a young child, is in a stall with a horse. Faulkner presents Vardaman's thoughts – using language – to recreate the child's perceptions of his surroundings, and in particular of the horse that Vardaman dimly perceives through the darkness:

> It is as though the dark were resolving him out of his integrity, into an unrelated scattering of components—snuffings and stampings; smells of cooling flesh and ammoniac hair; an illusion of a co-ordinated whole of splotched hide and strong bones within which, detached and secret and familiar, an *is* different from my *is*. I see him dissolve–legs, a rolling eye, a gaudy splotching like cold flames and float upon the dark in fading solution; all one yet neither; all either yet none. I can see hearing coil toward him, caressing, shaping his hard shape–fetlock, hip, shoulder and head; smell and sound.

The horse emerges to Vardaman through the darkness, not as a single, coherent whole, but in fragments, a 'scattering of components'. Faulkner brilliantly conveys how the horse seems to the child: Vardaman perceives the disembodied snuffings, the stampings and cooling flesh and the gaudy splotching. But while Faulkner attempts to convey Vardaman's thought processes in the dark stable using language, language is not the same as thought. After all, as I observed in Chapter 6, and in detail in *The Language Myth*, thought can proceed in the absence of language.

So here's the point: when Faulkner attempts to recreate Vardaman's *pure* thoughts, using language as the medium for doing so, he is in fact doing more than this. In this chapter, I will show that

our human meaning-making capacity is a consequence of the
symbiotic interaction between our conceptual system – the repository of our concepts, our units of thought – *and* language – our
linguistic system. Both are essential to produce the complex mental
simulations that Faulkner creates in the minds of his readers, as he
attempts to recreate Vardaman's thought processes. And in using
language to help coordinate and construct Vardaman's thoughts,
Faulkner is not in fact presenting pure, distilled thought. Language
is not the same as thought. Our linguistic and conceptual systems
work in tandem, to produce complex ideas that are more than the
sum of the linguistic or conceptual parts that give rise to them.

It is by virtue of co-creating a complex conception, using both
concepts and language, that Faulkner is able to conjure such a rich
experience: Vardaman experiencing the horse as through the
prism of darkness 'as though the dark were resolving him out of
his integrity'. To explain this process of perceiving the horse, the
animal being 'resolved' into 'an unrelated scattering of components' requires language. Pure thought, on its own, is insufficient to
provide this level of complexity: language plays an important role
in shaping and constructing the very thoughts it serves to express.

## A design feature for human meaning-making

In evolutionary terms, the embodied representations in the conceptual system preceded language. A conceptual system enables an
organism to represent the world it encounters, to store experiences,
to learn, and so to respond to new experiences as a consequence.
A conceptual system is what enables us to be able to tell friend from
foe, competitor from potential sexual mate, and to act and interact
in situationally appropriate ways. Our repository of concepts facilitates thought, categorisation of entities in the world and our action
in and interaction with our spatio-temporal environment.

While many other species have conceptual systems, humans are
unique in having language.[1] The range and complexity of human

conceptions, as we see with the quote from Faulkner's novel, appears to far exceed that of any other species. An obvious implication is that it is language that may provide, in part at least, a means of harnessing our conceptual systems, releasing its potential – a conclusion that has been reached by a number of leading cognitive scientists.[2]

The psychologist Lawrence Barsalou[3] has suggested that the function of language is to provide an executive control function, operating over body-based concepts in the conceptual system. And this view seems to be on the right lines. Language provides the framework that enables sophisticated composition of concepts, resulting in the rich meaning that a skilled practitioner, such as Faulkner, achieves.

Of course, language is not necessary to combine concepts – babies can perform rudimentary arithmetic way before they acquire their mother tongue.[4] And adults who suffer a catastrophic loss of language – known as aphasia – due to damage to specific brain areas retain otherwise normal intelligence.[5] So, it can't be the case that language is required in order to combine ideas and produce compositional thought. But language does enable us to combine concepts, in novel ways, allowing far more sophisticated conceptions than would otherwise be possible.

Language achieves this by virtue of constituting a grammatical system, with words and grammatical constructions cueing activations of specific body-based states in the brain. Their integration gives rise to complex 'simulations' – re-activations, by the brain, of stored embodied concepts – which is the stuff of thought. This means that language provides added value to our conceptual systems. It allows us to control and manipulate the very concepts that evolved for evolutionarily more rudimentary functions, such as object recognition and classification. Under the control of language, we can make use of body-based concepts in order to produce abstract thought, and to communicate with other minds – in the absence of telepathy, language both facilitates and enhances a rare and sceptred form of meaning-making.

To illustrate, read the following English sentence, then close your eyes and conjure up, in your mind's eye, exactly which hue of 'red' comes to mind: *The red fox (Vulpes vulpes) is the largest of the true foxes and the most abundant member of the Carnivora'.*[6] Now do the same with the following observation, uttered by none other than Gwyneth Paltrow: *Beauty, to me, is about being comfortable in your own skin. That, or a kick-ass red lipstick.*[7]

My bet is that the use of *red* in the fox example calls to mind a dun or browny red, but in the lipstick example what comes to mind is a vivid or true red. What we are doing, when we read these sentences, is activating a hue based on past experiences of different types of red. The perceptual hue is coming, in these cases, not from the word *red*. The precise perceptual hue – the meaning – of red doesn't reside there in the word: it can't, otherwise the word-form *red* would convey the same thing on each occasion of use. Rather, what we are doing when we read each sentence is re-activating a stored mental representation – a concept – one that is rich, vivid and detailed.

As you closed your eyes, you will have been able to visualise, in your mind's eye, exactly the shade you were imagining. This re-activation of a perceptual experience is made possible precisely because we each carry around with us a repository of concepts. This further reveals that what we mean when we use the word *red* is, strictly speaking, not a function of language. Of course, language, in these examples, is helping us to narrow in on the right kind of perceptual hue: the right kind of red. But much of this *narrowing in* is coming from the other words in each sentence, like *fox* and *lipstick*, which help us figure out what sort of hue to visualise. But whatever the linguistic function of the word *red* in these examples, the hue is most definitely not conveyed by the word itself.

What's going on is that, here, the word *red* is cueing that part of the colour spectrum that relates to the hue red. But here's the really important part. Each sentence is activating a different part of the red colour spectrum. We derive distinct simulations for *red*.

And this is achieved via language, which nuances which part of the red colour spectrum we should activate. These visualisations, while not as vivid as actually seeing a fox or, indeed, Gwyneth Paltrow's lipstick-adorned mouth in the flesh, are nevertheless rich experiences. More generally, concepts in the conceptual system are what we might refer to as 'analogue' in nature: they encompass the vivid, multimodal character of the experiences they are representations of – an idea I'll explore in more detail later in the chapter.

Language guides how our conceptual system is engaged in meaning construction: it shepherds the nature of the simulation that is derived. Linguistically mediated thought enables the re-activation of stored experiences: it shapes the simulations. To return to an analogy I introduced in Chapter 2, if the conceptual system is the orchestra, then language is the conductor, which coordinates and directs the way the instruments are played, and without which the full splendour of the symphony couldn't be realised.

Let's take another example, the by now familiar quotidian one: a cup of coffee, perhaps one that you've bought on the go, in a paper cup from a high-street coffee shop chain. You'll feel the cup in your hand: the warmth of the coffee coming through the cup. You'll sense its weight and the shape of the paper cup, as you clasp your hand around it. You'll also, inevitably, smell the aroma of the coffee perlocating through the lid up into your nostrils. And as you sip, carefully, from beneath the hot, foamy covering of the coffee, you experience the taste. Now, a number of different sense–perceptory modalities are engaged in even this simple act: of holding, raising to your lips and drinking a slurp of coffee. There is the motor action, as you grasp the cup, gauge its weight and move your hand and arm in synchronicity, so that the cup approaches your lips. And as you slurp, you are coordinating the pursing of your lips, the imbibing of the coffee, with the motor event of raising the cup to drink.

As we saw in Chapter 3, the way in which our brains construct even a relatively simple experience like this doesn't involve sending all this information to a single spot, where the brain integrates the information. Instead, different areas of the brain are specialised for processing various kinds of information: taste, touch and weight, sight, sound, and so on. And these different 'sensory modalities' are integrated in a *when* rather than a *where*: a place in the brain; synchronised oscillation of neurons in the different sensory processing areas of the brain allow coordination, and integration, of different aspects of the multimodal information associated with a single event: raising a coffee cup to your lips and tasting, and smelling the coffee.

And then later, when we remember what the coffee looked and tasted like, we reactivate this same body of sensory–motor experiences. In this way, our recollection of those experiences is analogue in nature: it recreates the diverse, sensory character of those experiences. And none of this depends upon language.

Accordingly, it is these sorts of reasons that characterise the representations available from the conceptual system as analogue concepts. They are analogous to the experience types of which they are representations. They are rich and multifaceted: they reflect all the aspects of the experience types of which that they are records.

So if concepts are analogue in nature, what are the representations like that language encodes? In slightly different terms, what, then, does language bring to the table in the meaning-construction process? While language provides a gateway to the conceptual system – one of its principal functions in the meaning-construction process – it is far more than a mere conduit to conceptual knowledge. After all, to shape the simulations we produce, when we use language to bootstrap analogue concepts, language must be bringing with it a type of representation that is different from those that inhabit the conceptual system.

One line of evidence for thinking that language does have a distinct type of representation – one that is qualitatively distinct from the analogue concepts in the conceptual system – is this: neuro-psychological conditions where patients suffer damage to parts of the brain responsible for encoding analogue concepts.

For instance, patients with Parkinson's disease display difficulty in carrying out motor movements, suggesting their motor representations are damaged. Nevertheless, these patients are still able to use and more or less understand corresponding action verbs, such as *to kick* and *to hammer*.[8] Likewise, patients with motor neurone disease are still able to process action verbs.[9] The conclusion from this, and the one I reached in *The Language Myth*, is that part of the concept remains, even in the absence of the corresponding body-based state. A conceptual representation must consist of more than simply an embodied analogue concept.

This is strikingly illustrated by patients suffering from apraxia. This is the condition where patients retain part of the knowledge associated with a concept; due to brain damage of the relevant motor area, they are unable to perform the corresponding action. For example, a patient with apraxia might know the word for *a hammer*, and even to be able to explain what hammers are used for, and what they are usually made of. In fact, such a person would be able to demonstrate quite a lot of knowledge about hammers via language. However, a patient suffering from apraxia would be incapable of demonstrating how to use a hammer: they would have no inkling of how to hold and how to swing a hammer. This reveals that we construct our conceptual representations from various sources, not exclusively body-based analogue concepts.

But in the absence of an analogue concept, something nevertheless remains: language would seem to provide a semantic contribution too – one that persists even in the absence of the corresponding analogue concept. In short, language must be providing representations – but of a different sort – that allow access to the analogue representations in the conceptual system. And more than that, these linguistic representations guide the way in which analogue representations become activated. After all, the different simulations for *red*, in the 'red fox' and 'red lipstick' sentences, are a consequence of being massaged by language to produce the correct interpretation. We can conclude from this that the essential ingredient for human-like meaning-making is the interaction between the conceptual system, on the one hand, and the linguistic system on the other.

## The meaning of grammar

So, to return to the question: what are the language-specific representations that persist in the face of the loss of corresponding analogue concepts? A direct window into the representations provided by language can be gleaned from examining the grammatical system of a language.

A common misconception is that the grammatical system is meaningless – that it provides a formal set of instructions, but that meaning resides elsewhere. But on the contrary, an investigation into what it is that grammar does shatters any illusions: human grammar provides grist to the meaning-making mill.

A central design feature of language is that it divides into two systems: the lexical and grammatical subsystems. To show you what I mean, consider the following sentence:

**The** poacher track**ed the** antelope**s**.

Notice that I have marked in boldface certain parts of this sentence – either whole words, like *the*, or meaningful sub-parts of words, like *–ed*, signalling past tense, and *–s*, the English plural marker. What happens when I alter those parts of the sentence? Have a look now:

**Which** poacher track**ed the** antelopes?
**The** poacher track**s the** antelopes.
**Those** poachers track **an** antelope.

The new sentences are still about some kind of tracking event, involving one or more poacher(s) and one or more antelope(s). But when I change the *little* words such as *a(n)*, *the* and *those*, and the sub-parts of words such as *–ed* or *–s*, we then, inevitably, interpret the event in different ways. The boldfaced elements provide information about number – how many poachers or antelopes are/were there?; tense – did this event happen before now or is it happening now?; old/new information – does the hearer know which poachers or antelopes we're talking about?; and whether the sentence should be interpreted as a statement or a question.

These little words, and word sub-parts such as –*ed*, are known as 'closed-class' elements: they relate to the grammatical subsystem. The term 'closed-class' reflects the fact that it is typically more difficult for a language to add new members to this set of linguistic forms. This contrasts with the non-boldface 'lexical' words which are referred to as 'open-class'. These relate to the lexical subsystem. The term 'open-class' captures the fact that languages typically find it much easier to add new elements to this subsystem, and do so on a regular basis.

In terms of the meaning contributed by each of these two subsystems, while 'lexical' words provide direct access to the analogue concepts in the conceptual system, and thus have a content function, 'grammatical' elements perform a structuring function in the sentence. They contribute to the interpretation in important but rather more subtle ways, providing a kind of scaffolding, which supports and structures the rich content accessed by open-class elements. The elements associated with the grammatical subsystem contribute schematic meaning, rather than rich contentful meaning. This becomes clearer when we alter the other parts of the sentence:

**The** supermodel kiss**ed the** designers.
**The** moonbeams illuminat**ed the** treetops.
**The** book delight**ed the** critics.

What all these sentences have in common with my earlier example – **The** poacher track**ed the** antelopes – is the 'grammatical' elements, again in boldface. The grammatical structure of all the sentences is identical: we know that both participants in the event can easily be identified by the hearer. We know that the event took place before now. We know that there's only one supermodel/moonbeam/book, but more than one designer/treetop/critic. Self-evidently, the sentences differ in rather a dramatic way, however. They no longer describe the same kind of event at all. This is because the 'lexical' elements – those not boldfaced – prompt for certain kinds of concepts that are richer and less schematic in nature than those prompted for by 'grammatical' elements. They prompt for analogue concepts.

The lexical subsystem relates to things, people, places, events, properties of things, and so on. In contrast, the grammatical subsystem encodes a special type of concept having to do with number, time reference, whether a piece of information is old or new, whether the speaker is providing information or requesting information, and so on.

To get a clearer sense, then, of grammatical meaning, now consider the following example that relates to renegade landscape gardeners, dubbed 'cowboys':

**These** cowboys **are** ruini**ng my** flowerbed**s**

Here the grammatical elements are again in boldface. And if we strip away the semantic contribution of the 'content' words – the nouns *cowboy* and *flowerbed*, and the verb *ruin* – we end up with something like: *these somethings are somethinging my somethings.* Although this meaning provided by the closed-class elements is rather schematic, it does provide the information that 'more than one entity close to the speaker is presently in the process of doing something to more than one entity belonging to the speaker'. This is actually quite a lot of information. And if we now exchange the content words for different ones, we end up with a description of an entirely different situation, but the schematic meaning provided by the closed-class elements remains the same:

**These** painters **are** defa**cing my** wall**s**

As this example illustrates, the meaning provided by closed-class elements remains constant despite contextual differences deriving from the content words relating to size, shape, and so on. For example, the demonstrative determiner *that* in the expressions *that flower in your hair* and *that country* encodes distance from the speaker regardless of the expanse of that distance. Equally, the modal verb *will* in the sentences *I will succeed!* and *The human race will become extinct* encodes future time regardless of the *distance* of that future time. As this shows, the function of the closed-class, or grammatical, system is to provide a pared-down, or highly abstract, representation. This structure provides a skeleton over which elements from the open-class system are laid in order to provide rich and specific conceptual content: a simulation.

This demonstration reveals that grammatical meaning is schematic in nature. It provides structural information. And so, the essential human design feature for meaning construction is to have two qualitatively distinct types of representations that play a complimentary role in the meaning-making process. While analogue concepts – directly accessed by open-class words, and housed in the non-linguistic, conceptual system – convey the *what* of a simulation, the closed-class elements encoded by human grammar – by language – provide the packaging that allows us to nuance how the analogue concepts are presented. Grammatical meaning mediates how our conceptual knowledge gets activated in the meaning-construction process: closed-class elements thus provide the *how* of a simulation.

## Parametric concepts

So, now that we've seen the way in which representations conveyed by the grammatical system of a language are qualitatively different from analogue representations – concepts – in the conceptual system, let's explore this notion in a bit more detail. It turns out that all linguistic units – whether open or closed-class – convey this schematic meaning. And this is so regardless of whether they directly index analogue concepts – as in the case of open-class words – or not – as in the case of closed-class elements.[10]

To begin to get at this idea, I want to illustrate using another aspect of grammar. While you may not always be aware of it, words are, in fact, divided into different 'lexical classes': nouns, verbs, adjectives, prepositions, and so on. And the distinction relates to a division of semantic labour. As we saw in Chapter 5, nouns, for instance, refer to things – most typically, objects, people and animals – while verbs concern relations that evolve through time. Another important lexical class is that of adjectives, which designate properties of things (nouns). So, let's examine the difference between adjectives and nouns.

Take the adjective *red*, and the noun *redness*. These words encode the semantic parameters 'property' and 'thing', an idea I informally introduced in Chapter 5. And unlike the body-based perceptual state – the hue: red – which is analogue in nature, 'property' and 'thing' are highly schematic notions: they are schematic or 'parametric' concepts. Unlike the rich, perceptual experience of different sorts of red which come to mind when we variously imagine lipstick, foxes, and so on, there is nothing about the parametric concepts 'property' or 'thing' which is like the perceptual experience of redness.

Parameters are abstracted from embodied states, filtering out all points of difference to leave highly schematic content: the parameter. The word-form *red* encodes the parameter 'property', while *redness* encodes the parameter 'thing'. This is another way of saying that *red* is an adjective – it describes a property of a thing – while *redness* is a noun – it describes a property that is reified in some way, and established as being identifiable in its own right, independent of other entities in a world of which it is a property.

So, let's look at how these different parameters package analogue content: multimodal information found in the conceptual system. Consider the following examples, which I've adapted from an advert for a skin care product:

> Treat <u>redness</u> with Clinique urgent relief cream.
> Treat <u>red</u> skin with Clinique urgent relief cream.

Both words, *red* and *redness*, which I've underlined, relate to the same perceptual state: the same analogue representation – that part of conceptual space corresponding to the colour spectrum usually identified as 'red'. But the words package the content in a different way, giving rise to distinct simulations. In the first example, *redness* leads to an interpretation relating to a skin 'condition'. In the second, *red* refers more straightforwardly to an unwanted property of the skin.

The different interpretations arising from these sentences are not due to a different hue being activated – the hue is presumably the same in both examples. Rather, the words – noun versus adjective – nuance our interpretation of the perceptual hue: they give rise to distinct simulations – an interpretation of 'skin condition' on the one hand, versus 'discolouration of skin', on the other.

In the case of *red*, this word encodes the parameter 'property'. This means that the word itself is telling us that whatever it is that it points to in the conceptual system, it has to be interpreted as a property of some entity. In contrast, *redness* encodes the parameter 'thing': whatever it is the word points to, it has to be interpreted as an entity, and in the case of colour, a property reified as a quality distinct from entities it might otherwise be a property of. And the consequence is that *red* versus *redness* leads to different interpretations.

What this all reveals is this: language has a representational format – parametric concepts – that is qualitatively different from the multimodal nature of the conceptual system – analogue concepts. And in turn, this has provided an evolutionary advantage not evident in other species. Words, and other units of language, provide instructions as to how simulations should be constructed: they provide the *how* to the *what* of the conceptual system (see Table 9.1).

## Meaning in the mix

The hypothesis I've been presenting is that meaning arises from the conjunction between language as a system – providing the *how* of meaning-making – and concepts residing in the conceptual system – providing the *what*. This conjunction provides our species with what we might liken to a crucible for meaning-making.

Table 9.1 *Parametric versus analogue concepts*

| Parametric concepts | Analogue concepts |
| --- | --- |
| • Specific to language. | • Specific to the conceptual system. |
| • Parametric (abstracted from embodied states, filtering out all points of difference to leave highly schematic properties or parameters). | • Analogue (i.e. rich, multimodal) representations of body-based states. |
| • Underpin all linguistic units (where a linguistic unit is a form/parametric content unit of any complexity). | • Arise directly from perceptual (conscious experience), and reside in the same neural system(s) as body-based states. |
| • Provide an instruction as to 'how' an analogue concept should be packaged during activation. | • Provide the content, the 'what' of a simulation. |

Language provides us with a means of tapping into and bootstrapping concepts – in the conceptual system – for creating meanings that can be communicated; and in the process, this combination greatly amplifies our potential for meaning-making. In this section, I explore how this admixture of concepts and language – our capacity to mean – works.

One way of thinking of our conceptual system is that it provides a meaning-making potential. The repertoire of analogue concepts to which words – especially open-class words – provide access is both complex and highly structured.[11] As we saw in the previous chapter, the word *book* provides access to a range of encyclopaedic knowledge structures – our analogue concepts – of different complexity. So let's consider what this meaning-making potential consists of, and how language provides a pathway through it when we use it to construct meaning.

To do so, let's examine a more complex idea, the word *France*, and the meaning-making potential to which it provides access.[12] Our knowledge system for *France* consists of – at the very least – the following analogue concepts: 'Geographical landmass',

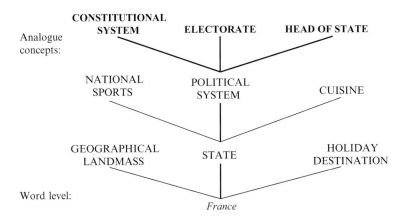

**Figure 9.1.** The meaning potential for *France*

'Nation state', and 'Holiday destination'. We develop complex bodies of knowledge for each of these knowledge units, via direct experience, for instance by holidaying in France, watching the news, and learning, though cultural transmission, about the state of affairs in France, which French President is having an affair with which well-known journalist, pop-star or actress, and also, through general knowledge about the world. And each of these analogue concepts provides access to further sets of analogue concepts.

In Figure 9.1, a flavour of this is given by virtue of the various analogue concepts, that, for many of us, are accessed via the 'Nation state' concept. These include 'National sports', 'Political system' and 'Cuisine'. For instance, we may know that in France, the French engage in national sports of particular types, for instance, football, rugby, athletics, and so on, rather than others. The French don't typically engage in American football, ice hockey, cricket, and so forth. We may also know that as a sporting nation, France participates in international sports competitions of various kinds, including the FIFA football World Cup, the Six Nations rugby competition, the rugby World Cup, the Olympic Games, and so on. In short, we may have access to a large body of knowledge concerning the sorts of sports French people engage in. We may also have some knowledge of the funding structures and

social and economic conditions and constraints that apply to these
sports in France, France's international standing with respect to
these particular sports and further knowledge about the sports
themselves, including the rules that govern their practice.

With respect to the analogue concept of 'Political system',
Figure 9.1 samples some of the further analogue concepts many
of us will have, stored in our minds, that populate our meaning
potential for *France*. For instance, 'Electorate' is an analogue
concept accessed via the 'Political system' concept. In turn, the
concept 'Political system' is accessed via the analogue concept
'Nation state'.

An important line of evidence for thinking that our conceptual
system for *France* is structured in this sort of hierarchical way
comes from language. Consider the following example sentences:

France is a country of outstanding natural beauty.
France is one of the leading nations in the European Union.
France beat New Zealand in the 2007 Rugby World Cup.
France voted against the proposed EU constitution in a 2005
    referendum.

In each sentence, we automatically interpret the word *France* to
mean something slightly different. In the first example, *France*
relates to a particular geographical region. For this to be the case,
we must be activating something like a 'Geographical landmass'
concept: we have knowledge about where the entity known as
'France' is located, its approximate shape, size and so on – individual language-users have knowledge potentially relating to the
physical aspects of France, including its terrain, and its geographical location.

In the second example, *France* activates a different part of our
semantic potential; in this sentence we activate information relating to our knowledge of France as a political entity. This is
achieved by activating the 'Nation state' concept, and what we
understand it to mean for a specified geographical region to
constitute an independent nation state, including our knowledge
of borders, passports, laws, political treaties and so on. For

instance, you may (or may not) know that a 16-year-old could, up until 2009, legally purchase beer in France and that it is still permissible to buy beer at 16 in Portugal, Germany and Austria, while the same person must be 18 in the United Kingdom and normally 21 in the United States of America.

In the third example, *France* relates to the group of fifteen French individuals who play as a team and thereby represent the French nation on the rugby field. This example activates the 'National sports' concept.

Finally, the fourth sentence relates not to a geographical land-mass, nor a political entity – a nation state – nor to a group of fifteen rugby players who happen to be representing the entire population of France. Rather, it relates to that portion of the French electorate that voted against ratification of the EU consti-tution in a referendum held in 2005. Accordingly, what is acti-vated here is the 'Electorate' analogue concept.

This last example provides an elegant illustration of the way in which an 'access route' proceeds through the conceptual seman-tic potential which a word, in this case *France*, connects with. The interpretation associated with *France* in this example has to do with the French electorate, and specifically that part of the French electorate which voted against ratification of the EU constitution. Here, the word *France* derives its interpretation by virtue of the path of activation which I've diagrammed in Figure 9.2, specific-ally those analogue concepts that I've highlighted in bold.

What this all demonstrates, then, is the way in which a word, such as *France*, connects with a range of analogue knowledge structures. Which knowledge structure – aka concept – becomes activated is, in part, determined by the linguistic utterance. A sentence provides a means of helping us to narrow in on the requisite part of the meaning potential for France, in our minds. And an access route is established, so that the correct concept is activated. Language, then, provides a set of instructions, enabling us to assemble the correct concepts from the vast network of knowledge that the word potentially connects with. And in so doing, this enables us to use our conceptual systems, to provide

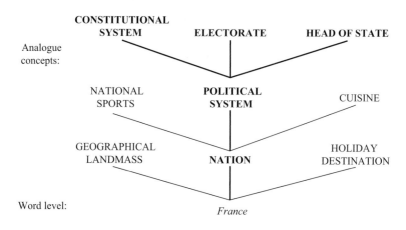

Analogue
concepts:

**CONSTITUTIONAL
SYSTEM**          **ELECTORATE**          **HEAD OF STATE**

NATIONAL          **POLITICAL**
SPORTS            **SYSTEM**                CUISINE

GEOGRAPHICAL                                HOLIDAY
LANDMASS          **NATION**                DESTINATION

Word level:                      *France*

**Figure 9.2.** Access route through the meaning potential for *France*

our words with rich content, when we think, speak and communicate with those around us.

## The anatomy of language

Having examined the way in which language interfaces with our conceptual system, what of language itself? If language is a system enabling us to bootstrap analogue knowledge for purposes of meaning-making, what does language, as a system, look like exactly? We carry around with us, in our heads, a 'mental' grammar. And this is made up of linguistic units known as 'constructions'. A linguistic unit is a construction in the sense that it is constructed from two components: a semantic pole – a meaning – and a phonological pole – a sound, or set of sounds. For instance, a particularly salient linguistic unit is the word, such as *dog* or *cat*. Words, like all constructions, are conventional pairings of form and meaning. They involve a sequence of one or more mental sound units, or phonemes (the form), and a concept (the meaning) that is conventionally associated with that sequence.

By way of example, let's take the English word *cat*. This involves three sound segments in a specific order which are associated, in the minds of English language speakers, with a particular type of meaning: a four-legged animal, with whiskers and tail, that says miaow. But the conventional relationship between the form and the meaning is symbolic in nature; this means that the motivation for associating a particular form with a meaning is arbitrary. For instance, Finnish uses the form *kissa* to refer to the same entity as the English *cat*, while it's *bushi* in the native American language Cree, *popoki* in Hawaiian and *macka* in Serbian – just to give you a flavour of some of the variety.

But as we have seen in this chapter, the meaning paired with a linguistic form consists of a parametric concept: a schematic unit of linguistic knowledge that conveys sparse details of the thing that it represents. For the form *cat*, this might include schematic information such as 'animal', 'behaviour' and 'habitat'. In addition, the construction points to a meaning potential – a region in our conceptual system – that embodies our rich analogue information associated with cats. This arrangement is captured in Figure 9.3.

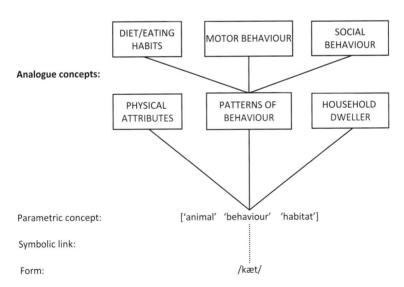

**Figure 9.3.** Linguistic construction for *cat*, and its access to the conceptual system

Figure 9.3 shows the following. The word-form /kæt/, using the International Phonetic Alphabet, is linked symbolically to the linguistic meaning associated with the form. This is signified by the dashed 'symbolic link'. The linguistic meaning is made up of semantic parameters. These comprise schematic atoms of meaning. They are in a representational format that is non-analogue in nature. This means that their content is in a more abstract form than the aspects of experience they are representations of. The rich details associated with what an animal is, the type of biological motion it can undergo, the nature of different patterns of animal behaviours and what it means to share a human dwelling – a house and home – are all left out. Language appears to draw on a system of meanings that abstract away from the rich embodied meanings. And it provides a system of parametric meanings that both allow us to package richer, analogue meanings in the conceptual system, and a means of linking to rich analogue concepts. In this way, language enables us to bootstrap the analogue concepts in our conceptual system for purposes of communicating, via language. The semantic parameters designated by 'animal', 'behaviour' and 'habitat', may not be all the parameters the form /kæt/ encodes. And further research is needed. But based on the evidence presented in this book, it seems incontrovertible that language does have an indigenous repository of meanings, ones that are qualitatively distinct from those in the conceptual system.[13] And finally, Figure 9.3 shows some of the analogue concepts that these semantic parameters correspond to. The analogue concepts, in this Figure, are enclosed in square boxes. As previously, the terms I am using in these boxes are a mnemonic: they are meant to represent the rich, multimodal experiences that make up our detailed, encyclopaedic knowledge concerning the physical attributes of a cat. Everything we know, and have acquired through direct experience, learning, cultural transmission and so on, makes up the rich information – the rich meaning potential – we potentially have access to, for cats. And finally, the analogue concepts form a network of representations in our minds, one that is partially shared across other minds, but partly constrained by individual experience: no two conceptual systems are the same. And of course, our analogue knowledge is in a continual state of modification. Each time we step out of the door and into the hustle-bustle of the world, we are perceiving new sights and sounds. Consequently, our analogue concepts are updated and modified, whether we want it or not, as we proceed through our daily lives. The range of analogue concepts in Figure 9.3 is, accordingly, probably highly partial, at best. And the sorts of concepts we hold in our minds for cat that I present here may turn out not to be fully accurate. But this, nevertheless, provides an indicative representation of the sorts of things we must know, to be able to successfully use the word in the range of ways we clearly do, on a daily basis.

## Constructions in the mind

In the previous chapter, we saw that words, like *over* and *time*, constitute a single category comprising a number of distinct, but related, meanings. But this is not a feature of language that is restricted merely to words. Other sorts of constructions, both below and above the level of words, exhibit the same behaviour.

The smallest unit of linguistic meaning is referred to by linguists as a 'morpheme'. And while a freestanding word such as *over* is a morpheme, some morphemes, like prefixes and suffixes, cannot stand on their own: they have to be combined with freestanding words, being what is sometimes referred to as 'bound' morphemes. For instance, the morpheme *un-* can be combined with *interested* to make *uninterested*. Or *-ed* can be combined with a freestanding verb to make the past tense form *kicked*. Nevertheless, both *un-* and *-ed* convey meaning: *un-* negates whatever it is prefixed to, while *-ed* encodes past time reference and denotes that whatever verb it is suffixed to is set in the past, relative to time of speaking. Similarly, above the word, more complex grammatical constructions also conventionally encode multiple meanings, as we also saw in Chapter 8, with the *(be) going to* construction.

In this section, I want to show you that constructions, both *above* and *below* the level of the word, also constitute single categories of distinct but related meanings. All constructions, no matter their stripe, are made up of webs of meanings in the mind.

So, let's begin, then, with a construction below the word-level: that of a bound morpheme. And in this case, I want to focus on the *-er* agentive suffix, which changes a verb into a noun, as when we add *-er* to the verb *teach* to create *teacher*: someone who teaches. Let's examine, then, what the *-er* suffix is contributing to the following words: *teacher, villager, toaster* and *best-seller*. In each of these examples, the *-er* suffix adds a slightly different meaning. In *teacher* it designates a human agent who regularly or by profession carries out the action conveyed by the verb: in this instance *teach*. But in contrast, a *villager* is not someone who carries out the actions of the verb; after all, there is no verb *to village*. Moreover, in the case of *villager*, the *-er* suffix is not referring to an action per se: for instance, someone who con-structs or builds villages. Rather, here, *-er* relates to a person who lives in a particular place – in the case of a *villager*, a village, although we can generate many other examples (e.g. *Londoner, New Yorker, Berliner, out-of-towner*, and so on).

In a word like *toaster*, *-er* relates to an artefact, rather than a person: the artefact that has the capacity designated by the verb, here *toast*. And in *best-seller,-er* relates to a particular quality associated with a type of artefact: the property of selling success-fully; notice that in the case of *best-seller*, the quality is a conse-quence not of anything the artefact actually does. Rather, it concerns what others do: in the case of a book that's a best-seller, customers purchase the book in such numbers that it outsells other comparable books.

Each of these usages is distinct: a *teacher* is a person (=a human) who teaches; a toaster is a machine (non-human) that performs a toasting function; a best-seller is an artefact such as a book that has the property of selling well; and a villager is a person who dwells in a village. Despite these differences, these meanings are intuitively related in terms of sharing, to a greater or lesser

Table 9.2 *The semantics of* -er

| Parametric meaning | Example |
|---|---|
| the human performance of a designated role or function | *a teacher* |
| the non-human performance of a designated role or function | *a toaster* |
| the attribute of living in a particular sort of dwelling | *a villager* |
| the attribute associated with an artefact as a consequence of human behaviour | *a best-seller* |

degree, distinct, albeit somewhat similar semantic parameters: 'the human performance of a designated role or function' (e.g. *teacher*); 'the non-human performance of a designated role or function' (e.g. *toaster*); 'the attribute of living in a particular sort of dwelling' (e.g. *villager*); and 'the attribute associated with an artefact as a consequence of human behaviour' (e.g. *best-seller*).

This shows, like freestanding words, that other linguistic units – sub-parts of words – also carry a range of distinct meanings. And these distinct meanings are related: they form a semantic network in our minds; we must know the distinct meanings associated with -*er* in order to be able to successfully use it in the range of everyday contexts with which we are familiar (see Table 9.2).

Now let's turn to the nature of constructions above the level of words. This level concerns grammatical constructions. And here, I want to focus on the construction exemplified by this sentence: *Joyce gave Jim her heart*. This kind of construction is known as the 'ditransitive', which I introduced in Chapter 8 of *The Language Myth*.[14] The term ditransitive gets at the idea that there are two ('di'-) direct objects following the verb – the only construction of this kind in English. And just as we have seen with the -*er* agentive morpheme, the ditransitive construction also has a number of distinct, albeit semantically related meanings associated with it. We will see that, just as we have networks of meanings in our minds for words and sub-parts of words, the same is also true for sentence-level grammatical patterns.

According to linguist Adele Goldberg, the 'X causes Y to receive Z' (or ditransitive) construction has six distinct variants.[15] The first is the schematic meaning we have already seen: the doer of the act of transfer causes the recipient to receive an object of transfer. This is exemplified by the sentence: *Jim gave Joyce the flowers.*

The second meaning involves sentences which use verbs like *guarantee, promise* and *owe*, as in the following: *Jim promised Joyce the flowers.* The difference from the previous meaning is that, here, the act of transfer is associated with conditions which determine the terms of the transfer. In the case of a promise, Joyce is guaranteed flowers (in the future) by virtue of Jim undertaking to provide her with flowers.

The third meaning involves actions where the doer causes the recipient not to receive the object of potential transfer. Here, verbs like *refuse* and *deny* prevent the transfer from taking place, as when we say: *Joyce refused Jim the cake.*

Another distinct meaning of the 'X causes Y to receive Z' construction involves transfer at some point in the future. This is represented by verbs of future transfer such as *leave, bequeath, allocate, reserve, grant*, for instance: *Joyce left Jim the cake,* or *Jim bequeathed Edith his African book collection.*

The fifth meaning centres on enablement, by the doer of the action, for the recipient to thus receive the object of transfer. This meaning is represented by verbs of permission such as *permit* or *allow*. And it's exemplified by the following: *Joyce allowed Freya the cake.*

And finally, the sixth meaning concerns intended, rather than actual, transfer. For instance, when we *bake, make, build, sew* or *knit* something for someone, we are often creating an entity for someone. And in so doing, we intend to cause the recipient to receive the entity we create, as when we say: *Joyce baked Jim the cake.* But notice, this meaning is not quite the same as examples where actual transfer takes place, as when we say: *Joyce gave Jim the cake.* When Joyce gives Jim the cake, transfer – self-evidently – takes place: Jim receives the cake. But when Joyce bakes Jim the cake, the transfer is not actually realised. Rather, Joyce, by creating

Table 9.3 *Distinct meanings for the ditransitive construction*

| Parametric meaning | Verbs employed | Example |
|---|---|---|
| X causes Y to receive Z | e.g. *give, pass*, etc. | *Jim gave Joyce the chocolates* |
| Conditions of satisfaction imply that X causes Y to receive Z | e.g. *guarantee, promise, owe*, etc. | *Joyce promised Jim the cake* |
| X causes Y NOT to receive Z | e.g. *refuse, deny*, etc. | *Joyce refused Freya the cake* |
| X acts to cause Y to receive Z at some future point in time | e.g. *leave, bequeath, allocate, grant, reserve*, etc. | *Jim bequeathed Vyv his entire collection of Koestler books* |
| X enables Y to receive Z | e.g. *permit, allow*, etc. | *Joyce permitted Freya the cake* |
| X intends to cause Y to receive Z | e.g. *bake, make, build, sew, knit*, etc. | *Joyce baked Jim the cake* |

the cake, is intending that Jim should receive it, once it's baked. Table 9.3 summarises the distinct, albeit related, parametric meanings associated with the ditransitive construction.

In essence, while each of the meanings associated with the 'X causes Y to receive Z', construction are distinct, they are clearly related: they all concern volitional transfer – or non-transfer, where transfer might have been a possibility. That said, the nature of the transfer, or the conditions associated with the transfer, vary across the different variants of the construction.

## To return to the beginning

To return to the beginning, how is it that Faulkner can recreate Vardaman's perceptions of the horse in the dark stall, a feat beyond the ken of all other species? While our mental capacities far outweigh those of other species, an important difference between human language and the communicative capacities of our nearest primate cousins appears to relate to our capacity for grammar. And specifically, the defining feature of grammar is that it encodes parametric concepts: grammatical meanings are schematic in nature, and allow us to shape our conceptual representations – analogue concepts – in order to produce complex and sophisticated meaning.

What is special, then, about grammar is that it enables us to package analogue concepts in divergent ways, as we saw in the distinction between *red* versus *redness* that I discussed earlier. And this can only be achieved if words can modify one another, and thereby nuance the way in which content from the conceptual system – analogue concepts – gets packaged for communicative purposes. With the development of parametric content, this allowed, for the first time, a humanly relevant scene to be constructed via language, as we saw with my discussion earlier of sentences such as *The poacher tracked the antelopes*.

What, then, is unique about human language is that it makes use of parametric knowledge, in order to coerce the analogue in order to express a wider array of meaning types. As we saw with the quote from the Faulkner novel at the outset of the chapter, language can help evoke a stream of consciousness. But it is only with the emergence of a full-fledged grammar that this has become possible. With the advent of parametric knowledge – aka the genesis of grammar – the full-blown meaning-making potential of modern humans was realised.

In this chapter I've been exploring the nature of meaning-making: the way in which language and our meaning-ready minds co-conspire to create meaning. The standard account of language, and the way it enables us to mean, has (too often) focused on language in isolation. But on the contrary – and the central argument of this book – language forms a complex with our meaning-ready minds, with our conceptual systems: providing a crucible for the creation of, on the face of it, something that is mystical – meaning. Language has co-opted, and hence repurposed, the repository of concepts we deploy for non-communicative functions, expressly for communication. Hence, a central design feature of language is that it provides a platform of ready-made parametric knowledge which can bootstrap the analogue knowledge in our minds, enabling us to convey meanings. In short, we cannot study the role of language in meaning-making without also considering in detail the way in which language hooks up with the conceptual system, allowing us to draw down on non-linguistic concepts when we interact with others on a daily basis.

But this conclusion, startling as it perhaps is, leads to other questions, concerning the evolutionary emergence of language and the development of parametric knowledge. In particular, what accounts for the complexity of our communicative system: one that allows language to engage with the human conceptual system, in order to produce meanings that are qualitatively unlike those of any other species? And this is the question to which we now turn in the remainder of the book.

# Chapter 10    The cooperative species

In the previous chapter, I focused on the relationship between language and the human conceptual system. But this is far from the end of the meaning-making story; there is a large infrastructure that not only supports our meaning-making prowess, but makes it possible in the first place. In this chapter I explore this *back office* support, which is what enabled our unique capacity for meaning in the first place. In so doing, I will seek to persuade you that language is, in some sense, an evolutionary by-product of more fundamental aspects of our species, and the evolutionary lineage that gave rise to us. It arose not as a means to an end, but as an indirect, albeit inevitable, consequence of what I shall dub our 'cooperative intelligence' – the subject of this chapter.

Until relatively recently, the infrastructure that led to the human meaning-making capacity, the result of over two and half million years of biological and cultural evolution, appeared, in the absence of a time-machine, to be too mysterious to be understood. This has changed in recent years, for a number of reasons. For one thing, we now know a lot more than we did even 20 years ago about the cognitive capabilities of great apes. And with that, we know far more about what very early ancestral humans were already equipped with, in terms of their mental capacities. We share many characteristics with other great apes – for instance, around 98 per cent of our DNA, we now know, is shared with chimpanzees. Moreover, advances in paleo-archaeology – the study of the fossil record of hominins, which I'll have more to say about in the final chapter – and advances in carbon and genetic dating, coupled with new computational modelling techniques, now mean that we are in a far better position than previous generations of researchers to say something meaningful about the evolutionary context that gave rise to our unique meaning-making capacity. In this chapter, I will show that our capacity for meaning – the symbiotic binding together of our contemporary conceptual and linguistic systems – is an outcome of a wider pro-social impulse. We are capable of language because we are, inherently and uniquely, *the* cooperative species.

## On the way to deeper matters

To start to get a better sense of the larger infrastructure that supports human meaning-making, let's begin with the following, quotidian example:

> John: 'It's chilly in here, Andy.'
> (Andy goes to close the window).

This seemingly unremarkable instance of language use reveals, paradoxically, something that, in fact, *is* highly remarkable; and this something, as it turns out, is a capacity which reveals that, mentally, we leave all other species in the dust.

In order for Andy to interpret what John *means* in making this utterance, and before even beginning to interpret the symbols – the words – Andy must, first and foremost, recognise the utterance as an attempt to communicate: to convey some meaning. This recognition is very definitely *not* dependent on actually understanding what the words themselves mean; it precedes language, both in evolutionary terms and also in the cognitive development of a pre-linguistic human infant.

Imagine being transported to some strange land, where people speak a language you don't understand. When a passer-by addresses you, jabbering away using words you fail to recognise, all you perceive is gobbledygook. But while you may not *understand* this foreign tongue, you nevertheless recognise that the foreigner *is* making an attempt to convey something: to communicate a message. It's just that you don't know what the message is! But *how* do you know that this is what they are attempting to do? How do you know there *is* a message, even when you don't recognise the meaning?

So, let's unpack what it is that you must be *understanding* – even when you don't *know* what the words themselves mean. To recognise a spoken utterance as an attempt to convey a message, we must, first of all, be aware that other members of our species are intentional agents: like you and me, they have thoughts and feelings, which they are trying to convey. But in addition, you must be recognising that language is a form of behaviour which enables us to try and influence the actions and mental states of others – even if you hadn't thought about it in this way before.

For instance, when I say to a child when crossing a busy road: 'Hold my hand, please', I'm attempting to influence the behaviour of the child, in order to make an aspect of the world – the child's continued safety – conform to my intentional state: my wishes. And so too, you must be aware, if only at a subconscious level, that the foreign passer-by is attempting to signal a communicative intention: to mean something.

More than that, you must also know, however implicitly, that the foreigner also recognises you to be an intentional agent: you are someone who can, perhaps, also be influenced by their communicative intentions. In short, even before we begin to interpret the specific meanings of words, we exhibit a powerful 'interactional intelligence' that must be in place for language itself to even get off the ground.[1] I, you, and everyone else we happen to engage in conversation with implicitly understands that the purpose of a linguistic exchange between two or more participants is to convey a communicative intention – a meaning – even if it's nothing more earth-shattering than making a casual comment on the weather. Without our interactional nous, our propensity for generating meaning couldn't begin to get off the ground.

Of course, your interactional intelligence will only take you so far in a foreign land: you'll be able to pick up a considerable amount of information from the gestures that accompany the speech of your foreign speaker, from their eye gaze and facial expressions. You'll also glean clues from their speech prosody – for instance, whether they are shouting, whispering or speaking with a normal volume. These cues will enable you to work out whether you're being welcomed or threatened; whether they are friend, foe, or something else. But as you don't *know* the foreign tongue, the mode of communication doesn't exhibit what linguists refer to as 'parity': the conversation is one-sided; your foreign passer-by knows what their words mean, but crucially, you don't – you may not even be able to decipher distinct words from the stream of gobbledygook you're hearing.

It is this foundational layer of meaning-making – our inter-actional intelligence – that enables us to recognise that other humans are attempting to communicate with us, that they are using language in an attempt to convey meaning. But a moment's reflection reveals that our interactional intelligence had to pre-cede, in evolutionary terms, the emergence of language. While language massively amplifies our intrinsic meaning-making potential – our conceptual system – it is an effect, rather than the cause of our interactional intelligence.[2] For instance, a cough can be a reflex behaviour, as when we suffer from hay fever, or a heavy cold. But it can also signal a communicative intention, when we cough to signal that our partner-in-crime should remain silent in a sticky situation – we see meaning in a host of behav-iours; we don't need the regal cloak of language to perceive communicative signals.

A famous example of interactional intelligence, one which proceeded without recourse to language, involved Lieutenant Cook, of His Majesty's bark *Endeavour*, during its journey of discovery around the Antipodes. In July 1770, the Endeavour, under Cook's command, had been beached for over six weeks on the banks of the Endeavour River, at the site of the modern-day Cookstown, in Australia. Captain Cook and naturalist Sir Joseph Bank were exploring the area when they came across strange-looking grey animals that moved around by hopping. The language of the local aboriginal people, Guugu Yimithirr, was one that neither Cook nor Banks spoke. Yet, Cook was able to make clear, using gestures to a local, that he was asking about the strange creature. The tribesman replied: 'gangurru'. The English word *kangaroo* derives from the Guugu Yimithirr word *gangurru*, referring to grey kangaroos.[3] The name was first recorded as *kanguru* on 12 July 1770 in an entry in the diary of Banks; and Cook referred to the creature in his diary entry of 4 August. Without possessing a mutually shared language, and with no shared culture, Captain Cook and the local tribesman were able to *converse* with one another: Cook wanted to know what the creature was, and the local understood Cook's communicative intention, in the absence of language.

John's utterance, 'It's chilly in here, Andy', involves a number of distinct words. Once we understand that an interaction pre-supposes an attempt to convey meaning – a communicative intention – our next task is to attempt to understand what these words mean. But to do so, we have to know what the words, individually, are usually taken to convey. As a speaker of English, you'll have access to the following information. You'll know that the word *chilly* usually refers to a low temperature, one that is slightly uncomfortable, rather than one inducing frost-bite. If you, then, like me, have been raised in an English-speaking speech community, and have acquired the linguistic conventions of this community, you'll readily access the conventional representation for *chilly*, due to a stable mapping in your mind between the word-form and the range of experiences you may have endured, involving different degrees of coldness.

But a word like *here* is slightly different. To understand it, you must know that *here* refers to a location that is defined, in part, by the location of the speaker. The meaning of *here* therefore shifts from speaker to speaker, location to location, and from each occasion of use to another. For instance, if I were to make a telephone call from the UK to a colleague based in the USA, my use of *here* might refer, somewhat vaguely, to the entire UK. But in the example above, *here* refers to a much more specific region of space: the room in which both John and Andy find themselves. Similarly, the word *it* refers to an entity or situation in a context-specific way – in this case, the relative temperature of the room – while *'s* – a contraction of *is* – refers to a stable state of affairs that persists through time. The point is, and one we've run into several times in this book, words don't have timeless 'dictionary-like' meanings; when we use language, what words refer to varies from situation to situation, and across contexts of use. For instance, the word *small* means quite different things when used to describe a mouse, versus an elephant, versus a galaxy. The properties associated with *small* vary in context-dependent ways; so, part of knowing what a word actually means in fact also entails understanding the context in which it is used, and how the context nuances the word. Words, on their own, don't convey meanings: they are always understood and interpreted in specific usage contexts.

But once Andy has worked out what the words, individually, might refer to, this is still not very useful on its own. We must also understand the complex and often subtle ways in which individual word meanings combine in order to give rise to the global meaning of an utterance. And as we saw in the previous chapter, in part, this comes from recognising the relative contribution of the *little* words in a sentence, words like *it's* and *in*, and how they combine with words like *chilly* and *here*. Part of this entails understanding the relative semantic contribution of the parametric knowledge conveyed by different words, and in particular the function they provide in constructing a grammatical scaffolding for our interpretation of the utterance – for drawing down from analogue knowledge in the conceptual system.

In the example, above, the contracted verb, *'s,* links *chilly* with the subject of the sentence *it*, so that the *chilly* describes a facet of whatever *it* refers to – in this case, an aspect of a particular state of affairs having to do with the room's temperature. And *in here* helps clarify what that state of affairs might be: the nature of the room in which John and Andy find themselves. Part of the resulting meaning comes from how the words combine – figuring out that *it* refers to the temperature inside the room – but also from more stable aspects of global meaning. The expression *It's chilly* is an instance of what linguists perplexingly refer to as the 'predicate adjective construction'. While the label itself doesn't matter, and needn't confuse us, what does matter is that part of our semantic knowledge includes knowing that multi-word units have parametric meaning independent of the specific words that make up the multi-word unit, as attested by the 'He died' interpretation of the idiom *He kicked the bucket* – after all, this idiom doesn't mean what it literally says: there's no actual tantrums and physical kicking of buckets involved.

To correctly understand the utterance, we must know that in John's exchange with Andy, *chilly* refers back to the subject of the sentence, to *it*, rather than something that comes later in the utterance. *Chilly* is an adjective. But in this example, chilly doesn't refer, as adjectives usually do, to a following noun, as when we say, for instance, *bald head, red knickers* or *greedy bankers*. In each of these examples, the adjectives, *bald, red* and *greedy*, are influencing our interpretation of the nouns – *head, knickers* and *bankers* – in rather specific ways. But in the exchange between John and Andy, *chilly*, governed by the grammar of the multi-word unit in which it's embedded, refers back to *it*. We have to know this in order to be able to make sense of the utterance. Hence, both grammatical and semantic rules of word composition – rules that you may not even have been aware you *are* aware of – provide the necessary linguistic context, allowing Andy to begin to make sense of the utterance.

A further design feature of our uniquely human capacity for meaning-making is the drawing of inferences based on what is said (and not said). Not only does Andy understand John's utterance; he also recognises that John is attempting to convey something more than a simple observation about the temperature in the room. Andy takes John's utterance to imply that there is a specific reason for the room being chilly, *and* he proceeds to do something about it.

This amounts to our capacity for recognising what the philosopher Daniel Dennett refers to as different 'orders of intentionality'.[4] When Andy interprets the utterance, and accordingly comes to believe that John is cold, this shows that Andy can cope with one order of intentionality. But when Andy believes that John is cold (something Andy knows), and that in making the utterance, John thus believes Andy to also know that he is cold (something that John knows), Andy can cope with two orders of intentionality. In addition, Andy also knows that John is most likely cold due to the open window, which is three levels of intentionality. And finally, Andy recognises that the utterance is not being made by John simply to communicate his physical warmth index: it's not a random utterance; there is situated relevance in making the utterance: there is an open window in the room, and it's a chill, autumnal day outside.[5] Andy, accordingly, recognises an implied request, on the part of John, to close the source of John's chilled demeanour. This is four levels of intentionality. Indeed, humans regularly manipulate five orders of intentionality.

This sophisticated embedding of intentionality is something beyond the ken of all other species. Most animals cannot cope with more than one order of intentionality. And even chimps, smarter than most, only appear to regularly manage two orders of intentionality.[6] Andy's ability to recognise and interpret different levels of intentionality is what enables him to infer that John is chilly because there is a window open.

But once he's recognised John's implied meaning – that it's the open window that's to blame – Andy doesn't sit idly by. Andy helps John out: Andy's response to hearing John's complaint is to close the window. And so, here's the million-dollar question: how does Andy know to do this? After all, nowhere does John specifically request that Andy close the window. Nor does John say that he's chilly *because* the window is open. So *how does* Andy *know* to close the window?

This illustrates the final, and arguably most decisive, cognitive dimension underpinning the human meaning-making capacity: we exhibit a pro-social impulse. It would be fairly pointless to recognise an implied request but to do nothing about it. What would our communicative smarts otherwise be for? Our species is inherently cooperative. By this, I don't mean that we always get on with one another, or even that we all get on most of the time. Nevertheless, we appear to have a deep-seated impulse for cooperation. In recognising the communicative intention, Andy does more than this: he altruistically closes the window. Altruism is an especially human characteristic. With no potential gain for himself, and moreover without expectation of gain, Andy helps John out.

In the animal kingdom, genuine altruism is vanishingly rare: when chimpanzees – our closest primate cousins – interact in their social groupings, motives are largely egocentric, selfish even.[7] Even assistance given to other chimps is contingent on self-serving motives. It serves as a device for maintaining social relationships that are critical to the long-term well-being and even survival of the individual. For example, male chimps have even been observed to donate meat to female chimps. But in fact, this is not done out of the goodness of their hearts: what they are in fact doing is *buying* sexual privileges.[8]

In a human context, altruism is evidenced on a daily basis, from the stranger on a railway platform who volunteers an explanation as to why and by how long your train has been delayed, to holding open a door for others coming through, to the celebrated biblical story of the Good Samaritan. Moreover, some human institutions make cooperation a central facet of their activity. The Boy Scout movement, for instance, requires its members to perform a 'good deed' – or a 'good turn' – every day. This altruistic tendency – which I am calling our cooperative intelligence – provides the platform for meaning-making; without both interactional and cooperative intelligence, there could be no spark for our admixture of concepts and language, no combustion and no explosion of meaning.

As a coda to my discussion of John being chilly, and the complexity involved in Andy doing his good deed, I can't resist relating an old joke that the late, great social psychologist Leon Festinger used to tell. An old Jewish couple are 'lying in bed when the wife says, 'Harry, close the window. It's cold outside'. Harry gets up and closes the window, turns to his wife, and says, 'So now it's warm outside?'[9] Of course, the humour here is a consequence of our capacity for meaning-making, and the cooperative intelligence that underpins it.

## Intelligence, tools and other minds

Our understanding of the mental capabilities of our nearest primate cousins, chimpanzees and bonobos, has undergone a revolution in the last two decades or so. Our hominin lineage separated from the African great apes – tailless primates, that evolved for life amid the arboreal canopy of sub-Saharan Africa – some six million years ago.[10] But we now know that many of the essential ingredients, in terms of, at the very least, aspects of our interactional intelligence, are something that we share with other great apes.

An important symptom of intelligence, and hence of a sophisticated conceptual system, is tool use. In the earliest stage of human prehistory, *Homo habilis* ('handy man'), a very early species of ancestral humans living in what is today Ethiopia, developed the ability to manufacture rudimentary stone tools. In particular, ancestral humans worked out that by striking or 'knapping' a hard stone against the fault line on other stone materials, such as flint, quartz, or obsidian, a sharp, flake-like edge could be created. And these flakes could be used for cutting the skin, flesh and even bone of dead game. By around 1.8 million years ago, with the advent of the more advanced *Homo erectus* ('upright man'), ancestral humans began creating other tools, out of wood, bone or antler, to work the flakes, creating more effective cutting edges. Archaeological finds dated to this period include stone hand-axes and cleavers.

Tools are also widely deployed by a wide array of species for acquisition of food and water, grooming, construction and even defence.[11] This ranges from sea otters, who have been observed to transport small rocks to break open clams and shell-fish,[12] to moulting brown bears that use rocks to exfoliate,[13] to elephants who use sticks and leaves held in their trunks to swat away flies.[14] But it is among apes and monkeys that we witness the most sophisticated non-human tool use. In the past couple of decades, primatologists and comparative psychologists have made important breakthroughs in the study of the cognitive tool-manufacturing capabilities of great apes, especially chimpanzees.

Chimpanzees are particularly adept tool users: they regularly use stone tools to crack nuts. But not only do chimps make use of objects they find; they often fashion tools from naturally occurring entities. Chimps carefully strip leaves off twigs they find or break from trees and use the stems to *fish* for termites or other insects in the ground.[15] Moreover, we now know that chimps can make use of several tools to help them prepare food for consumption. For instance, chimps from the Nimba mountains in Guinea, Africa make use of both stones and pieces of wood to act as cleavers to cut up treculia fruits – about the size of a melon – into more digestible portions. Intriguingly, they additionally make use of stone *anvils* as a chopping surface – combining two tools for food preparation, a feat once thought to be beyond the ken of all non-human species.[16] Chimps even create tools for hunting. For instance, chimps from Senegal have been observed to manufacture rudimentary spears to hunt for bushbabies.[17]

Up until the 1980s, ethologists thought that of the great apes, it was only chimps that were capable of *manufacturing* tools in this way. However, we now know that a range of species are capable of this. Both bonobos and chimpanzees are known to create *sponges* from moss and leaves. They use these sponges to absorb water before washing themselves.[18] Like chimps, orang-utans also manufacture tools to fish for termites. They do this by fraying the end of a twig and then inserting it into termite nests in trees.[19] Moreover, mandrills – Old World monkeys closely related to baboons – have been observed to manufacture tools for personal grooming. In the wild, mandrills regularly create tools to clean their ears. And in one instance, a mandrill was even filmed stripping down a twig before using it to clean away dirt from under its toenails.[20]

Another feature, and arguably the hallmark of interactional intelligence, is the ability to recognise that, like you and me, others have thoughts, feelings and wishes that are not dissimilar from our own. This amounts to an understanding that other members of one's species are intentional agents. Until relatively recently, it wasn't clear whether the great apes – gorillas, orangutans, chimpanzees and bonobos (pygmy chimps) – understood other members of the same species to be intentional agents. In philosophical circles this idea is sometimes referred to as having a 'theory of mind': understanding others in one's species as having minds which, like our own, we can attempt to interact with and influence via communicative strategies. Moreover, having a theory of mind means that we can recognise the intentions of others, based on visual cues such as facial expressions, body posture and so on. Recognising others as intentional agents affords an intention-reading ability: we can modify our own behaviour, and attempt to influence the behaviour of others, as a consequence of *reading* their intentions. For instance, recall my example from earlier in the chapter: if I were to see a small child at the edge of a busy road, seemingly about to step out, I might react by inviting the child to wait, or to find a safer place to cross. And this unremarkable act arises precisely because I recognise the child's intention – its desire to cross the road – and the potential harm that might arise due to the child's relative immaturity, and hence its failure to fully anticipate the potential danger.

However, chimps, we now know, appear to have, on the face of it, something approaching a theory of mind. The psychologist Dale Peterson recounts a telling example of chimp deception, which betokens an ability to gauge what other chimps may be thinking. One young chimp, nicknamed Dandy, was courting a female. The form that courtship takes among chimps is to directly reveal just how arousing a male chimp finds a female to be. So, Dandy revealed to his paramour his erect penis. But just then, a higher-ranking male approached, making advances towards Dandy's love interest. As Peterson reports: 'For Dandy, that meant big trouble. Worse, the young male's forbidden interest in the female was being communicated honestly by something he seemed to have little control over, an erect penis – which he quickly covered with his hands, apparently hoping thus to deceive the higher-ranking male'.[21]

What this strikingly reveals is that while Dandy had no voluntary control over his erection, nevertheless, in the presence of an older, stronger male, his sexual arousal, and the potential threat it suggests to the older male's attempt at sexual activity, is unwelcome. Moreover, Dandy's aroused state might even be detrimental to Dandy's well-being, given the older male's physical prowess and prior territorial claim. The only explanation available for Dandy's subsequent behaviour – attempting to hide his erection from the competing male – is precisely that Dandy understands that fellow chimps have wishes and desires of their own – that other chimps are intentional agents. Dandy wished to avoid both causing offence and being physically chastised as a consequence. Chimps seem to understand that other members of their species have minds of their own, with their own wishes, desires and beliefs.[22] And as we saw earlier, recognising a member of one's own species as a minded creature – an intentional agent – is foundational to the human meaning-making capacity: our interactional intelligence – and its distillation, in the human lineage, as a sophisticated cooperative intelligence – depends on it.

## The cooperative species

Interactional intelligence is a necessary precursor to the emergence of a genuine cooperative intelligence, with the concomitant pro-social impulse evident in our species. For reasons that are, perhaps, self-evident, something like language would not have been possible without the cooperative turn that emerged at some point in the minds of our forebears, sometime in the past two million years or so. After all, while we now know that chimps understand that other members of their species are intentional agents with whom they can interact, their lifestyle remains primarily individualistic, rather than cooperative. And they don't have language.

In contrast, our species is inherently cooperative: we achieve far more working together than we ever could alone. Our societies are inherently cooperative – in modern society, we pay taxes to ensure the upkeep of welfare states of various stripes, to maintain a free state education system and, in the United Kingdom, a publicly funded National Health Service, free at the point of access. There is the rule of law, overseen by a police service, a judiciary and other state-run agencies. We share streets where we live, laid out by adherence to and sanction by public planning bodies – and pay local taxes for refuse removal, street lights and so on. We drive on communal roads, adhering to a highway code and other traffic laws, and we agree upon a political infrastructure – sometimes through democratic elections and sometimes through other means, such as monarchic–feudal governance structures, or a combination of the two: the UK, for instance, has an unelected sovereign as Head of State. And these cultural institutions administer and drive many aspects of our national life, which ultimately affect each of us in our daily lives. This cooperative mode of living is qualitatively distinct from any other extant species.

My claim is that language could only have arisen in such a cooperative milieu. It isn't sufficient just to understand that other members of our species are intentional (and sometimes rational!) agents with whom we can engage. Cooperative intelligence entails more than merely co-action alongside others. It additionally involves shared and devolved responsibilities for the greater good, which we all, ultimately, hope to benefit from. It requires pooling resources and agreeing who will do what in order to facilitate obtaining and then the sharing of resources – food, shelter and the opportunity to mate being chief among these.

But cooperation entails more than interaction and the division and sharing of labour in order to achieve common goals. It requires a means of communication, not least to ensure coordination of the goals we cooperatively attempt to achieve. In short, without this new, cooperative way of living, there would – and probably could – not have been language. And this is why our species – and lineage – developed language, while our nearest primate cousins have not. Our lineage, and species, developed a new form of cooperative intelligence built upon the interactional intelligence shared, more or less, with our great ape cousins. And consequently, what is different about our species is not just the nature and range of concepts that we hold in our conceptual systems; we additionally have language that allows us to make use of these self-same concepts for meaning-making and communication.

The comparative psychologist Michael Tomasello proposes that the development of cognitively modern humans, with our contemporary smarts, has followed an evolutionary trajectory in terms of the stages that have led to our cooperative intelligence.[23] And, crucially, Tomasello's natural history of human thinking centres on the notion of intentionality – our awareness of the thoughts, wishes and feelings of others – and how far and to what extent we engage with the intentionality of others.

For the most part, chimps, and other great apes, operate at the level of 'individual intentionality'. Chimps, for example, spend most of their waking hours 'in small bands foraging individually for fruit and other vegetation, with various kinds of social interaction'.[24] While chimps are social creatures, and recognise hierarchical and social relationships – all essential for group living – their interactions are primarily self-centred and self-serving, as in the case of Dandy's attempt to hide his erection. Moreover, when chimps do engage in collaborative hunting, their actions remain largely individualistic, rather than truly collaborative. For instance, chimps sometimes engage in group hunting of monkeys.[25] In this situation, when a monkey has become separated from its group, the chimps opportunistically surround and proceed to capture the monkey, a strategy that can only work through collaboration. While one chimp initiates the chase, others move to block possible routes of escape. But only one chimp actually captures the monkey, and that is the chimp who consumes most of the meat.

Tomasello argues that 'chimpanzees are engaged in a kind of co-action in which each individual is pursuing his own individual goal of capturing the monkey'.[26] The pursuit can only be achieved by collaborating in a cooperative way. But the fact that the meat is not shared – those that don't actually do the capturing are left with scraps and remnants – suggests that chimps are not quite operating beyond a single intentionality mode. The hunt is not fully cooperative. Chimps recognise the need for interactional co-action, but not full-fledged cooperation, which involves performing specific individual roles in the hunt, in exchange for the promise of a fair share of the spoils.

At stage two, individuals achieve what Tomasello calls 'joint intentionality'. This involves an agreement – or at least a recognition – that the greatest spoils can be achieved by, for instance, hunting in a truly collaborative manner. But of course, if individuals are to work as a team, there can still only be one captor. But to work as a team, and to be able to bring down large game, requires those individuals that are not actually involved in the kill being rewarded appropriately: their role is, after all, crucial to the successful hunt, such as driving the game into a trap where it can be subdued and killed. And it is this understanding – greater spoils result from pooling resources, and subsequently sharing food – that betokens this more cooperative cognitive strategy.

Tomasello proposes that following the separation of hominins from the great apes, and for the first several million years of the hominin lineage, through the genus *Australopithecus* – essentially an upright ape – the cognitive strategy was essentially individualistic. It most likely operated on a similar plane to that of other great apes. While australopithecines most likely had some aspects of human-like interactional intelligence, they lacked the essential ingredient of being able to set aside their individualistic motives for a more cooperative approach to procuring food. They were still operating at the level of single, rather than joint, intentionality.

During the emergence of the genus *Homo*, beginning around 2.8 million years ago, ancestral humans began the move to joint intentionality, and a full-fledged cooperative intelligence. According to Tomasello, this most likely culminated with the species *Homo heidelbergensis*, the presumed common ancestor of our species, *Homo sapiens*, and *Homo neantherthalensis*.[27] Fossils for *Homo heidelbergensis* (or a closely related species, *Homo antecessor)*, date from 800,000 years ago, at a site in Spain; this suggests the species may have existed perhaps over a million years ago in Africa.[28] Archaeological finds of weaponry, such as sophisticated, wooden throwing spears, also reveal that *Homo heidelbergensis* may have been the first human species to be able to bring down large game through collaborative hunting. And this could only have been possible if they hunted cooperatively. Moreover, there is archaeological evidence that this species of ancestral humans brought the food back to a base to be shared out, including by those, especially women and children, that hadn't taken part in the hunt.[29] Behaviour of this kind would, indeed, seem to suggest the kind of cooperative intelligence that Tomasello associates with joint intentionality.

Our capacity for joint intentionality appears to be a defining feature of human cognitive organisation. It is for this reason that we share in the collective upbringing and education of our children. Chimps and other great apes don't. We point things out to others, in an unsolicited fashion: those things that we believe might be helpful for them. Again, chimps don't do this. And as I observed earlier, we take collective decisions about our shared and individual lives, a feature absent from the lifestyle of chimps. These types of behaviour, as well as language, are only possible with the advent of cooperative intelligence – joint intentionality.

While language is not something that we are born with – it is not innate[30] – human cooperative intelligence is. Numerous experiments in the psychology lab demonstrate that pre-school children – children with little or no language – are naturally cooperative, in a way that chimps in the same lab settings just aren't. For instance, in one study, children aged just three were invited to play a game with one adult. Once they were engaged in the game, a second adult invited them to join in another even more compelling game. Before leaving for the new game, the infants either paused or handed the instrument they were using to the first adult, seemingly sensing that a joint activity entails a joint commitment to see the game out.[31] In contrast, there is no evidence that chimps of the same or indeed any age perceive joint activities in this way.[32]

In the third and final evolutionary stage of cooperative intelligence, our lineage has developed what Tomasello terms 'collective intentionality'. This type of cooperation involves the extrapolation of joint intentionality in order to develop rituals and other social structures that support, maintain and even constrain our collaborative way of life. Social constructs such as money, marriage and so on are all cultural artefacts that result from intelligence of this kind. And with this final, extended type of cooperative intelligence, evident in *Homo sapiens*, and arguably in the social behaviour of the extinct *Homo neanderthalensis*, full-blown language of the kind we recognise today would have had to be in place, in order to support the rich culture that this sort of collaborative living entailed.

In the final analysis, our species is uniquely cooperative in the way that no other species is. Once ancestral humans began the move away from single intentionality – the type of interactional intelligence which early hominins shared with great apes – rudimentary forms of communication, perhaps via gesture and pantomiming, would have already been on the march.[33] And the way of life that this gave rise to would have further selected for enhanced collaboration, leading, ultimately, to the development of full-blown language.

## Crossing the symbolic threshold

But if developing joint intentionality paved the way for simple communication systems, and in time language-like behaviour, how might this have proceeded? In his monumental 1997 book, *The Symbolic Species*, the biological anthropologist Terence Deacon proposes that the eventual emergence of language in the ancestral human mind resulted from crossing what he dubs the 'symbolic threshold'.

Human language is symbolic in the sense that a language, any language, consists of a series of symbols – words, idioms and other grammatical constructions, as we saw in the previous chapter – that have an arbitrary connection with the object or idea they signify. The father of modern linguistics, the Swiss linguist Ferdinand de Saussure, argued that the hallmark of language is that it makes use of an arbitrary relation between a sign – for instance, a word – and the entity or idea it signifies or points to.[34] This is exemplified by the idea designated by the English word *dog*, for instance, in our minds. The word – composed of three distinct sound segments, sequenced in a fixed order, making the word *dog* – designates the concept for dog. When you or I hear the word *dog*, it is the four-legged creature with a tail, and for many, the notion of man's best friend, that comes to mind. This relation is symbolic in the sense that the sign employed – the word *dog* – doesn't have to otherwise look, sound like or otherwise invoke the entity that it signifies, as evidenced by the diverse ways in which other languages evoke the same idea. To give you a sense of the diversity, the same creature signified by the English word *dog* is *góshe* in Apache, *kalb* in Arabic, *gou* in Mandarin, *koira* in Finnish and *skyli* in Greek.

Figure 10.1 illustrates the nature of symbolic reference. What this shows is that distinct signs, such as spoken words, symbolically refer, via convention, to a specific idea in our mind, for instance *love*, or an entity in the world, such as *dog*.

But symbolic reference – the strategy deployed by human language – is not the only way, in principle, that a communicative system could pick out the ideas it attempts to signal. The American philosopher Charles Sanders Peirce distinguished the symbolic reference strategy employed by language from other referential strategies, notably 'iconic reference' and 'indexical reference'.[35]

Objects and events in the mind/world

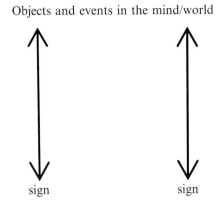

sign                       sign

**Figure 10.1.** Symbolic reference

Each of these three types of reference describes a type of relation between a sign – the physical representation that does the signalling, such as a word – and the 'signified' – the idea or physical entity that the sign – or symbol, in the case of language – represents. A sign can refer by virtue of the type of relation – iconic, indexical or symbolic – holding between the sign and the thing it signifies.

For instance, while language primarily relies on symbolic reference, there are nevertheless some instances where it does make use of iconic reference. The English word *buzz*, as in a buzzing bee, is a case in point. It is iconic in the sense that the word actually resembles the sound emitted by bees. Buzz is in a class of 'onomatopaeic' words: words that resemble the things they represent by emulating the sound associated with the referent. And this notion of reference by similarity is the hallmark of iconic reference: compare with the icon for a recycle bin on a computer desktop that I discussed in Chapter 7. In a conventional office, we discard unwanted papers and files by placing them in the recycle bin. And in the desktop metaphor that many computer interface systems make use of, the 'desktop' metaphor allows us to manipulate the computer, by selecting particular icons based on the office frame. The recycle bin icon therefore iconically *resembles* the location and function it provides a sign for: the placing of an unwanted file in a location where it will be deleted.

In contrast to icons, other signs convey indexical reference: the relation between the sign and thing signified arises from a factual basis, often from a causal or physical link between the sign and the entity represented. For instance, pointing to a specific object is an instance of indexical reference: the pointing gesture establishes a physical link between the sign (the pointing gesture) and the entity being referred to by the pointing. Similarly, rising smoke indexes a fire – after all, there's no smoke without fire, as the saying goes. And when I say, idly: 'Those clouds mean rain', the reference is again based on an indexical relation; dark, brooding clouds overhead are factually, and indeed, causally, related to rain, and hence can index or point to the imminent arrival of a downpour.

But the overwhelming majority of words, and other referring expressions in a language, are symbolic, in the sense that the referential relation is established by convention: a rule, norm or habit, rather than by a natural connection – as in the case of a rain cloud – or an icon – as in the case of a computer desktop recycle bin. Speakers of English agree that the sounds that combine to make up the word *dog* refer to the same entity that Greek speakers use *skyli* to express. Symbolic reference is, thus, a more abstract way of referring to things. In the case of symbols, there is no obvious connection between the sign and the thing it refers to; and this contrasts with icons (iconic reference) and indices (indexical reference), where there is.

In his influential book, Deacon proposes that the emergence of human language was dependent upon the ability of ancestral humans to cross the symbolic threshold: to figure out the utility of making use of signs with no obvious or otherwise motivated connection to the thing they refer to. The advantages of symbolic reference should perhaps be obvious. If I wanted to tell you that there is a fire, and our lives are in danger, I could hope you might notice rising smoke – this is iconic reference: the smoke is given off from the smouldering fire and hence, in part at least, resembles the source the smoke relates to and emanates from. Or alternatively, I could point to the smoke, or indeed the fire, drawing your attention to it. This is, of course, indexical reference. But in many situations, the things we wish to refer to don't announce themselves so helpfully in the here-and-now – imagine trying to persuade a reluctant lover to come out on a dinner date with you without recourse to symbolic reference (language), by using iconic and indexical reference alone. The object of your affections would no doubt end up thinking you were just plain weird, following your outbreak of ad hoc pantomimed gesturing. In such a case, without recourse to symbolic reference, how do we convey the subtlety of our desires and aspirations, the fun and excitement that we hope will ensue during the course of the evening, the tasty food we will consume, the fun and laughter we'll share? We could obviously take our prospective date to the restaurant and point to the menu in the window with images of the tasty delights on offer, hoping they'll hence be persuaded. But most dinner dates would never get started if we had to take our prospective partner to see a physical menu.

The power of symbolic reference is that there doesn't need to be any natural or obvious connection whatsoever holding between the sign – the symbol doing the signifying – and the entity signified. We just have to agree that a particular sign – for example, the sounds that make up the word *dog* – will refer to a particular entity – the animal that has four legs, a wagging tail, and the pet of choice for many. And this solution to the referential problem opens up a huge communication potential, allowing us, in principle, to refer to all manner of objects, events, experiences and feelings, from doorknobs, to unrequited love, to mediaeval musicology, to phlogiston. The words and expressions refer to particular things, experiences or ideas, because we've grown up in a particular socio-cultural milieu where it is widely accepted that these expressions will have relatively stable referential counterparts: both the concrete and more abstract things they refer to.

But Deacon's argument is that once we crossed this symbolic threshold, once our hominin ancestors – creatures that, like us, walked upright on two legs – began to deploy symbolic reference of this sort, this opened up a design-space possibility for the later emergence and evolution of language. A symbolic relation between a sign – for instance a word-form, or whatever signs preceded spoken language, perhaps pantomimed gestures in early ancestral human proto-languages – and an object or entity in the world presumes an interactional intelligence, which could only have arisen in a rich socio-cultural context that supported and necessitated cooperative interaction. After all, symbolic reference would have had little utility unless there was a context that facilitated, and perhaps also necessitated, communication. Ancestral humans therefore already had to have something approaching the joint intentionality of Tomasello, or what I am calling cooperative intelligence, which would have been a pre-requisite, at least in the earliest stages, for ancestral humans to begin to cross the symbolic threshold. Cooperative intelligence entailed the development of more complex symbolic abilities, leading to the development of a conventional system of signs, precisely because symbolic reference provides a more powerful means of referring in a cooperative milieu than iconic or indexical reference strategies alone.

## Towards abstract symbolic reference

One of the achievements of Deacon's research is that he demonstrates this: once ancestral humans began crossing the symbolic threshold, this led to a raft of co-evolving changes in the brain organisation of ancestral humans. Not only did ancestral human brains get bigger than their forebears; they became configured in different ways, specialising for this new symbolic reference strategy. In humans, the prefrontal cortex of the brain is way more pronounced than in any of the other great apes, for instance. Deacon claims that this region of the brain is particularly adept at performing the associative learning necessary to relate signs to referents in a symbolic way. Hence, what led to us becoming more than merely upright apes was the ability to establish relationships between symbols on one hand, and entities in the world to which the symbols could be used to refer on the other.

But wait. What might it mean to say that human language developed by crossing the symbolic threshold? After all, many other species are capable of communication employing symbolic reference. One example concerns the alarm calls made by vervet monkeys. Vervets live in southern and eastern Africa. As I observed in *The Language Myth*, they make specific and distinct calls upon sight of different predators: a chutter when they see snakes, and different calls when they spot eagles or leopards. Tellingly, other vervets take an appropriate form of evasive action, even if they haven't seen the predator.[36] For instance, upon hearing a leopard call, other vervets run towards trees and begin climbing. Upon hearing an eagle alarm call they look up into the air. And upon hearing a snake call they look down at the ground, often by standing on their two rear legs. The vervet alarm calls are, in one sense, clearly symbolic – there's nothing about a chutter that calls a snake to mind.[37]

While this approaches the human capacity, using language for evoking things that aren't present, there nevertheless remains a connection to the present, relating to a potential threat in the here-and-now. In contrast, symbolic reference in human language moves quite decisively beyond the here-and-now. It provides a referential strategy that is no longer strait-jacketed by things that can be pointed to or perceived. And in so doing, it allows much greater flexibility in the range of things that can be conveyed. Moreover, symbolic reference also implies a level of abstraction that goes well beyond icons and indices: it implies that its users understand the nature and referential power of signs. After all, symbolic reference strips signs of their natural, fact-based meaning. Symbols don't have any obvious connection to the referents they signify; they are wholly arbitrary, relying on convention – and hence agreement within a group – for how they should be interpreted.

But Deacon goes further than this. He argues that for a language-like system to have emerged, it wasn't sufficient for symbols to refer to *just* entities in the natural world. Signs had to also come to refer to other signs, which gave rise to the emergence of grammar. To show you how this works, consider the following attested example (note that 'GP' refers to a type of medic known as a general practitioner in a UK context):

> The Government's **aim** is to make GPs more financially accountable, in charge of their own budgets, as well as to extend the choice of the patient.[38]

In this sentence, I've placed in bold the noun *aim*. Moreover, this noun refers to a complex idea, which I've underlined. In this example, the speaker presents a particular idea ('to make GPs more financially accountable, in charge of their own budgets, as well as to extend the choice of the patient') as an 'aim'. The linguist Hans-Jorg Schmid labels nouns like *aim*, which refer to a more complex idea, as 'shell nouns': they provide a shell, or case, which carries, or refers to, a complex idea. The shell noun encapsulates the various components contained in the idea I've underlined as a single, relatively stable – albeit temporary – concept. It does so by casting 'this complex piece of information into one single noun phrase'.[39] But this meaning of *aim*, the underlined noun phrase, is not an inalienable property of *aim*. Rather, *aim* takes on this property in this extract of discourse by virtue of symbolic reference: *aim* refers to the underlined segment of the utterance. Evidence for this comes from the next sentence in the discourse:

> The Government's **aim** is to make GPs more financially accountable, in charge of their own budgets, as well as to extend the choice of the patient. Under **this new scheme**, family doctors are required to produce annual reports for their patients...[40]

Here we see that once the complex idea has been encapsulated by the shell noun *aim*, it can be glossed with a different characterisation, as signalled by a new shell noun phrase, *this new scheme*, which I've also marked in bold. In essence, the function of the expression *aim* is to establish reference to a complex idea, the underlined expression, which can then be picked up in ongoing discourse and referred to by a new shell noun phrase: *this new scheme*. This demonstrates the ability of language not just to refer, symbolically, to ideas outside the language system, but additionally to aspects internal to the system itself. The noun *aim* is referring to a grouping of other words. And in so doing, the meaning of *aim* derives from that grouping.

Hence, we can usefully distinguish between two qualitatively distinct types of symbolic reference. On the one hand we have a 'words-to-world' strategy, as when the word *dog* refers to the animal in our everyday lives, and when vervet monkeys, for instance, use a distinct alarm call to refer to a particular type of predator. But on the other we have a new type of symbolic reference, one indigenous and unique to human language: a 'word-to-word' reference strategy, as exemplified, in my example above, by shell nouns. I have captured these two types of symbolic reference in Figure 10.2.

Figure 10.2 illustrates that symbolic reference – signalled by the double-headed arrows – can proceed in two directions. On the one hand, signs (words) can refer outside the language system to ideas or entities in the world. But on the other hand, signs (words) can also refer to other signs (words) within the language system itself. And human language, unlike extant animal communication systems, makes use of both: the more concrete word-to-world strategy, as well as the more abstract word-to-word relation.

Deacon has proposed that crossing this 'symbolic threshold' – the move from symbolic relationships that I characterise as the word-to-world type, to the word-to-word type – led to a range of

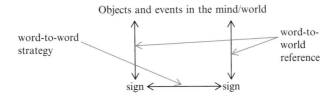

**Figure 10.2.** Two types of symbolic reference

adaptations to the basic ape brain-plan our forebears inherited; these gave rise, ultimately, to a language-ready brain in our ancestral human forebears. And ultimately, this paved the way for the emergence of grammar, and the parametric representations that enable our species to bootstrap analogue concepts in the conceptual system, producing the most sophisticated natural meaning-making system that has ever existed on this planet. But of course, this is not the end of the story. We still need to figure out how language, and meaning-making more generally, emerged.

# Chapter 11    The crucible of language

Until relatively recently, it was not considered good form to speculate on the origin of language. And in part, this was a sound position to adopt. By the time that Charles Darwin published *On the Origin of Species* in 1859, and his subsequent publication *The Descent of Man* in 1871, all manner of exotic theories had been put forward to explain the origin of language, replete with some equally ludicrous names. My personal favourite is the 'ta-ta' theory of Sir Richard Paget.[1] Paget, who was influenced by Darwin, proposed that language may have arisen as an unconscious, vocal imitation of specific body movements – for instance, the way my tongue sticks out when I attempt a task that leaves my thumbs-for-fingers confused, such as trying to thread a needle or play the guitar. Indeed, Darwin himself was not immune, speculating that spoken language may have arisen from our ability to produce song – but it seems unlikely that singing gave rise to language. Recent research, for instance, demonstrates that 'amusia' – an impairment of the brain that results in the inability to process musical cadences and recognise music, and 'aphasia' – the loss of language – are unrelated. A person can lose the ability to use or comprehend language, but still retain, perhaps counterintuitively, the ability to recognise music.[2] Indeed, the nature and organisation of music and spoken language appear to diverge in a host of ways[3]– although some scientists do see value in Darwin's musical origins of language hypothesis.[4]

When the Linguistic Society of Paris was founded in 1865, it famously included a prohibition against speculating on the origin of language in its constitution: 'Article 11: The Society will accept no communication ... dealing with the origin of language'. This stance made good sense at the time, being later adopted by the Philological Society of London. In 1873, the President of the

Philological Society, Alexander Ellis, declared that 'We shall do more by tracing the development of one work-a-day tongue, than by filling waste-paper baskets by reams of paper covered with speculations on the origins of all tongues'.[5]

Speculation on the evolutionary basis of language remained off-limits for over a century. But by the 1970s, scientists began to again speculate on the origin of language. Today, the scientific literature is brimming at the seams with a whole host of theories about how language may have come into being. But this hasn't necessarily resulted in clarity. As one leading expert puts it: 'The current state of the field is largely one of chaos, to the point that some observers might be tempted to think the ban should be reinstated'. [6] The cacophonous din of different accounts of language origins ranges from the sublime – language evolved to enable us to engage in gossip, proposed by Professor Robin Dunbar[7] – to the ridiculous – the aptly named Bow Wow Theory, attributed to the German philosopher Johann Gottfried Herder.[8] This contends that language may have arisen from sounds used to identify animals, perhaps based on onomatopoeia, which eventually became their names. But, in the past decade or two, new findings, some of which I review below, have begun to shed light on this most thorny of issues.

In the previous chapter my conclusion was this: inheriting the essential interactional intelligence of the great apes, something changed in the way of living among our very early hominin forebears. And this led to a shift from the interactional intelligence of our great ape ancestors to a new type of cooperative intelligence. But cooperative intelligence entailed, indeed it required, communication. This pro-social impulse led early species of the genus *Homo* to begin to cross the symbolic threshold. Our early ancestors would have shared, with a great many other species, basic symbolic abilities, notably in a words-to-world direction. But what changed, probably relatively early in the ancestral human lineage, was the development of symbolic reference in a words-to-words direction. And over evolutionary time, this would have paved the way for the emergence of lexical classes – a distinction between nouns and verbs, and later more esoteric parts of speech – eventually giving rise to more complex syntax – word order. And later still, as syntax became more complex, this would have resulted in the human ability to produce recursive thought – our ability to combine and embed grammatical units within one another, to produce grammatically well-formed sentences of, in principle, great complexity. With the emergence of rudimentary grammar – of words-to-world symbolic reference – parametric knowledge was born. Finally, the emergence of this new type of representation enabled the rise of the human meaning-making capacity in evidence today: language provided a means of bootstrapping our conceptual systems – the repository of our analogue concepts – enabling ancestral humans to begin to utilise language to construct complex simulations by encoding and externalising analogue concepts in order to create rich meanings.

The development of language as an executive control system, working in conjunction with the human conceptual system, has emerged in just over two million years. While this is several times greater than the 100,000 years or less that some scientists have estimated for the emergence of language, it still represents but a flash in the pan in evolutionary terms.[9] It's sobering to reflect, for instance, that over 50 million years were required, in comparison, for the evolution of birdsong.[10] Hence, the human capacity for meaning, of which language is an integral part, must have been cobbled together relatively quickly, by adapting pre-existing ape-like structures in the ancestral human brain.[11] And this has led to a whole suite of other changes, especially the emergence of our ability to produce language via the spoken medium. That said, I won't consider here the evolution of speech. One reason for this is that it is language, rather than speech, that is the essential ingredient of our capacity for creating meaning. After all, the 130 or so recognised sign languages used today manage perfectly adequately without recourse to the oral–auditory medium.[12] So in principle, meaning-making is not contingent on one medium or another. And so, it is the origins of language – regardless of its medium of expression – and the larger meaning-making capacity that I focus on in this final chapter. In so doing, I complete the last part of the meaning-making story by examining what may have happened in this evolutionary process, resulting in a full-fledged linguistic system; and this, ultimately, has afforded our species with an exquisitely sophisticated capacity to mean.

## The long and winding road

Our evolutionary beginnings are associated with primate ancestors that lived in the trees of tropical forests around 85 million years ago. With the exception of humans, most primate species today are still wholly or partly arboreal, exploiting the adaptations that enabled life in this formidable tree-top environment. Primates range in size from the tiny mouse lemur, weighing around 30 g, to the Eastern Lowland gorilla, with some males weighing in at over 200 kg. And, humans excepted, primates are restricted to tropical and subtropical forest regions of Africa, Asia and the Americas. Primates have large brains relative to their body size, compared to other mammals, and have an increased reliance on stereoscopic vision as opposed to smell and hearing, the most important senses for many other mammals. Most primates have opposable thumbs, enabling grasping, an important adaptation to the challenge of inhabiting tree-top canopies.[13]

Humans are descended from the great African apes, with the smallest living species being the bonobo – the so-called 'pygmy' chimpanzee – at 30–40 kg in weight, and the largest being the gorillas.[14] In all great apes, the males are, on average, larger and stronger than the females, although the degree of 'sexual dimorphism' – the bodily difference between males versus females – varies greatly among species. Although most living species are predominantly quadrupedal, they are all able to use their hands for gathering food as well as for manufacturing and deploying simple tools.

The gestation period for Great Apes is 8–9 months, which is long compared to many other animals. And when offspring are born they are helpless and need a sustained period of being cared for. Moreover, there is a lengthy period of adolescence in the great apes, with infants only being weaned after several years, and maturity not being achieved until the individual is between 8–13 years of age – longer in humans. Consequently, great apes typically only produce one infant at a time, and the typical time-span between babies is 2–3 years, as is also the case in humans. While all great apes are omnivores, in all species except humans, fruit is the preferred food. In contrast to other great apes, human teeth and jaws are smaller for their body size. This is likely to be an adaptation to eating cooked meat for well over a million years.[15]

Ever since Darwin's proposal that our species is descended from African apes,[16] scientists have been preoccupied with the so-called 'missing link'. After all, if humans really are descended from apes – this is confirmed by genetic evidence showing that over 98 per cent of our DNA is shared by chimps and bonobos[17] – then we would expect to find evidence for an early hominin species – a creature that could get around by walking, not just some of the time, like chimps can, but habitually – that had the body structure to enable walking upright on its hind legs. Such a creature would have, presumably, exhibited other features that were close to the apes from which the first upright creature emerged.[18]

One of the most celebrated fossil finds is that of Lucy, a 3.2 million-year-old skeleton of a small female hominin, attributed to the species *Autralalopithecus afarensis* – the genus of hominin is indicated by the first word 'Australopithecus', using an initial capital letter, while the species is indicated by the second 'afarensis', with a lower-case initial letter. Australopithecus means 'southern ape', while 'afarensis' relates to 'dweller of Afar', the harsh Afar desert region where Lucy was found. The fossil find was discovered by archaeologists Donald Johanson and Tom Gray in Hadar, Ethiopia, in 1974. And famously, at the post-find party, The Beatles track *Lucy in the Sky with Diamonds* was playing, hence the name 'Lucy'.[19] As one wag has observed: 'Might we have been just one record flip away from knowing *Australopithecus afarensis* as 'Lovely Rita?'[20]

The striking feature of Lucy's skeletal morphology is that the pelvis is far more human-like than ape-like, demonstrating an evolutionary re-modelling compared to other apes, enabling bipedalism. For instance, Lucy's pelvic blades are short and wide, and the pelvic sacrum – the triangular bone at the base of the spine – is positioned, like in humans, directly behind the hip joint.[21] This would have meant that the thigh bone connects directly to the knee joint, enabling habitual walking on two legs, as in modern humans.[22] Moreover, spacing of prehistoric footprints found at Laetoli, in modern-day Tanzania, which have been attributed to *Australopithecus afarensis* suggests that Lucy and her kin were able to walk on two legs at a pace of around 1 m/s, about the pace of a gentle stroll by modern adult humans around town.[23]

In other respects, Lucy retains features that would have allowed her ancestors to inhabit the tree-top canopy from which apes developed. For instance, the structure of Lucy's hands, such as the curvature of her fingers and toes, is similar to modern apes. This suggests an ability to grasp branches and climb efficiently. However, while Lucy, like modern humans, retained the opposable thumb on her hand, she appeared to have lost the opposable big toe – a feature of all modern-day tree-climbing apes – which meant that, like humans, she would have been unable to grasp with her feet, a hindrance to tree-climbing.[24]

Twenty years after Lucy was uncovered, an even older hominin fossil was discovered just 46 miles from where the *Australopithecus* remains were found, by archaeologist Tim White. This creature belonged not only to a different species, but to a different genus named *Ardipithecus ramidus*, preceding Lucy by over a million years, being dated to 4.4 million years ago.[25] By 2009, scientists had painstakingly reconstructed 'Ardi', as the fossil was nicknamed. And interestingly, Ardi exhibited a mix of more advanced characteristics as well as more primitive traits, including the opposable big toe. In particular, while Lucy was most likely primarily a ground-dwelling ape, Ardi had features that allowed it to walk upright *as well as* climb trees – Ardi was, in an important sense, intermediate between the tree-inhabiting apes and the exclusively ground-dwelling austrolepthecines, such as Lucy, that came later. Together, these various fossils provide evidence for the transition from tree-dwelling apes to creatures that could operate on the ground.

Of course, one question centres on how this came about. For instance, today modern apes, particularly gorillas and chimps, deploy a knuckle-walking technique for walking across the ground, using all four limbs. This involves clenching the fists of the forelimbs and using the knuckles as *footpads*, enabling quadrupedal motion. One possibility is that ancestral humans developed into upright creatures by first engaging in knuckle-walking. But the discovery and subsequent analysis of Ardi suggests this not to have been the case. After all, Ardi had a body structure that enabled arboreal climbing as well as bipedalism, without the need to engage in knuckle-walking. Knuckle-walking was probably not, then, an intermediate step giving rise to bipedalism. Rather, Ardi may have evolved from a form of bipedalism used in specific arboreal contexts.

Finally, a third pre-*Homo* genus was discovered in 2000: *Orrorin tugenensis*, which means 'original man', and was discovered in the Tugen Hills in Kenya. While advances in genetics mean that scientists were able to figure out that early humans had to have diverged from chimps at least 5 million years ago, this find was the first hard evidence for the split, and pushed the date back by around a million years.[26] While these creatures were the size of a chimpanzee, they have some human-like features, including the smaller teeth with thick enamel common to later hominins. Moreover, their leg bones, especially the bone build-up of the femur, provided evidence for bipedalism.

One thing we have to be aware of is that the path that led to our genus, *Homo*, is not a direct one. In 1999 a team of archaeologists led by Maeve Leakey discovered a new genus named *Kenyanthropus Platyops*, the so-called 'flat-faced man of Kenya'.[27] Although a contemporary of Lucy and sharing some similarities with Lucy's species, such as the structure of the cranium and brain size, this species featured important differences. This has led to the specimen being classed as belonging to a different genus; in fact, it is likely that there were various species of early hominins, that were taxonomically diverse, for much of the period leading to the emergence of the genus *Homo*. Moreover, some archaeologists consider this species – the flat-faced man of Kenya – to provide evidence for Darwin's proposal that when one species makes an adaptive change, other species will get on the bandwagon, adapting in a similar fashion to an accommodating ecosystem. Importantly, the existence of several quite different species of hominins, living at roughly the same time and in the same region, reveals that the evolution of ancestral humans is less than straightforward.

## Becoming human

While pre-human species, such as the australopithecines of which Lucy was a member, were essentially upright apes, from around 2.8 million years ago a new genus emerged: the genus *Homo*.[28] One of the earliest members of this new line was dubbed *Homo habilis* 'handy man'. *Homo habilis* exhibited a larger brain size than the australopithecines, ranging from 550 cm$^3$ to 687 cm$^3$. In some respects, *habilis* resembled australopithecines, with short bodies and disproportionately long arms. But in other respects, *habilis* was more human-like, with a less protruding jaw. Nevertheless, for some archaeologists, *habilis* may be better classified as a more advanced species of the *Australopithecus* genus.[29]

An important new behaviour associated with *Homo habilis* was its use of stone tools. While this may be a far cry from the mitre saws and drills that you and I might use for our household DIY chores, this was a very important evolutionary development. *Homo habilis*, the handyman, was among the earliest habitual tool users. *Homo habilis* appears to have used rudimentary stone tools, specifically created for the purpose, for opening up carcasses and animal bones in order to obtain marrow.[30]

The tools developed by *Homo habilis* made use of rocks and large pebbles that were chipped away to form crude, flake-like blades. This type of technique is often referred to as the Oldowan industry, named after the Olduvai Gorge in Tanzania, where fossils of such tools were found in abundance by the archaeologist Louis Leakey in the 1930s.[31] There appear to have been a number of main uses for Oldowan tools: they were used for chopping meat, as well as for scraping and pounding foodstuffs.

The relationship between *Homo habilis* and later species of the genus *Homo* is unclear. At one time, archaeologists thought that *Homo habilis* evolved into the more advanced *Homo erectus*, 'upright man'. But in 2007, Mary Leakey discovered evidence that *habilis* and *erectus* co-existed, suggesting that they may in fact have been overlapping species, rather than one evolving into the other.[32]

Whatever their relationship, by around 1.8 million years, *Homo erectus* had emerged, the first clear exemplar of ancestral humans, with relatively long legs, shorter arms and a larger brain, at about 900 cm$^3$ on average.[33] And strikingly, a further feature that is human-like is the reduced difference in sexual dimorphism, compared to other great apes.

The earliest fossil find of *Homo erectus* was discovered by a Dutch army surgeon, Eugène Dubois, in 1891 in Java, giving rise to the moniker Java Man.[34] Later, older *Homo erectus* fossils were found in Africa, confirming Darwin's proposal for an African genesis.

*Homo erectus* exhibited many human-like behaviours.[35] Fire was probably used for food preparation, for protection and for warmth. Moreover, *erectus*, for the first time, was an explorer, and, despite its African origins, travelled the world, quite literally – making its way from the African tropics, across Europe, through South Asia and southeast Asia, creating rudimentary seafaring vessels to discover new lands, as in the case of Java Man. *Homo erectus* fossils have been discovered ranging from England to Georgia, from China to Indonesia, and continued to exist in parts of the world until relatively recently, with the most recent fossil finds having been dated to about 300,000 years ago, perhaps later.[36] And *Homo* erectus may have exhibited surprisingly modern human-like behaviour: there is evidence, for instance, that *Homo erectus* settlers in Trinil, Java, may have engaged in decorating sea-shells by engraving them, perhaps as long as half a million years ago. To date, this appears to provide evidence for the earliest apparition of art in the *Homo* lineage.[37]

One of the clearest indicators of the move from *Homo habilis* to *Homo erectus* is in the manufacture of tools. The Oldowan tools of *Homo habilis*, and indeed earlier australopithecine species, involved the creation of rough flake tools. *Homo erectus* inherited the tool-making techniques of the Oldowan industry but modified them in rather significant ways, giving rise to what archaeologists refer to as the Acheuelean industry – a term based on the site Saint-Acheul, near Amiens, in northern France where the first fossils of these new tools were unearthed.[38] The key difference is that flakes were worked symmetrically on both sides, giving rise to bifacial cutting and chopping tools such as bifacial handaxes. These tools were worked using tools made from bone and antler specifically created to work flakes into sharp cutting implements. While this particular stone-age technology began in Africa, finds have now been located in many regions of the world.[39]

By possibly as early as around 1.4 million years ago, perhaps later, African *Homo erectus* had evolved into a more advanced species of ancestral humans, *Homo Heidelbergensis* – so-called after the first fossil find was discovered in Heidelberg, Germany in 1907.[40] *Homo heidelbergensis* had a brain size of between 1100–1400 $cm^3$, which overlaps with the contemporary human brain average of 1350 $cm^3$.[41] Based on a find of extensive bones for this species found in Atapureca in Spain, archaeologists have been able to reconstruct what *Homo heidelbergensis* would have looked like.[42] Adult males averaged about 1.75 m tall, while females were around 1.57 m tall on average, making this species slightly taller than the later *Homo neanderthalensis*.[43]

*Homo heidelbergensis* was an adept tool user and probably fashioned sophisticated tools used for hunting, such as javelins, enabling this ancestral human species to bring down large quarry. There is evidence of the use of fire and burial of the dead. Moreover, red ochre was probably employed to create a type of paint; remains of the pigment have been found at various locations, including East Africa and excavations in the south of France.

Moreover, 500,000-year-old hafted stone points used for hunting have been discovered in South Africa.[44] This suggests that our species, *Homo sapiens*, as well as the species *Homo neanderthalensis*, about which I will have more to say later, may in fact have inherited the stone-tipped spear, rather than developing the technology independently.

By about 300,000 years ago, groups of *Homo heidelbergensis* that had migrated to Europe had evolved, on some accounts, into *Homo neanderthalensis*.[45] Those that remained in Africa embarked on a slightly different evolutionary trajectory, leading to our species, *Homo sapiens*. Complicating the picture is the fact that, in at least one area of Indonesia, a few *Homo erectus* remained until at least 53,000 years ago, and the little understood dwarf *Homo floresienses* persisted until about 18,000 years ago.[46]

## What happened?

The million-dollar question is this: what happened? What was it that led the earliest hominins, the genus *Australopithecus* – an upright ape that had moved down from the trees – to begin to hone the interactional intelligence that would lead to a cascade of neuro-biological changes resulting in the genus *Homo*, and a full-fledged cooperative intelligence, an awareness of joint intentionality, in the parlance of Michael Tomasello?

A plausible scenario involves a change in the ecological niche that early hominins inhabited.[47] While archaeologists once believed that stone tools first emerged with the genus *Homo*, and specifically *Homo habilis*, which lived from at least 2.3 million years ago, and persisted until around 1.6 million years ago, we now know that tool use in fact preceded our genus, *Homo*, by over half a million years. Recent fossil finds from Ethiopia of animal bones dated to around 3.4 million years ago bear compression and cutting marks.[48] These animal bones therefore date from around the time that Lucy, recall, a member of the species *Australopithecus afarensis*, was roaming the African savanna. This points to a change in lifestyle. Although no stone tools have actually been found (so far), and hence there is no direct evidence that australopithecines manufactured tools, nor that that they used tools for hunting, the evidence of butchered carcasses suggests that at the very least australopithecines were supplementing their primarily vegetarian diet with meat.

The teeth and jaws of australopithecines were intermediate between other great apes and the later *Homo* species, for instance *Homo erectus*. In particular, the canines were reduced in size compared to other apes, but larger than in modern humans.[49] One reason for this change may have been the reduced importance of baring teeth in displays of aggression; with the advent of bipedalism, and the consequent freeing up of the hands, male-to-male aggression displays and combat may have been achieved via hands and perhaps the use of stone tools, for example sticks and rocks.[50] That said, based on microscopic analysis of the tooth enamel of australopithecine fossils, the australopithecine diet appears to have mainly consisted of fruit and leaves, rather than meat.[51] Moreover, australopithecines had a cone-shaped rib cage.[52] This suggests they had large stomachs adapted to a low-quality, high-bulk, largely vegetarian diet.

According to Deacon, a 'kind of adventituous hunting and scavenging probably characterised the precondition for the evolution of stone tool-assisted hunting, which appears to have begun about 2.8 million years ago. The transition to stone tool technology is evidence of a major change in the way meat was incorporated as a food resource'.[53] But the move from a foraging to a scavenging/hunting lifestyle would have required changes resulting in a more cooperative lifestyle. After all, while women, and even children, can contribute to foraging for leaves and fruits, hunting for meat would, at the very least, have precluded pregnant females and those nursing small infants. And it is highly plausible that the shift from a primarily vegetarian lifestyle to one involving greater incorporation of meat would have resulted in social–cooperative changes that led to – moreover, required even – a shift from the single intentionality associated with the socio-cognitive strategies evident in modern chimpanzees, to the sort of joint intentionality abundantly evident in later species of the genus *Homo*. For one thing, australopithecines, like modern humans, appear to have lived in social, mixed-sex groups, where males and females as well as children lived alongside each other. And not only would hunting having required cooperative inter-action; such a living arrangement would have required cooper-ation so that the individualistic impulses were overcome and that spoils of the hunt were shared with members of the community unable to participate. More than that, new social structures would have been required, to ensure that mating rights were respected: the males away on a hunt would have needed a guarantee that they would not be cuckolded by other males, while absent. Deacon proposes that early forms of a marriage contract may have been developed, which would have required a means of developing rudimentary communicative mechanisms allowing males to be confident that not only would their mating partners not stray, but also that other males would respect their exclusive, monogamous mating privileges. Hence this new mode of coopera-tive interaction, required to exploit a new ecological niche rendered possible by bipedalism, and the freeing up of the hands for tools and weaponry would have led to new ways of symbolis-ing and communicating ever more complex social structures, structures required to support the new lifestyle.

Evidence that such a scenario may indeed have led to the emergence of cooperative intelligence comes from the sexual dimorphism exhibited by humans, compared to australopith-ecines, and indeed other apes. Australopithecines, like today's gorillas and orang-utans, were highly sexually dimorphic; the latter exhibit a difference such that males are, on average, more than 50 per cent bigger and stronger than females – essential for male-to-male competition, to protect mating and food resources. But with the advent of *Homo habilis*, sexual dimorphism had dramatically reduced, leading to a difference of only around 15 per cent.[54] And this reduction in sexual dimorphism has persisted throughout the human lineage; if anything, it has reduced further. For instance, recent data suggests that in the United States adult males are, on average, just 8 per cent heavier than adult females[55] and just 4 per cent taller.[56] One interpretation of these facts is that, due to newly created social structures, resulting from the advent of a genuine cooperative intelligence, the need for sexual dimorphism to protect resources in male-to-male competitive contexts was no longer required to the extent necessary in ape-like scenarios. Increasingly, ancestral humans would have developed symbolic representations, used for communication, to support and sustain the new cooperative cognitive mode of operating and the new ecological niche to which they had adapted. In turn, this would have driven a cascade of other neurobiological changes, resulting in full-blown joint intentionality and, most likely, the gradual emergence of full-blown language, which, as we shall see, may have already begun to emerge by the time of the last common ancestor of humans and Neanderthals.

Hence, it is likely that a change in australopithecine ecology set in train a raft of changes that not only necessitated a more cooperative lifestyle, but also set in motion other developments. The result would have been that ancestral humans developed a truly cooperative intelligence, leading, irrevocably, to our forebears crossing the symbolic threshold. And once that began to happen, a suite of other neuro-biological changes would have followed.

For one thing, the brain size of ancestral humans has shown an increase over successive species of our genus. But in certain respects, it's not brain size per se that has given us our modern smarts.[57] Rather, it's what we've been able to do with a bigger brain that counts: how effectively a larger brain is organised. In particular, a key change in the brain anatomy throughout our lineage has been the increase in the prefrontal cortex. Deacon proposes that this was necessary to accommodate the raw, computational processing capability associated with symbol use. Other changes would have required better auditory perception, to accommodate speech as the preferred medium for language – in later species of the genus *Homo* – as well as the musculature and nerve control to produce well-articulated speech, a process that has been ongoing for around two million years.

It is also likely that for much of the almost 3-million-year history of our lineage, the symbol use made possible by an enhanced capacity for cooperative intelligence was multimodal in nature. Compelling arguments have been put forward for the use of pantomiming and gesture in the early stages of language use,[58] supported by mirror neurons, which enabled ancestral humans to co-opt their emerging cooperative intelligence to mime actions for communicative purposes.[59] But later, and most likely by the time of *Homo heidelbergensis*, full-blown spoken language, if not fully modern-like, was probably on the march, as I spell out later in the chapter. In short, it's conceivable that gesture and spoken capabilities competed as the primary medium for the outward expression of our meaning-making capacity, namely language. And even today, many thousands of language-users function perfectly effectively without recourse to the spoken medium, as attested by the 130 or so documented sign languages in the world today.

## How old is language?

Aficionados of the BBC TV science fiction series *Doctor Who* will be familiar with its novel approach to the concept of time travel: the eponymous Doctor is a Time Lord from the now extinct planet Gallifrey. The Doctor travels through time in his *Tardis* – a time-travelling spaceship, which is famously larger on the inside, a feat made possible by Time Lord technology. Until relatively recently, in lieu of a Tardis, it was almost impossible to say anything meaningful about the evolution of language, as

I observed at the outset of the chapter. But in the past decade or so, with more recent fossil finds and with advances in the genetic dating of ancient DNA, the picture has begun to change.

Until recently, it had been fairly widely assumed that human-like language was a very recent evolutionary development.[60] One important reason for thinking this was that it had been assumed that language was absent in *Homo neanderthalensis* ('Neanderthal man'). And if Neanderthals lacked language, then the last common ancestor of humans and Neanderthals, *Homo heidelbergensis,* must also have lacked language. Consequently, the emergence of language must have been a uniquely human innovation.

Genetic evidence for early modern humans points to our species being around 200,000 years old. Moreover, from around 50,000 years ago – the period referred to by archaeologists as the Upper Palaeolithic – an unprecedented cultural explosion began to manifest itself in human communities. This resulted in art work, sophisticated jewellery, advanced stone tool technology, evidence of complex ritual systems and social structures, fishing and boat-building, the manufacture of projectile javelins for hunting and other trappings of a relatively sophisticated material culture. The conclusion was clear: language must have emerged sometime after 200,000 years ago and prior to this cultural 'big bang', some 50,000 years ago.[61]

There were three main reasons for thinking that Neanderthals lacked a (spoken) language capacity. For one thing, Neanderthals were robust creatures, which implied great physical strength, but at the expense of smarts. Moreover, early reconstructions of the fossil vocal tract of Neanderthal specimens, in the 1960s and early 1970s, seemed to suggest that they lacked speech capacities, implying a lack of language full stop. And finally, there appeared to be a large gap between the cultural products and capabilities of Neanderthals, compared with Upper Palaeolithic humans – again implying reduced mental acuity, and hence, a lack of language. But as the evidence has come in, it is now becoming clear that Neanderthals may, in fact, have had a spoken, human-like, language capacity; and from that, it also follows that the common ancestor of humans and Neanderthals also had language: spoken language may be older than previously suspected.[62] Moreover, this conclusion fits with Michael Tomasello's proposal that *Homo heidelbergensis* was the first species of Homo to have a fully optimised joint intentionality cognitive strategy, as I discussed in the previous chapter.

Recognisable Neanderthal fossils have been found in Europe from around 400,000 years ago. Their physique was shorter and stockier than the more gracile, later arriving *Homo sapiens*, most likely an adaptation to the severe glacial European environment of the last ice age.[63] They occupied regions, at various points in their existence, ranging from as far north as sub-arctic regions of Europe, as far east as Siberia and as far south as the Middle East.[64]

In contrast, the earliest modern-looking human fossils have been found in Omo from around 200,000 years ago and in Herto – both in modern-day Ethiopia – dating to around 160,000 years ago.[65] Human fossils have been discovered in the Middle East from around 100,000 years ago, suggesting the beginning of an out-of-Africa dispersal. And by around 70,000 years ago, humans began to disperse around the Old World, reaching glacial Europe sometime before 40–50,000 years ago.[66]

Scientists once thought that Neanderthals and *Homo sapiens* were completely different species. But with advances in genetic testing techniques, and the mapping of the Neanderthal genetic sequence based on ancient DNA samples, we now know that the picture is far more complicated. Moreover, it's now becoming clear that Neanderthals may have been, in many ways, the cognitive and linguistic equals of the new influx of early *Homo sapiens*, entering Europe for the first time.

It appears that early modern humans regularly interbred with the prior existing communities of Neanderthals they came across in Europe. Evidence for this comes from genetic testing of modern humans and comparing it to Neanderthal DNA. It turns out that non-African living humans have a higher admixture of characteristically Neanderthal genetic material, consistent with an interbreeding pattern for those early humans who had left Africa. On average, non-African adults share between 1 and 4 per cent of their DNA with Neanderthal DNA, with an admixture of 6.4 per cent in European adults, and an even higher admixture ratio of nearly 10 per cent in Asian adults.[67] Moreover, different Neanderthal genes are found, to varying extents, in different individual adult humans today. According to one prominent expert, what this means is that 'the number of [breeding] contacts was not very small – more like low thousands or high hundreds than dozens'.[68]

Other evidence for an interbreeding scenario comes from the fossil record. In one famous find, the fossils of a child's burial were discovered in Arbrigo de Lagar Velho, in Portugal. This child exhibited features intermediate between humans and Neanderthals, suggesting that it shared one human and one Neanderthal parent.[69] Moreover, the nature of its burial suggests that it was a fully integrated member of its community: there appears to have been no evidence of stigma attached to this 'mixed race' child. This indicates that human/Neanderthal interbreeding was commonplace.[70] In terms of the widely accepted definition of a biological species introduced by the evolutionary biologist Ernst Mayr, a species is one that can only successfully breed among its own members. On this definition, the horse and the donkey are distinct species as their offspring, the mule, is typically infertile and incapable of reproduction. But in contrast, genetic and fossil evidence of successful interbreeding between humans and Neanderthals strongly suggests that these two groups were not distinct species, from a biological perspective. Indeed, today, many archaeologists and biologists treat them as related sub-species rather than distinct species. The upshot, of course, is that if humans and Neanderthals successfully interbred, and otherwise interacted to facilitate breeding, then the neuro-biological differences are likely to have been less significant than was at one time suspected.

The second line of evidence indicating that Neanderthals had modern, speech-like capabilities comes from new evidence relating to their articulatory and auditory capacities. Species with sophisticated communication systems – as in the case of modern humans – have broadcast capacities (e.g. speech) that match reception capacities (e.g. hearing).[71] For instance, human auditory capabilities are particularly attuned to the sound range for speech production, with unrivalled sensitivity among other primates in the 1–6 kHz range.[72] In recent reconstructions of the outer and middle ears of five fossil *Homo heidelbergensis* specimens, it was found that *heidelbergensis*, the presumed common ancestor of both humans and Neanderthals, would have exhibited an auditory capacity in the modern human range.[73] Moreover, analysis of fossil human and Neanderthal ear ossicles, found in Qafzeh and Amud, in the Middle East and around 50–100,000 years old, are essentially identical to those of humans. This implies that Neanderthals had a modern hearing capacity.

In the early 1970s, reconstruction of the Neanderthal vocal tract led scientists to believe Neanderthals to have been incapable of spoken language. The argument was based, in part, on the reconstruction of the tiny hyoid bone, essential for controlling and coordinating tongue movements in human-like speech. In Neanderthals, it was believed the hyoid bone hadn't yet descended to its human-like resting place, making human-like speech impossible.[74] However, since then, it has been established that the assumptions underpinning this reconstruction may have been flawed.[75] In fact, a hyoid bone located higher in the skull is associated with an evolutionarily earlier feature exhibited by ancestral humans, namely air sacs connected to the vocal tract. The presence of air sacs reduces the ability to produce articulate speech. This was likely to have been a feature of the anatomy of the much earlier *Homo erectus* (1.8. million years ago), but had most likely disappeared by the time of *Homo heidelbergensis*. This reveals that while *Homo erectus* had at best a limited speech capacity, later species of *Homo*, including *Homo heidelbergensis*, may have already developed some speech-like capacity.

A further line of evidence comes from the size of the thoracic vertebral canal. Spoken language requires voluntary control of the lungs, and breathing, enabling, in modern humans, the expulsion of air from the lungs to produce speech sounds. But while breathing is under involuntary control in most species, humans have a larger thoracic vertebral canal. And this is a direct result of additional nerve control of the intercostal muscles and diaphragm, enabling voluntary control and hence speech. A well-preserved *Homo erectus* specimen, the so-called Nariohotome boy, lacks an enlarged vertebral canal, suggesting lack of the voluntary control required for the articulatory apparatus. However, Neanderthal fossils, like modern humans, provide evidence of an enlarged canal, suggesting that Neanderthals were also capable of the voluntary control of breathing, a pre-requisite for speech.[76]

Finally, recent archaeological finds cast considerable doubt on the received view that Neanderthals produced a meagre material culture, lacking in sophistication compared to that of *Homo sapiens*. For one thing, there is emerging archaeological evidence, based on analysis of finds in Border Cave in southern Africa, that some elements of the later Upper Palaeolithic culture in Eurasia were already present in Africa 75,000 years ago, prior to *Homo sapiens* entering Europe.[77] This includes evidence for pigment use, beads, engravings and sophisticated stone and bone tools. Moreover, the material culture that produced such artefacts disappears from the archaeological record around 60,000 years ago, before reappearing later. This suggests a non-linear development of a rich material culture. Moreover, it also means the assumption that the apparent cultural explosion in Eurasia around 50,000 years ago may not have been a unique event, nor necessarily unique to modern humans.

As one team of experts has observed, it is becoming increasingly clear that Neanderthals 'exhibited many complex behaviours (pigment use, funerary practices, complex hafting techniques, wood-working, personal ornamentation, and bone tool manufacture) before or at the very moment of contact with modern humans'.[78] They possessed, and made use of, a sophisticated stone-tool technology. The manufacture of stone tools of this type involved up to fifty distinct actions. And in modern training experiments, it takes adult humans several months of training to master the techniques that would have been deployed by

Neanderthals to fashion their stone-age tools.[79] Neanderthals manufactured clothing as well as footwear by sewing animal skin.[80] They buried their dead,[81] and may well have left grave offerings.[82] They manufactured jewellery by painting shells with red ochre which they then perforated to be worn.[83] Moreover, decorated pendants found in sites occupied by a Neanderthal community and dating to 50,000 years ago have been discovered in Spain, long before Neanderthals had contact with early humans in that region of Europe.[84] Neanderthals appeared to live in small, social communities, with married couples living with the husband's parents. They built huts with complex foundations; they used pitch to haft their tools, which they extracted by fire,[85] and even mined materials to manufacture their tools, with mines up to 2 m in depth.[86]

There is also recent evidence of cultural borrowing by Neanderthals from the influx of *Homo sapiens*. In the late Neanderthal period, the Neanderthal Mousterian stone-age industry was giving way to a more complex technology, dubbed the Châtelperronian, from the location in France where these more advanced artefacts were first discovered.[87] This particular technology was a blend of the older Neanderthal technology and the more advanced techniques that were arising in the human populations at that time, dubbed the Aurignacian industry. None of this could, presumably, have been possible without some linguistic basis. And of course, if Neanderthals had a modern spoken language-like capacity, then it stands to reason this derived from the presumed common ancestor they shared with humans: *Homo heidelbergensis*.

A question that has preoccupied many scientists has been the demise of the Neanderthal populations, from around 30,000 years ago. The received narrative, that Neanderthals were brutish and essentially dumb cavemen, fits with this scenario: the smarter humans who entered Europe with better weapons, smarts and language easily wiped out the cognitively inferior Neanderthals. But again, this now appears to be overly simplistic. Neanderthals had only about a tenth of the population size of the incoming humans. And, as we have seen, interbreeding must have been fairly common. While we may never know exactly why the Neanderthals died out, there may not have been a single cause: Neanderthals appear to have had a low population size relative to Homo sapiens; interbreeding may also have been a factor, as well as the challenging climactic conditions in which they lived, and possibly also genocide.[88] But in the final analysis, two prominent experts, Dan Dediu and Stephen Levinson, conclude that 'nothing like Neandertal culture with its complex tool assemblages and behavioral adaptations to sub-Arctic conditions would have been possible without recognizably modern language.'[89]

## The birth of grammar

So, having considered the complex, evolutionary emergence of our species, *Homo sapiens*, what of our unique capacity for meaning-making, and of course language? In the previous chapter, I proposed that the evolutionary conditions for the emergence of a linguistic capacity would have derived from a prior cooperative intelligence. But this still doesn't account for the emergence of the *sine qua non* of language, its body of parametric knowledge – its grammar. And this is the issue with which we must now grapple.

A communicative system – a language – could, in principle, function effectively without a grammar; and this was the probably the route that human language took. Ancestral humans most likely began with an inventory of signs (words), but no grammar, which only developed later. A grammar, we've seen, provides a conceptual scaffolding across which rich, meaningful words can be draped. But with a grammatical system, a greater range of complexity and subtlety is added to the range of meanings that can be expressed. In a simple or proto-language, the sole reference strategy would have been to use signs to refer to entities outside the system, in the world – this is the words-to-world referential strategy I discussed in the previous chapter, and which is the preserve of animal communication systems. The meaning of the sign derives largely from the referent it points to. For instance, in human language, the meaning of the word *dog* derives from the idea or entity it points to.

But the shift from referring to entities outside the language system – from words-to-world – to reference within it – words-to-words – most likely didn't happen as a single jump, but rather in incremental stages. And the first stage in the process was likely to have been associated with the initial emergence of grammar.

The first stage in the development of a grammar, a shift from a straightforward inventory of signs without grammatical differentiation to a rudimentary grammatical system, would have been the emergence of lexical categories: categories such as noun, verb, adjective and adverb. The significance of this development was that, for the first time, signs or words came to have significance *in addition to* the external referents they pointed to. Words came to refer, symbolically, to other words. And in a words-to-word reference strategy, signs (or words) simultaneously also refer in a words-to-world direction. Another way of thinking about this is that, by virtue of there being a convention associating the sounds that make up the word *dog* with the four-legged entity in the world, a natural connection is established: the word-form also points to the entity, by virtue of the word being symbolically linked, in our minds, with the idea of dogs from our interaction with them in the world.

The division into lexical categories, for instance a noun versus a verb, would have arisen by virtue of a shift such that while symbolic reference was maintained in the words-to-world direction, indexical reference was established in the word-to-word direction. To show you this, consider the distinction between *redness* (a noun) and *red* (an adjective). Both words refer to an entity outside language: that part of the colour spectrum which has the frequency associated with the range of hues associated with the designation 'red'; this covers that part of the colour spectrum continuum ranging from all the shades from dark orange, to bright red, through to light purple. But in addition, the words *redness* and *red* also refer to other signs within the system, and in a rather special way. These words enable us to combine them with other words, because part of their meaning is system-internal.

Let's examine the adjective *red* in a bit more detail. Part of the meaning of this word is that portion of the colour spectrum to which it symbolically refers. But in addition, part of the meaning concerns what the word conveys within the language system – its parametric meaning: red refers to a property of a thing-like entity. It is for this reason that *red* can be used to modify nouns: nouns designate thing-like entities that, in principle, have properties. And it is because of this that *red* can be combined with a vast array of nouns in English, ranging across *lipstick*, *fox* and *sweater* making, variously, *red lipstick*, *red fox* and *red sweater*, where *red* designates a salient property of the entity it modifies.

In contrast, as *redness* is a noun, it can be combined with words that speak to other properties of nouns – for instance, their ability to undergo changes over time, encoded by verbs. For instance, redness can combine with verbs such as *oozed* and *seeped*, as in expressions like: *Redness oozed (under the door)*; *Redness seeped (from the wound)*. Another way of approaching this is that both adjectives, such as *red*, and verbs, such as *ooze* and *seep*, have slots that can be elaborated.[90] Part of the meaning of an adjective, then, is that it calls for a thing-like entity to complete its meaning: a property is, of necessity, a property of something. And so an adjective specifies an 'elaboration site': that part of its meaning which relates to a thing whose property it designates.[91] The parametric meaning of an adjective such as *red*, that it constitutes a property, can thus be completed by the parametric meaning of a noun, a thing, whose property the adjective specifies.

What I am saying, in essence, is that a grammar entails our ability to combine words, in order to produce complex combinations of words. But the combinatorial power of grammar is a consequence of different lexical categories completing, or filling in, the meaning of other lexical categories. Evidence for this comes from the quite different semantic contribution of different lexical categories, for instance a noun versus an adjective, when they refer, symbolically, to ideas and entities outside the language system. Reconsider the following examples, which I discussed in Chapter 9:

> Treat <u>redness</u> with Clinique urgent relief cream.
> Treat <u>red</u> skin with Clinique urgent relief cream.

Both words, *red* and *redness*, which I've underlined relate to the same perceptual state: that part of conceptual space corresponding to the colour spectrum usually identified as 'red'. But the words – *red* and *redness* – package the content in a different way. In the first example, *redness* leads to an interpretation relating to a skin 'condition'. In the second, *red* refers more straightforwardly to an unwanted property of the skin. The different interpretations arising from these sentences are not due to a different hue being activated – the hue is presumably the same in both examples. Rather, the words –noun versus adjective – nuance our interpretation of the perceptual hue: they give rise to distinct readings: an interpretation of 'skin condition' on one hand, versus 'discolouration of skin' on the other.

In the case of *red*, this word, an adjective, tells us that whatever it is that red symbolically refers to, it must be interpreted as a 'property' of some entity. In contrast, *redness* tells us that whatever it points to outside the language system, it must be interpreted as a 'thing'; and, in the case of colour, a property reified as a quality distinct from entities it might otherwise be a property of. The consequence is that *red* versus *redness* lead to different interpretations. With *red*, the interpretation for the second sentence is that we are dealing with a, presumably, unwanted property of the skin, an unusual colouration that is perceived as *red skin*. In contrast, in the first example, the use of *redness* tells us that the colouration symbolically referenced is an entity in its own right: this suggests an interpretation in which we are dealing with more than merely a skin discolouration, but in fact a skin *condition*. While the difference in interpretations across the two sentences is subtle, there *is* nevertheless a distinction: a skin condition interpretation (in the first example) and skin discolouration (in the second). And this is directly attributable to the use of *redness* versus *red*. In short, evidence for a distinction in the semantic character of nouns versus verbs is illustrated by these examples.

This also illustrates a further property of lexical categories, such as nouns, verbs and adjectives. By virtue of referring to other words within the language system, they also encode schematic meaning – their parametric information. As we have just seen, using *redness* versus *red* nuances the overall interpretation of a sentence. The adjective *red* instructs us to interpret 'red' as a property of something else, while *redness* tells us to interpret 'red' as an entity independent of the entities it happens to be a property of. After all, *redness* is a noun; hence, *redness* reifies the colour 'red' as if it were an abstract entity, divorced, conceptually at least, from all red things.

This semantic capability of lexical categories reveals two design features of grammar which are rather remarkable. First, the meaning associated with lexical categories, such as nouns and adjectives, is parametric. After all, the meaning of the lexical categories *red* (adjective) and *redness* (noun) is not reliant on whatever it is the words themselves symbolically point to outside the language system. There, the symbolic meaning has to do with red in all its glory. But within the language system, the meaning doesn't relate to the details of how we perceive or recall red. It is much more sketchy, delineating whether we are dealing with a property (of a thing), or a thing.

Second, by virtue of being highly schematic, this type of meaning is qualitatively distinct from the type of symbolic reference achieved by words when calling to mind entities in the real world. The relation is referential not in the sense that it refers to an idea in the mind or an entity in the world. Rather, it picks out a specific class of lexical category. For instance, the adjective *red* can, in principle, pick out pretty much any noun in English. That said, some lexical categories are more restrictive. For instance, the indefinite article, *a*, picks out a sub-class of the lexical category *noun*, the so-called count nouns of English: count nouns are those nouns which can be pluralised, and hence counted, such as *table, man* or *love* – and a sub-set of this class: just those count nouns which are singular: *a man*, but not *\*a men* (recall that linguists use an asterisk before an expression to show that the phrase or utterance is ungrammatical).

And what this also reveals is something rather special about lexical categories: the relation between different lexical categories is motivated. An adjective, by virtue of designating a property, carries a schematic slot for a thing: the thing that it is designated as the property of. The combinatorial potential of an adjective and a noun derives from this relation: an adjective is elaborated by a thing, which thereby completes its schematic meaning potential. Hence, this kind of meaning, by virtue of being motivated, is qualitatively distinct from the relation holding between signs in a sign-to-world direction.

In the final analysis, what this all suggests is that once ancestral humans crossed the symbolic threshold, once they began using symbols in a words-to-world fashion, it would only have been a matter of time before symbols began to be used in a more abstract way: adopting a words-to-words referential strategy. It is likely that a large vocabulary of signs, or proto-words – words not yet assigned to an inventory of lexical categories – would have developed before a distinction in lexical categories began to emerge. And it may be that developing a complex body of proto-words, based on symbolic reference, was a pre-requisite before a grammar, based on lexical categories, could begin to develop – with more complex grammatical strategies, such as recursion, entailed by grammatical complexity emerging only later.

## The emergence of grammatical complexity

We have seen that the defining feature of grammar is that it encodes parametric concepts: grammatical meanings are schematic in nature, and allow us to shape our conceptual representations – analogue concepts – in order to produce complex and sophisticated meaning. This is, of course, the essential internal logic of the human meaning-making capacity. Language has evolved as a means of using parametric knowledge to access, nuance and externalise analogue representations in our conceptual systems for purposes of communication. So, once lexical classes began to emerge, as I proposed in the previous section, how might the development of early human grammar have proceeded? In slightly different terms, what were the stages in the emergence of our repository of parametric concepts?

While we cannot know for certain, the recent discoveries in 'grammaticalisation' – the study of the way in which grammar develops and evolves – offer compelling insights into what the process might have been like. There can be little doubt that languages evolve. And not just in terms of their vocabulary. Their structure changes, often beyond recognition, in a surprisingly rapid fashion. For instance, the English spoken in England about 1,000 years ago is, to all intents and purposes, a foreign language – contemporary speakers of English today wouldn't recognise it as English, and are still less able to understand it. Consider the following poem fragment from Aelfric's *The Fisherman* written about 1,000 CE:

> Hwelcne cræft canst þu?
> *Ic eom fiscere.*
> Hu gefehst þu þa fiscas?
> *Ic ga on minne bat, and rowe ut on þa ea.*

Here's the modern English translation:

> What craft do you know?
> *I am a fisherman.*
> How do you catch the fish?
> *I go in my boat, and row out into the sea.*

What's striking is just how different Old English was. And in fact, one millennium has been sufficient for English to undergo a wholesale reconfiguration of its grammatical system and vocabulary, many times faster than biological evolution. So, what accounts for the dramatic change to the grammatical make-up of English? The answer is the natural process of grammaticalisation. Grammaticalisation affects all of the world's languages, and in this regard English isn't special. The move from Latin to the modern Romance languages of French, Spanish, Italian and so on, also in the space of around 1,000 years, is also accounted for by this process.

Grammaticalisation involves three aspects. First and foremost, there is a change in the meaning of the linguistic unit undergoing the process. The semantic change involves a move away from a more concrete meaning to a more schematic one. In short, it involves a move away from analogue knowledge to parametric knowledge. Consider the Old English verb *willan*. Around a 1,000 years ago, *willan* was a full lexical verb, meaning 'to want' or 'to desire' something. But over the course of its history, it has come to be used as a marker first of intention, and latterly as a marker of futurity, as embodied in the modern English *will*, as in: *It will rain tomorrow*. This reveals that the richer meaning associated with *willan* has given way to more schematic, parametric meaning.

In addition, *willan* has undergone a second, simultaneous change: it has shifted its lexical class. While Old English *willan* was a full lexical verb, one that could take various tense affixes, the modern *will* is referred to by linguists as a 'modal' marker. It is used alongside lexical verbs, as in *will rain*: modals such as *shall*, *should*, *might*, *may*, and so on, all of which also evolved from full verbs, designate necessity or possibility. But they now belong to a different lexical class: they are no longer lexical verbs. This is a common pattern of grammaticalisation found across the world's languages: full verbs evolve into modal markers.

And finally, *willan* has undergone a process whereby its phonological content has become ever more compact. In Middle English *willan* evolved into the shorter form *will*. In modern English, a further shift has occurred so that *will* now typically occurs, in spoken language, as an *-ll* attached to the main verb: *It'll rain tomorrow*, with the full form now reserved solely for emphasis.

A consequence of these three types of grammaticalisation processes, and widely attested in the world's 7,000 or so languages, is
that a grammar emerges from full-blown vocabulary items. And
as a consequence of our relatively recent understanding of how
grammaticalisation proceeds, it is now possible to reconstruct
how grammar may have evolved from early human language.
After all, if modal markers consistently evolved from verbs, then
it stands to reason that verbs must have preceded modal markers
in terms of grammatical evolution. Moreover, similar findings
relating to other lexical items can be used to reconstruct the
genesis of grammar.

The linguists Bernd Heine and Tania Kuteva have argued, based
on the sorts of changes to language I've just outlined, that human
grammar developed in a number of stages.[92] The first stage most
likely involved the emergence of common nouns: in evolutionary
terms, our primitive grammatical elements. Nouns typically
denote tangible and/or visible entities which can be identified in
the real world – although, as we saw in Chapter 5, they can also
relate to more abstract notions such as *love*, *alphabet*, and so on.
The second stage involved the emergence of verbs, which may have
evolved from nouns. Evidence from grammaticalisation, in
modern languages, reveals that verbs often do evolve from nouns –
as evidenced by English, for instance, in which historically prior
nouns, such as *editor*, have given rise to new verbs such as *to edit*.

With the emergence of a second distinct lexical class, grammar
was born: the distinction between nouns and verbs would have
provided, for the first time, a distinction in parametric knowledge
not apparent with a single lexical class. As we saw in Chapter 5,
nouns encode a parameter relating to a region in some domain,
while verbs encode a process that evolves through time. And so,
with the advent of a distinction in lexical classes, it would have
been possible to combine words of different lexical classes, providing a rudimentary word order, or syntax. In time, this ordering
of words would have developed schematic significance, giving rise,
later, to grammatical constructions, such as the ditransitive construction I discussed in Chapter 9.

## The crucible of language and meaning

Until relatively recently, before there was much in the way of evidence that might help us sort out the wood from the chaff in terms of language origins, one's view of what language is and how it works determined a scientist's position on language evolution.[93] The dominant Anglo-American linguist of the second half of the twentieth century was Noam Chomsky, and he was very clear. Language is a uniquely human endowment, with which we are born: we don't learn language – or at least, not the essential grammatical framework that, on Chomsky's view, underpins all the world's 7,000 or so living languages; we have it programmed into our genetic code: we inherit it.[94] Hence, language must have arisen, quite suddenly, as a random genetic mutation. And once the new 'grammar' gene had propagated through our ancestors, hey presto, humans had language.

In my earlier book, *The Language Myth*, I argued that this view is wrong, flying in the face of well over a century of findings concerning the processes at play in evolution: as Tomasello writes, 'language did not come out of nowhere. It did not descend on earth from outer space like some stray asteroid'.[95]

While one challenge, in accounting for where language came from, is undoubtedly uncovering how the shift from words-to-world to words-to-words reference came about, this move didn't occur in isolation. The larger challenge is to account for the precursors that made language possible to begin with: all the other changes that must have taken place before language could even have got off the ground – enter the interactional and cooperative intelligences I discussed in the previous chapter. These were the necessary precursors for a symbolic–representational system, for language, to emerge in the first place. And this entailed several million years of adaptation to a new ecological and later social-biological niche. Chomsky's improbable intellectual handstand is to discount the role of natural selection, of evolution itself, in the emergence of language.[96]

In cognitively modern humans, we exhibit an unprecedented capacity to use a symbolic–representational system – language – to encode, shape in the process and externalise thoughts and ideas from our conceptual systems – our mental repository of concepts; and in the absence of telepathy, the function of language is to enable us to communicate *and*, thereby, interact with and influence one another. But what supports this unique capability? And what has been the evolutionary trajectory that has given rise to the meaning-making complex?

As we saw in the previous chapter, chimpanzees, and possibly other species of ape, understand that other members of the same species are intentional agents – intentional agents that they can attempt to influence. So early hominins, by necessity, were starting from a base involving a basic interactional competence. In our lineage this interactional ability has been honed into a cooperative intelligence. And only within this crucible of rudimentary social interaction could a symbolic system – language – begin to emerge. But even then, it took over a million years for the emergence of muscular and breath control to develop, allowing spoken language to arise. I suggested earlier that *Homo erectus*, around 1.8 million years ago, most likely had some form of proto-language, but very limited – if any – capacity for speech. But by the advent of *Homo heidelbergensis* – the presumed common ancestor of modern *Homo sapiens* and *Homo neanderthalensis* – the spoken capacity had emerged or was emerging.

The proposition that language resulted from a sudden genetic mutation flies in the face of everything we have learned about evolution since Darwin. After all, it would have required more than a single change to the human genome, the arrival of a grammar gene, to enable language. We now know that humans have a much larger prefrontal region of the brain, compared to other apes. This, most likely, is required to process the associative memory that allows our sophisticated form of symbolic learning and use, and to string words together in a grammatical sequence.[97] We also have exquisite breath and voluntary motor control, resulting from a wholesale change in both the motor areas of the ape brain-plan, nervous system and anatomy of the mouth, jaw and neck, enabling speech production. Such changes, required by language, have affected brain and body development through-out the *Homo* lineage, at least 2.8 million years. There was nothing abrupt about the emergence of language.

The essential problem in debates on the origin of language is that language is too often viewed as a single discrete entity, one that is unrelated to the rest of human cognition *and* culture. But the interactional, and later cooperative, intelligence which gave rise to language most likely arose in a specific ecological and, later, socio-cultural niche. It emerged from the honing of interactional and cooperative intelligence, giving sophisticated external expression to a deep-seated meaning-making ability that arose in African contexts around three million years ago; these required more sophisticated communicative interaction than had been required prior to that point. Language is not, from this perspective, a discrete speciation event, a singularity that emerged abruptly. It represents the gradual fulfilment of our unique facility for creating meaning in communicative contexts; such contexts required sophisticated interpersonal negotiation. Language has emerged from the long, slow unweaving of our capacity for making-meaning. But a more specific stumbling block in attempting to figure out how language evolved is failing to see the social–cultural context in which language most likely emerged.

What makes it now possible to begin to have an approximate sense of the outlines of the story arc leading to language, and meaning-making more generally, is that we are no longer inhabiting the netherworld of speculation. The volume of discoveries in palaeo-archaeology, and new techniques allowing extraction and mapping of ancient DNA found in fossils, and computer simulations by computational evolutionary biologists and linguists, now allow us to model different scenarios. And this means that, today, we can hazard more than just wild flights of fancy. We have a basis for a realistic guesstimate as to the time-depth of language, the time-depth of human meaning-making and the changes that must have led to these developments.

In the final analysis, language in its current, variegated splendour is the (end) product of our long, evolutionary trajectory to produce and convey meaning – and, of course, language continues to change and evolve. Meaning, our capacity to signal an idea – a wish, feeling, belief, instruction – and be understood to be signalling that idea, did not originate with language. But it has led, irrevocably, to (spoken) language, which greatly facilitates and, in its modern form, helps create meaning.

# Epilogue: The golden triangle

In this book, I've focused on the relationship between language and mind in creating meaning. I've argued that meaning arises in the mix, from the complex interplay of analogue knowledge in the mind's conceptual system and the parametric knowledge embedded in the grammatical system of a language. But there's a third factor that contributes just as significantly to meaning: namely, culture. Daniel Everett, an anthropological linguist and one of the world's leading authorities on the relationship between language and culture, has observed that, in certain respects, language itself appears to be a cultural invention. For Everett, language is a tool, moulded and honed by culture, in order to facilitate the shared values and ideas that form the backdrop to the collective lives of the individual members of any given community. And just as language is, in part, shaped by culture, so too are the concepts that it helps express: 'Living in a culture and acquiring cultural knowledge enables us to gain meaning from the world around us and from each other'.[1] Hence, no account of the unprecedented capacity exhibited by our species to create meaning would, or could, be complete without considering the role of culture in giving rise to meaning.

A moment's reflection reveals that language *is* a repository of cultural knowledge, one that captures and provides effective cues to a complex body of shared values, experiences and even a common past. For instance, Everett discusses the use of the word *Dickensian* in the following utterance: *The living conditions were Dickensian.*[2] The word itself amounts to a label – a shorthand cue – pointing to a complex body of knowledge shared by all literate native speakers of English. It evokes the inequality and moral decrepitude of aspects of Victorian England: the poor sanitation, overcrowding, and the misery of the have-nots compared to their lords and masters, as brilliantly captured in the didactic works of Charles Dickens. The word itself neatly 'packages' this body of shared knowledge and the value-laden judgements, both implicit and explicit, in Dickens' oeuvre. Moreover, even those who haven't read Dickens' novels will nevertheless understand the term, through shared cultural knowledge of the Victorian world of Dickens. The word, then, neatly labels a large and diffuse web of culturally shared and culture-specific information, and the values that apply.

In the same way, the Korean word *nunchi* relates to a cultural body of knowledge and set of shared values, arguably alien to English-speaking cultures. The term might best be translated, in English, as 'eye-measure'. It relates to Korean values of propriety and, in part, hospitality; for example, a good host is judged by virtue of their ability to *read* their guest's desires, by offering sustenance without the guest having to make a request for food or drink, thereby embarrassing the guest – in Korean culture requesting something, such as food or drink, is perceived as impolite. Hence, *nunchi* concerns, in part, the host's responsibility for, as well as their ability to assess, a guest's unspoken needs, by *reading* their body language; and in so doing, this reflects well on the host, as the guest is not potentially faced with the loss of face that being impolite – making a request for something – would entail. In short, the word serves as a shorthand mnemonic for a complex set of shared cultural values, which form a complex matrix of social norms, behaviours and expectations that guide daily interpersonal encounters and interactions, and imbue, in part, Korean social contexts with their meaning.

The discipline of anthropological linguistics is concerned with the study and description of language in a cultural context, especially the complex interplay between language, culture and thought. These three aspects of human cognitive and social life – language, mind (or thought) and culture – I liken to a 'golden triangle'. A full account of the evolutionary development of the meaning-making capacity of our species, as well as the realisation of meaning and communication in our everyday world of experience, must, ultimately, grapple with their intersection. They fulfil complementary and often overlapping roles, enabling us to make sense of our interactions with others, and ultimately ourselves.

The modern discipline of linguistic anthropology – at least in the Anglo-American tradition which informs my own perspective on language – can be traced to the work of the German-born anthropologist Franz Boas, working at the beginning of the twentieth century. Boas famously emphasised the 'psychic unity of mankind'[3]: roughly, the idea that commonalities across the world's languages reflect shared aspects of human cognition (thought). Whether you live in a tribe of Kalahari bushman, in an Inuit settlement in sub-Arctic Canada, or are a city-dweller in the heart of London, we all share a common cognitive apparatus – an embodied cognition, a consequence of shared neuroanatomical architecture, irrevocably fused with similar bodies. We are also co-participants in a shared physical environment – the physical world is broadly similar the world over. For instance, the laws of gravity are the same whether you live in the Arctic, an African desert or the south-east of England. For Boas, commonalities across human languages and cultures arise from this common psychic unity. But variation nevertheless abounds; and this arises from the specific sets of values and histories of a given community – a culture – which interprets this psychic unity in community-specific ways, imbuing it, often, with considerable local variation.

Those who followed Boas, especially the influential linguist Edward Sapir[4] and, later, Benjamin Lee Whorf,[5] essentially reversed this line of argument, emphasising the ability of habitual patterns found in a language to influence and even transform key aspects of thought.[6] This idea, based on the work of Whorf in particular, is sometimes referred to as the Principle of Linguistic Relativity, which I discuss in some detail in Chapter 7 of *The Language Myth*. And indeed, while language does appear to influence aspects of the way we think – findings from contemporary neuroscience reveal that perceptual processes can even be restructured as a consequence of habitual differences across languages – culture can also be instrumental in influencing and shaping both thought *and* language.

To my mind, what this reveals is that the points on the golden triangle are inextricably linked; our unprecedented capacity to mean and to communicate must ultimately arise from the symbiotic relationship between all three. And language science must, of necessity, grapple with their complex interplay if we are to fully account for the nature of meaning. As Everett puts it: 'all human languages are tools. Tools to solve the twin problems of communication and social cohesion. Tools shaped by the distinctive pressures of their cultural niches – pressures that include cultural values and history and which in many cases account ... for the similarities and differences between languages'.[7]

So, to give a flavour of the relationship between language, thought *and* culture, here I dwell on the way in which culture – a system of shared values, norms, behaviours, practices and history – can influence both language, and thought. Take the domain of TIME, and in particular conceptual metaphors for time, which I examined in Chapter 4. There we saw that Aymara, an indigenous Andean language spoken in Bolivia, Peru and Chile, conceptualises the future as located behind, and the past as in front. In short, the Time Orientation conceptual metaphor appears to be structured, in Aymara, in a way that is at odds with conceptual systems for time in many other known languages.

So what might be the explanation for this? The rationale appears to be cultural. The Aymara culture places great value on information that has been witnessed at first hand, privileging information directly witnessed with one's own eyes, rather than gleaned through hearsay.[8] A linguistic reflex of this is that Aymara features a rich evidential system: Aymara speakers are obliged by their grammatical system to signal whether an assertion has been perceived at first hand or learned about indirectly. And consequently, it is likely that the Time Orientation metaphor is also organised due to this cultural logic: an event that has been experienced, such as a past event, has been *seen*, while one that has yet to be experienced, one that lies in the future, has not yet been *seen*. Given the organisation of the human body – our eyes are located at the front of the head – what can be seen is the terrain in front of us, while what lies behind us remains unseen. And in light of this cultural privileging of *evidence* – especially visual evidence – experiences, like the past, that have been experienced at first hand, are metaphorically conceptualised as lying in front, while the future lies behind.[9]

But as a conceptual metaphor concerns a structural principle of thought, embedded in the human conceptual system, in this case culture is influencing conceptual organisation, albeit revealed symbolically in language and gesture. The cultural privileging of visual experience leaves an indelible mark on the mind, shaping the way Aymaran conceptual metaphors for time are structured. So, what about cases where culture influences representations in language?

A particularly famous example concerns the Pirahã, an indigenous tribe of around 400 hunter-gatherers living on the banks of the Maici River in the Amazonian rain forest, in the Brazilian state of Amazonas. The Pirahã people refer to themselves as the *Hi'aiti'ihi*, which means 'the straight ones'. And they refer to all other languages as 'crooked/twisted head', a designation both reflecting the Pirahã's perception of the inferiority of other languages and their playful sense of humour.

The Pirahã language is remarkable in a number of ways; while languages across the world exhibit great diversity in terms of the number of sounds that are used – up to 144 distinct sounds in some, such as the Khoisan languages of southern Africa; these are the languages that feature clicks on their consonants, made famous in the 1960s by the Click Song of Miriam Makeba – Pirahã has one of the fewest. Male Pirahã speakers make use of eleven distinct sounds, and female Pirahã just ten. Moreover, given the prosodic patterns used, and the fact that Pirahã is a tone language, it can also be hummed – as Pirahã mothers do to their babies, or to disguise what one is saying – or whistled rather than spoken, a technique used to great effect by Pirahã men while on hunting sorties in the deep Amazon jungle. For the interested reader, there's an excellent documentary covering some of these aspects of this intriguing people and language, *The Grammar of Happiness*.[10]

Daniel Everett, together with his wife and young family, spent many years living with the Pirahã, and learning their language. He documents his life living in the Amazonian jungle in the hugely entertaining book *Don't Sleep, There are Snakes*. It's an exhilarating and at times poignant story, recounting the mischievous Pirahã as well as covering the missionary zeal that took Everett to the remote Amazon jungle in the first place, and his subsequent loss of faith.

The Pirahã language also appears to be unique in a number of other ways. It's the only known language without numbers, numerals or a concept of counting – it even lacks terms for quantification such as *all*, *each*, *every*, *most* and *some*. It lacks colour terms, and has the simplest pronoun system known. Moreover, and more generally, Pirahã culture lacks creation myths, and exhibits no collective memory beyond two generations. Even more curious, Pirahã seems to lack the ability to embed grammatical phrases within other phrases: for instance, a noun phrase inside another noun phrase, or a sentence within a sentence.

This grammatical ability, deemed by many linguists to be a universal, and indeed on some accounts the criterial feature of human grammar, is often referred to as recursion, which I briefly discussed in Chapter 11. Recursion provides a grammar with a means of combining grammatical units to build complex clauses and sentences, enabling the construction of complex syntactic assemblies, giving rise, in principle, to sentences of infinite complexity.

For instance, take the following English sentence, which I used to illustrate this property of grammar in *The Language Myth*: *Death is only the beginning*, uttered by Imhotep in the 1999 movie *The Mummy*. This phrase can be embedded in the grammatical frame 'X said Y', providing a more complex sentence: *Imhotep said that death is only the beginning*. This sentence can then, itself, be further embedded in the same frame recursively: *Evelyn said that Imhotep said that death is only the beginning.* But, based on his many years of working with the Pirahã, Everett has found this sort of embedding to be impossible in Pirahã.[11] The lack of recursion in fact reflects a more general prohibition in the grammar of the language; unlike a language like English, and many – perhaps most – of the world's languages, the Pirahã language only permits one event to be encoded in each sentence. And this keeps each grammatical sentence discrete, circumspect and short.

So what might lie behind the lack of grammatical recursion in the grammar of the language? And might it be related, somehow, to wider aspects of Pirahã culture, such as the lack of creation myths – itself also highly unusual – and the absence of collective memory beyond two generations? Everett has argued in detail that the common denominator is Pirahã culture, which influences and shapes the nature and organisation of the Pirahã language.

Pirahã culture appears to exhibit a preference for immediacy of experience, 'which values talk of concrete, immediate experience over abstract, unwitnessed and hence non-immediate topics'.[12] Everett's conclusion is that you need to know the Pirahã culture to know its language: the culture, in a profound sense, influences and constrains the way the language works. The lack of recursion – the lack of relative grammatical complexity – and the consequent prohibition against expressing more than one event per sentence appears to be a constraint imposed by the Pirahã culture. And this suggests that the meaning-making potential of the language is constrained, in important ways, by the system of values that make up the Pirahã culture. As Everett puts it, 'language is in the first instance a tool for thinking and communicating', which is consonant with the central argument of this book. But, and in addition, 'it is crucially shaped from human cultures. It is a cultural tool as well as a cognitive tool'.[13]

In the final analysis, meaning-making arises from the confluence of language and the mind's concepts. But collective intentionality – the culturally sophisticated cooperative strategy exhibited by modern humans – has created systems of rich material and ideational cultures, within which the confluence of languages and minds are embedded and construe each other. And as meaning arises in a cultural context, a full account of meaning-making ultimately needs to include all three points of this golden triangle: together, the golden triangle – language, mind and culture – underpin our unique prowess for creating meaning, everyday.

# Notes

## Chapter 1

1 Evans (2014).

## Chapter 2

1 Julian R. (2005). See also the John Dee website: www.johndee.org
2 Linden (2003).
3 Newman and Principle (2002).
4 MacIntosh, J.J. and P. Anstey (2014).
5 Jakobson (1942).
6 Geeraerts (2009).
7 Fodor (1975).
8 Andrew Sparrow, 'Gordon Brown's use of the word "depression" was a slip of the tongue, says No 10.' *The Guardian*, 4 February 2009.
9 Bentonville, Arkansas; 6 November 2000.
10 Poplar Bluff, Missouri; 6 September 2004.
11 Stanovich (2011).
12 Fodor (1983).
13 Evans (2014) for a review.
14 Thierry et al. (2009).
15 Levinson (2003).
16 See, for instance, Barsalou (1999); Clark (1997); Evans and Green (2006); Johnson (1987); Lakoff (1987); Mandler (2004); Shapiro (2010); Varela et al. (1991).
17 See Evans and Green (2006) for a review.
18 Varela et al. (1991).
19 Tyler and Evans (2003).
20 Examples drawn from Lakoff and Johnson (1980: 32).
21 Evans (2013).
22 Barsalou et al. (2008), for example.
23 See Chomsky (1965), and Fodor (1975, 1998).

## Chapter 3

1 The initial development of Conceptual Metaphor Theory was presented in Lakoff and Johnson (1980). The most recent version of the theory is presented in Lakoff and Johnson (1999). See also Lakoff (1987), Johnson (1987) and Lakoff (1993). For an excellent survey of a range of contemporary treatments of metaphor see the papers in Gibbs (2008). See also Kövecses (2010) for a useful primer.
2 Examples derived from Lakoff and Johnson (1980).
3 See Grady (1997a, 1997b, 1999).
4 Grady (1997a); Lakoff and Johnson (1999).
5 Hebb (2002).
6 The Event Structure metaphors were discovered by George Lakoff and his students, and first reported on in Lakoff (1993).
7 From an article entitled: 'Microsoft's grinning robots or the Brotherhood of the Mac. Which is worse?', which appeared in *The Guardian* on 28 September 2009.
8 Tomasello (2008).
9 For further details on the role of conceptual metaphor in poetry and literature see Lakoff and Turner (1989), Stockwell (2002) and Gavins and Steen (2003).
10 Lakoff and Turner (1989); Turner (1996).
11 President Bush at a joint session of US Congress, 20 September 2001.
12 Jeffrey Record, a strategy expert at the US military's Air War College in Alabama. Reported in *The Guardian* newspaper, Wednesday 25 March 2009.
13 Lakoff (1991); see also Lakoff (1999, 2008).

## Chapter 4

1 See Casasanto (2010).
2 *The Onion*, 16 October 2007. Issue 43/42.
3 Flaherty (1999: 52).
4 Flaherty (1999: 60).
5 Campbell (1986).
6 Siffre (1964).
7 Loftus et al. (1987).
8 Fraisse (1984).

9 See Evans (2004) for a review of the relevant evidence.

10 Evans (2004, 2013); Pöppel (1994, 2009).

11 Chafe (1994: 69).

12 Chafe (1994: 61–2).

13 Turner and Pöppel (1982).

14 Pöppel (2009: 1891).

15 Varela (1999).

16 Pöppel (2009: 1891).

17 In this I am following Lakoff and Johnson (1999).

18 The discussion of the Moving Time Metaphor is based on Lakoff and Johnson (1999).

19 Recent research has shown that the Moving Time metaphor is in fact divided into two distinct metaphors with different reference points (see Moore 2006). Behavioural evidence for such a distinction is provided by Rafael Núñez and colleagues (Núñez et al. 2006).

20 For surveys of time in other languages see, for example, Alverson (1993), Núñez and Sweetser (2006), Shinohara (1999) and Yu (2001). For a detailed study of time in English see Evans (2004).

21 Nunez and Sweetser (2006).

22 See Sinha et al. (2011).

23 Talmy (2000).

24 While space has no inherent asymmetry, Galton (2011) points out that some directions in space do nevertheless exhibit asymmetry. For instance, the vertical plane is asymmetric by virtue of the gravitational pull of the Earth, which provides an asymmetry between up and down. Analogously, there is an asymmetry between North and South, a consequence of the magnetic core of the Earth.

25 See Coveney and Highfield (1991).

26 Le Poidevin (2003).

27 See Galton (2011).

28 See Gentner et al. (2002). See also Boroditsky (2000), and Casasanto and Boroditsky (2008).

29 Gentner et al. (2002).

30 In fact, sentences such as this are motivated by a slightly different conceptual metaphor: RELATIVE SEQUENCE IS RELATIVE LOCATION ON A PATH (see Moore 2006).

31 A further potential problem with Boroditsky's work is that it has become clear that the linguistic expressions Boroditsky took to relate

to the Moving Time Metaphor in fact relate to a different conceptual metaphor (see Moore 2006 and for experimental evidence Núñez et al. 2006).

32 Cai and Connell (2012); Cai and Connell (2015).
33 Kranjec et al. (2013).
34 See Evans (2013) for a review.
35 Wiener et al. (2010).
36 Buhusi and Meck (2005).
37 Abraham et al. (2008); Schacter et al. (2007).
38 Moore (1977); Ratliff and Hartline (1974).
39 Kubovy (1988).
40 Lakoff and Johnson (1999: Chapter 10).
41 Evans (2004, 2013).
42 Langone (2000: 7).
43 Fraser (1986).

## Chapter 5

1 Prinz (2002: 1).
2 Fodor (1975; 1981).
3 Fodor (1998).
4 Lakoff (2004).
5 Dawkins (1976).
6 Ryle (1949).
7 Hofstadter (1979).
8 Fodor (1975).
9 Turing (1950).
10 Harnad (1990). See also Barsalou (1999), Cisek (1999); Taylor and Zwaan (2009); Viglioccio et al. (2009).
11 Harnad (1990).
12 Talmy (2000).
13 It has been argued that not all of the world's language may exhibit grammatical categories corresponding to nouns and verbs. An example is Straits Salish, as argued by Jelinek (1995). However, nouns and verbs do appear to be quasi-universal based on findings from linguistic typology.
14 Langacker (1987, 2008).
15 Langacker (1987, 2008).

16 Langacker (e.g. 1987).
17 Talmy (2000: 412).
18 Barsalou (1999); Taylor and Zwaan (2009); Vigliocco et al. (2009).
19 Isenberg et al., (1999); Martin and Chao (2001); Pulvermüller (1999); see also Buccino et al. (2005). For a review see Taylor and Zwaan (2009).
20 Isenberg et al. (1999).
21 Dahan and Tanenhaus (2002); Stanfield and Zwaan (2001); Zwaan and Yaxley (2003).
22 Dahan and Tanehaus (2002).
23 Zwaan (2004); see also Clark (1997).
24 Talmy (2000: 139).
25 Damasio (1995).
26 Deacon (1998).
27 Damasio (1995).
28 Damasio (1995: 45).
29 See Plutchik (1980; see also 2002). A further distinction of tertiary emotions is often also made. Secondary emotions are often thought of as combinations of pairs of primary (or 'basic') emotions, while tertiary emotions consist of combinations of three primary emotions.
30 Damasio (1995).

## Chapter 6

1 Johnson (1987: 331; my italics differ from those of Johnson).
2 Mandler (1988, 1992, 1996, 2004).
3 Mandler (2004: 13).
4 Vandeloise 1994: 173.
5 Early evidence for the development of concepts, and most notably containment, was reported in Freeman et al. (1980), and Sinha (1982). For discussion see Sinha (1988).
6 Hespos and Baillargeon (2001).
7 Mandler (1996, 2004).
8 Based on Johnson (1987); see also Cienki (1997), and papers in Hampe (2005).
9 Lakoff (1987).

10 See Tyler and Evans (2003) for discussion.
11 Johnson (1987: 43).
12 Derived from Johnson (1987: 45–8).
13 Johnson (1987); Lakoff (1987, 1990, 1993).
14 Fodor (1975, 1981, 1983).
15 Fodor (1981: 315).
16 Fodor (1975, 2008).
17 Fodor (1975, 1995, 2008); Pinker (1997).
18 Fodor (1995); Jackendoff (1987, 1992).
19 Fodor (1975: 27).
20 Mandler (2004: 41).
21 Mandler (2004: 63).
22 Mandler (2004: 63).
23 Julesz (1981).
24 Biederman (1987).
25 This discussion is based on the work of Wertheimer (1923).
26 Gregory (1998).
27 Gregory (1998: 98).
28 Gibson (1986).
29 Johansson (1973).
30 Johansson (1973).
31 Mandler (2004) refers to this as 'perceptual meaning analysis'.
32 Kellman and Spelke (1983).
33 Berthental (1993); Arterberry and Bornstein (2001).
34 Frye et al. (1983); Legerstee (1992); Watson (1972).
35 Leslie (1982, 1984).
36 Grady (1997a); see also Grady and Johnson (2000).
37 Johnson (1999).


## Chapter 7

1 Koestler (1964: 33).
2 Koestler (1964: 33).
3 Boden (1990, 1994a, 1994b; see also 1995, 1996).
4 Fauconnier and Turner (2002).
5 Fauconnier (1994, 1997).
6 See Fauconnier (1994, 1997).
7 Fauconnier and Turner (1994, 1998, 2002). See also Coulson (2000).

8 www.dailykos.com/story/2007/07/28/363487/–We-re-all-wearing-the-blue-dress-now# (published 27 July 2007 at 10:11 PM PDT).

9 'Fish shrink to avoid the plate', *The Sunday Times*, 20 May 2012, p. 11.

10 Fauconnier and Turner (2002)

11 Source UW Geoscience: http://www.geology.wisc.edu/homepages/g100s2/public_html/history_of_life.htm (accessed 6 August 2012).

12 http://www.geology.wisc.edu/homepages/g100s2/public_html/Geologic_Time/Time_Clock.gif (accessed 13 June 2014).

13 See Hulme (2008).

14 www.fightglobalwarming.com

15 The discussion and analysis of low carbon diet in this section is based on Nerlich, Evans and Koteyko (2011).

16 *The Augusta Chronicle* [Georgia], 28 March 2006; also in *Pittsburgh Tribune Review*, 2 April 2006.

17 The Associated Press State & Local Wire, 16 September 2007; see also *Milwaukee Journal Sentinel* [Wisconsin], 16 September 2007; *The Capital Times* [Madison, Wisconsin], 17 September 2007.

18 www.irr.org.uk/news/the-media-war-against-migrants-a-new-front/. Comment piece posted 21 January 2004 (accessed 13 June 2014).

19 Boden (1994a).

20 See http://markturner.org/blending.html

21 Fauconnier and Turner (2000).

22 See Zbikowski (2001).

23 www.ethnologue.com

24 Sandler et al. (2011).

25 Fauconnier and Turner (2008).

26 Dediu and Levinson (2013); Villa and Roebroeks (2014).

27 See Mithen (1996); Deacon (1997).

## Chapter 8

1 Aitchison (1996: 39–40).

2 Atkins (1987); Dąbrowska (2009); Gries (2006).

3 Taylor (2012).

4 Crystal (1998).

5 Tyler and Evans (2001, 2003).

6 Tyler and Evans (2001).

7 This way of modelling word meanings was pioneered by George Lakoff (1987).
8 Rosch (1978).
9 Evans and Green (2006); Lakoff (1987); Taylor (2003).
10 Sandra and Rice (1995); Tyler (2012).
11 Tyler (2012).
12 Lakoff (1987: case study no. 2).
13 Heine *et al.* (1991); Sweetser (1988).
14 Examples drawn from Evans (2004).
15 Sinha et al. (2011).
16 Evans (2009); Langacker (1987); Taylor (2012).
17 Williams (2012).
18 Williams (2012: 651).

## Chapter 9

1 Although see Evans (2014).
2 See for example Evans (2009) and Mithen (1996).
3 Barsalou (2005); Barsalou et al. (2008); see also Evans (2009).
4 Wynn (1992, 1995).
5 Evans (2014).
6 http://en.wikipedia.org/wiki/Red_fox (accessed 2 April 2014).
7 www.imdb.com/name/nm0000569/bio (accessed 2 April 2014).
8 Boulenger et al. (2008).
9 Bak et al. (2001).
10 Evans (2009).
11 Barsalou (1992).
12 This discussion is based on Evans (2009) and Evans (2013: Chapter 2).
13 See Evans (2009), which presents the Theory of Lexical Concepts and Cognitive Models (or LCCM Theory for short), and which spells out the details of this proposal.
14 Goldberg (1995).
15 Goldberg (1995).

## Chapter 10

1 Lee et al. (2009); Levinson (2006).
2 Levinson (2006).

3 Haviland (1974).
4 Dennett (1989).
5 Sperber and Wilson (1995).
6 Mithen (1996).
7 Tomasello and Call (1997); Tomasello (2014).
8 Gomes and Boesch (2009).
9 Gazzaniger, M. (2006). I am grateful to David Kemmerer for pointing this reference out to me.
10 Klein (2009).
11 Shumaker et al. (2011).
12 Haley, D. (1986).
13 Deecke (2012).
14 Hart et al. (2001).
15 Boesch and Boesch (1990).
16 Koops et al. (2010).
17 Pruetz and Bertolani (2007).
18 Boesch and Boesch-Achermann (2000).
19 Van Schaik, Fox and Sitompul (1996).
20 Pansini and de Ruiter (2011).
21 Peterson (2011).
22 Pika et al. (2005); Call and Tomasello (2007, 2008); Schmelz, Call and Tomasello (2011); Lurz (2011); Tomasello and Call (1997).
23 Tomasello (2014); see also Tomasello (1999, 2008).
24 Tomasello (2014: 30).
25 Boesch and Boesch (1989); Watts and Mitani (2002).
26 Tomasello (2014: 35).
27 Mounier et al. (2009).
28 Arsuaga et al. (1999).
29 Klein (2009).
30 See Evans (2014).
31 Gräfenhaim et al. (2009).
32 Tomasello (2014).
33 Arbib (2012); Tomasello (2008, 2014); see also Hurford (2012).
34 Saussure (1916).
35 Pierce (1903).
36 Seyfarth, Cheney and Marler (1980).
37 Further examples of the symbolic referential strategies of other species are reviewed in Evans (2014: Chapter 2).

38  Schmid (2000).
39  Schmid (2000: 7).
40  Schmid (2000).

## Chapter 11

1   Paget (1930).
2   Peretz (2006).
3   Patel (2008).
4   Although see discussion in Fitch (2009a).
5   Quoted in Kendon (1991: 199).
6   Corballis (2008).
7   Dunbar (1996).
8   Müller (1861).
9   Dediu and Levinson (2013).
10  Dediu and Levinson (2013).
11  Deacon (1997).
12  Evans (2014).
13  Kingdon (2004).
14  Kingdon (2004); see also Klein (2009).
15  Deacon (1997).
16  Darwin (1859).
17  Wildman et al. (2003).
18  Dawkins (2012).
19  Johanson and Edey (1981).
20  Robert Lamb: www.discovery.com/tv-shows/curiosity/topics/9-aus
    tralopithecus-afarensis/
21  Stern Jr. and Susman (1983).
22  Rak et al. (2007); Tomkins (1998).
23  Raichlen et al. (2010).
24  Green and Alemseged (2012)
25  White et al. (2009).
26  Reynolds and Gallagher (2012); Senut et al. (2001).
27  Leakey et al. (2001); Lieberman (2001).
28  Klein (2009); DiMaggio et al. (2015).
29  Spoor et al. (2007).
30  Clark et al. (1994).
31  Leakey (1981).

32 Spoor et al. (2007).

33 Klein (2009).

34 Shipman (2001).

35 Klein (1999).

36 Antón (2003); Klein (2009).

37 Joormens et al. (2014).

38 Bar-Yosef and Belfer-Cohen (2001); Tattersall (2012).

39 Gamble and Marshall (2001).

40 Mounier et al. (2009).

41 Cartmill and Smith (2009).

42 Lozano et al. (2009).

43 Carretero et al. (2012).

44 Wilkins et al. (2012).

45 Klein (2009).

46 Brown et al. (2004).

47 Deacon (1997); Tomasello (2014).

48 McPherron et al. (2011).

49 White et al. (2000).

50 Deacon (1997).

51 Ungar (2004).

52 Deacon (1997).

53 Deacon (1997: 393).

54 Larsen (2003).

55 United States National Health and Nutrition Examination Survey, 1999–2002.

56 National Health Statistics Reports 10. 22 October 2008.

57 Deacon (1997).

58 Corballis (2002); Hurford (2012); Tomasello (2008).

59 Arbib (2012).

60 Berwick et al. (2013); Bickerton (1990, 2002); Chomsky (2010); Mithen (1996).

61 Mithen (1996).

62 Dediu and Levinson (2013); see also Villa and Roebroeks (2014).

63 Hublin (2009).

64 Hublin (2009); Green et al. (2010).

65 Klein (2009).

66 Klein (2009).

67 Dediu and Levinson (2013).

68 Hawks (2013; cited in Dediu and Levinson 2013: 4)
69 Bayle et al. (2010).
70 Zilhão and Trinkaus (2003).
71 Lafon (1968); Kojima (1990).
72 Martinez et al. (2004, 2008).
73 Martinez et al. (2004, 2008).
74 Lieberman and Crelin (1971).
75 Falk (1975); DuBrul (1977); Houghton (1993); Fitch (2009b); Dediu and Levinson (2013).
76 Dediu and Levinson (2013).
77 d'Errico et al. (2012).
78 d'Errico et al. (2012: 1).
79 Dediu and Levinson (2013).
80 Sørensen (2009).
81 Pettit (2002).
82 Lalueza-Fox et al. (2010).
83 Zilhao et al. (2010); d'Errico and Soressi (2002); d'Errico and Vanhaeren (2009); Watts (2009).
84 Zilhao et al. (2010).
85 Roebroeks and Villa (2011).
86 Verri et al. (2004).
87 Floss (2003).
88 Villa and Roebroeks (2014).
89 Dediu and Levinson (2013: 9).
90 Langacker (1987).
91 Langacker (1987, 1991).
92 Heine and Kuteva (2007).
93 Jackendoff (2010).
94 See Evans (2014) for detailed discussion, and references therein.
95 Tomasello (1999: 94).
96 See discussion in Deacon (1997), as well as recent critical reviews of Chomsky's position, Behme (2014), and Lieberman (2015).
97 Deacon (1997).

## Epilogue

1 Everett (2012: 192).
2 Everett (2012).

3 Boas (1911).
4 Sapir (1921).
5 Whorf (1956).
6 Lucy (1992).
7 Everett (2012: 6).
8 Miracle and Yapita Moya (1981).
9 For discussion, see Evans (2004); Moore (2013); Núñez and Sweetser (2006).
10 Available on The Smithsonian Channel by downloading the free app:
   www.smithsonianchannel.com/videos/grammar-of-happiness-
   sneak-peek/16905
11 Everett (2005).
12 Everett (2012: 262).
13 Everett (2012: 18–19).

# References

Below you will find an alphabetic listing of all primary research works referred to in the book.

Abraham, A., R.I. Schubotz and D.Y. von Cramon. (2008). Thinking about the future versus the past in personal and non-personal contexts. *Brain Research*, 1233: 106–19.

Aitchison, J. (1996). *Words in the Mind: An Introduction to the Mental Lexicon*. Oxford: Blackwell.

Antón, S.C. (2003). Natural history of *Homo erectus*. *American Journal of Physical Anthropology*, 122: 126–70.

Alverson, H. (1994). *Semantics and Experience*. Baltimore, MA: Johns Hopkins Press.

Arbib, M. (2012). *How the Brain Got Language: The Mirror System Hypothesis*. Oxford: Oxford University Press.

Arsuaga, J.L., L. Martínez, C. Lorenzo, A. Gracia, A. Muñoz, O. Alonso and J. Gallego. (1999). The human cranial remains from Gran Dolina Lower Pleistocene site (Sierra de Atapuerca, Spain). *Journal of Human Evolution*, 37/3–4: 431–57.

Arterberry, M.E. and M.H. Bornstein. (2001). Three-month-old infants' categorization of animals and vehicles based on static and dynamic attributes. *Journal of Experimental Child Psychology*, 80: 333–46.

Atkins, B.T.S. (1987). Semantic-ID tags: Corpus evidence for dictionary senses. In *The Uses of Large Text Databases: Proceedings of the Third Annual Conference of the New OED Centre*, pp. 17–36. University of Waterloo, Canada.

Bak, T.H., D.G. O'Donovan, J.H. Xuereb, S. Boniface and J.R. Hodges. (2001). Selective impairment of verb processing associated with pathological changes in Brodmann areas 44 and 45 in the motor neuron disease-dementia-aphasia syndrome. *Brain*, 124: 103–20.

Bar-Yosef, O. and A. Belfer-Cohen. (2001). From Africa to Eurasia – early dispersals. *Quaternary International*, 75: 19–28.

Barsalou, L.W. (1992). *Cognitive Psychology: An Overview for Cognitive Scientists*. Hillsdale, NJ: Erlbaum.

(1999). Perceptual symbol systems. *Behavioral and Brain Sciences*, 22/4: 577–609.

(2005). Continuity of the conceptual system across species. *Trends in Cognitive Sciences*, 9: 309–11.

Barsalou, L.W., A. Santo, W.K. Simmons and C.D. Wilson. (2008). Language and simulation in conceptual processing. In M. De Vega, A.M. Glenberg and A.C. Graesser (Eds.), *Symbols, Embodiment, and Meaning*, pp. 245–83. Oxford: Oxford University Press.

Bayle, P., R. Macchiarelli, E. Trinkaus, C. Duarte, A. Mazurier and J. Zilhão. (2010). Dental maturational sequence and dental tissue proportions in the early Upper Paleolithic child from Abrigodo Lagar Velho, Portugal. *Proceedings of the National Academy of Sciences*, USA, 107: 1338–42.

Behme, C. (2014). A Galilean science of language. *Journal of Linguistics*, 50/3: 671–704.

Berthenthal, B. (1993). Infants' perception of biomechanical motions: Intrinsic image and knowledge-based constraints. In C. Granrud (Ed.), *Visual Perception and Cognition in Infancy*, pp. 175–214. Hillsdale, NJ: Erlbaum.

Berwick, R.C., A.D. Friederici, N. Chomsky and J.J. Bolhuis. (2013). Evolution, brain, and the nature of language. *Trends in Cognitive Sciences*, 17: 89–98.

Bickerton, D. (1990). *Language and Species*. Chicago, IL: University of Chicago Press.

(2002). From proto-language to language. In T. Crow (Ed.)., *The Speciation of Modern Homo Sapiens*, pp. 103–20. Oxford: Oxford University Press.

Biederman, I. (1987). Recognition-by-components: A theory of human image understanding. *Psychological Review*, 94: 115–47.

Bickerton, D. and W.H. Calvin. (2000). *Lingua ex Machina: Reconciling Darwin and Chomsky with the Human Brain*. Cambridge, MA: MIT Press.

Boas, F. (1911). The Mind of Primitive Man. London: Macmillan.

Boden, M.A. (1990). *The Creative Mind: Myths and Mechanisms*. London: Weidenfield and Nicholson.

(1994a). Précis of *The Creative Mind: Myths and Mechanisms*. *Behavioral and Brain Sciences*, 17/3: 519–70.

(1994b). Creativity: A framework for research. *Behavioural and Brain Sciences*, 17/3: 558–570.

(1995). Modelling creativity: Reply to reviewers. *Journal of Artificial Intelligence*, 79: 161–82.

(1996). What is creativity? In M.A. Boden (Ed.), *Dimensions of Creativity*, pp. 75–118. Cambridge, MA: MIT Press.

Boesch, C. and H. Boesch-Achermann. (2000). *The Chimpanzees of the Taï Forest: Behavioural Ecology and Evolution*. Oxford: Oxford University Press.

Boesch, C. and H. Boesch. (1989). Hunting behavior of wild chimpanzees in the Tai National Park. *American Journal of Physical Anthropology*, 78: 547–73.

(1990). Tool use and tool making in wild chimpanzees. *Folia Primatology*, 54: 86–99.

Boroditsky, L. (2000). Metaphoric structuring: Understanding time through spatial metaphors. *Cognition*, 75/1: 1–28.

Boulenger V., L. Mechtou, S. Thobois, E. Broussolle, M. Jeannerod and T.A. Nazir. (2008). Word processing in Parkinson's disease is impaired for action verbs but not for concrete nouns. *Neuropsychologia*, 46: 743–56.

Brown, P., T. Sutikna, M.J. Morwood, R.P. Soejono, E. Jatmiko, W. Saptomo and A.D. Rokus. (2004). A new small-bodied hominin from the Late Pleistocene of Flores, Indonesia. *Nature*, 431: 1055–61.

Bruner, J. (1976). From communication to language – a psychological perspective. *Cognition*, 3: 255–87.

Buccino, G., T.L. Riggio, G. Melli, F. Binkofski, V. Gallese and G. Rizzolatti. (2005). Listening to action-related sentences modulates the activity of the motor system: A combined TMS and behavioral study. *Cognitive Brain Research*, 24: 355–63.

Büchel, C., C. Price and K. Friston. (1998). A multimodal language region in the ventral visual pathway. *Nature*, 394: 274–7.

Buhusi, C.V. and W.H. Meck. (2005). What makes us tick? Functional and neural mechanisms of interval timing. *National Review of Neuroscience*, 6/10: 755–65.

Bybee, J. (2010). *Language, Usage and Cognition*. Cambridge: Cambridge University Press.

Cai, Z.G. and L. Connell. (2012). Space-time interdependence and sensory modalities: Time affects space in the hand but not in the eye. In N. Miyake, D. Peebles and R.P. Cooper (Eds.), *Proceedings of the 34th Annual Conference of the Cognitive Science Society*, pp. 168–73. Austin, TX: Cognitive Science Society.

(2015). Space-time interdependence: Evidence against asymmetric mapping between time and space. *Cognition*, 136: 268–81.

Call, J. and M. Tomasello. (2007). *The Gestural Communications of Apes and Monkeys*. Mahwah, NJ: Lawrence Erlbaum.

(2008). Does the chimpanzee have a theory of mind? 30 years later. *Trends in Cognitive Sciences*, 12/5: 187–92.

Campbell, S.S. (1986). Estimation of empty time. *Human Neurobiology*, 5, 205–7.

Cartmill, M. and F.H. Smith. (2009). *The Human Lineage*. London: John Wiley.

Carretero, J.M., L. Rodríguez, R. García-González, J.L. Arsuaga, A. Gómez-Olivencia, C. Lorenzo, A. Bonmatí, A. Gracia and I. Martínez. (2012). Stature estimation from complete long bones in the Middle Pleistocene humans from the Sima de los Huesos, Sierra de Atapuerca (Spain). *Journal of Human Evolution*, 62/2: 242–55.

Casasanto, D. (2010). Space for thinking. In V. Evans and P. Chilton (Eds.), *Language, Cognition, and Space: State of the Art and New Directions*, pp. 453–78. London: Equinox Publishing.

Casasanto, D. and Boroditsky, L. (2008). Time in the mind: Using space to think about time. *Cognition*, 106: 579–93.

Chafe, W. (1994). *Discourse, Consciousness, and Time: The Flow and Displacement of Conscious Experience in Speaking and Writing*. Chicago: University of Chicago Press.

Cheney, D.L. and R.M. Seyfarth. (1990). *How Monkeys See the World: Inside the Mind of Another Species*. Chicago: University of Chicago Press.

Chomsky, N. (1965). *Aspects of the Theory of Syntax*. Cambridge, MA: MIT Press.

Cienki, A. (1998). STRAIGHT: An image schema and its metaphorical extensions. *Cognitive Linguistics*, 9/2: 107–50.

Cisek, P. (1999). Beyond the computer metaphor: Behaviour as interaction. *Journal of Consciousness Studies*, 6/11–12: 125–42.

Clark, H. (1996). *Using Language*. Cambridge: Cambridge University Press.

Clark, A. (1997). *Being There: Putting Brain, Body and World Together Again*. Cambridge, MA: MIT Press.

Clark, J., J. de Heinzelin, K. Schick, W. Hart, T. White, G. WoldeGabriel, R. Walter, G. Suwa, B. Asfaw and E. Vrba. (1994). African Homo erectus: Old radiometric ages and young Oldowan assemblages in the middle Awash Valley, Ethiopia. *Science*, 264/5167: 1907–9.

Corballis, M. (2002). *From Hand to Mouth: The Origins of Language.* Princeton, NJ: Princeton University Press.

 (2008). Not the last word. Book review of *The First Word: The Search for the Origins of Language by* Christine Kenneally in *American Scientist,* Jan-Feb, Scientist's Nightstand, available online at www.americanscientist.org/bookshelf/pub/not-the-last-word

Coulson, S. (2000). *Semantic Leaps: Frame-Shifting and Conceptual Blending in Meaning Construction.* Cambridge: Cambridge University Press.

Coveney, P. and R. Highfield. (1991). *The Arrow of Time: The Quest to Solve Science's Greatest Mystery.* London: Flamingo.

Croft, W. (2001). *Radical Construction Grammar.* Oxford: Oxford University Press.

Crystal, D. (1998). *The Cambridge Encyclopedia of English.* Cambridge: Cambridge University Press.

Dąbrowska, E. (2009). Words as constructions. In V. Evans and S. Pourcel (Eds.), *New Directions in Cognitive Linguistics,* pp. 201–24. Amsterdam: John Benjamins.

Dahan, D. and M.K. Tanenhaus. (2004). Continuous mapping from sound to meaning in spoken-language comprehension: Evidence from immediate effects of verb-based constraints. *Journal of Experimental Psychology: Learning, Memory and Cognition,* 30: 498–513.

Damasio, A. (1995). *Descartes' Error: Emotion, Reason and the Human Brain.* London: Vintage.

Darwin, C. (1859). *On the Origin of Species* (First ed.). London: John Murray.

 (1871). *The Descent of Man and Selection in Relation to Sex* (First ed.). London: John Murray.

Dawkins, R. (1976). *The Selfish Gene.* Oxford: Oxford University Press.

 (2010). *The Greatest Show on Earth: The Evidence for Evolution.* London: Black Swan.

Deacon, T. (1997). *The Symbolic Species: The Co-evolution of Language and the Brain.* New York: W.W. Norton & Co.

Deecke, V. (2012). Tool-use in the brown bear (*Ursus arctos*). *Animal Cognition*, 15/4: 725–30.

Dennett, D. (1989). *The Intentional Stance*. Cambridge, MA: MIT Press.

d'Errico, F., L. Backwell, P. Villa and colleagues. (2012). Early evidence of San material culture represented by organic artifacts from Border Cave, South Africa. *Proceedings of the National Academy of Sciences*, USA, 10.1073/pnas.1204213109.

d'Errico, F. and M. Soressi. (2002). Systematic use of manganese pigment by the Pech-de-l'Azé Neandertals: Implications for the origin of behavioural modernity. *Journal of Human Evolution*, 42: A13.

d'Errico, F. and M. Vanhaeren. (2009). Earliest personal ornaments and their significance for the origin of language debate. In R. Botha and C. Knight (Eds.), *The Cradle of Language*, pp. 16–40. Oxford: Oxford University Press.

DiMaggio, E.N., C.J. Campisano, J. Rowan, G. Dupont-Nivet, A.L. Deino, F. Bibi, M.E. Lewis, A. Souron, D. Garello, L. Werdelin, K.E. Reed and J. Ramón Arrowsmith. (2015). Late Pliocene fossiliferous sedimentary record and the environmental context of early *Homo* from Afar, Ethiopia. *Science*, 347/6228: 1355–9.

DuBrul, E. (1977). Origins of the speech apparatus and its reconstruction in fossils. *Brain and Language*, 4: 365–81.

Dediu, D. and S.C. Levinson. (2013). On the antiquity of language: The reinterpretation of Neandertal linguistic capacities and its consequences. *Frontiers in Psychology*, 4: 397.

Dunbar, R.I.M. (1996). *Grooming, Gossip and the Evolution of Language*. London: Faber and Faber.

Evans, V. (2004). *The Structure of Time: Language, Meaning and Temporal Cognition*. Amsterdam: John Benjamins.

   (2009). *How Words Mean: Lexical Concepts, Cognitive Models and Meaning Construction*. Oxford: Oxford University Press.

   (2010). Figurative language understanding in LCCM Theory. *Cognitive Linguistics* 21/4: 601–62.

   (2013). *Language and Time: A Cognitive Linguistics Approach*. Cambridge: Cambridge University Press.

   (2014). *The Language Myth: Why Language is Not an Instinct*. Cambridge: Cambridge University Press.

   (2015). What's in a concept? Analogue versus parametric concepts in LCCM Theory. In E. Margolis and S. Laurence (Eds.), *The*

*Conceptual Mind: New Directions in the Study of Concepts,*
pp. 251–90. Cambridge, MA: MIT Press.

Evans, V. and M. Green. (2006). *Cognitive Linguistics: An Introduction.*
Edinburgh: Edinburgh University Press.

Everett, D. (2005). Cultural constraints on grammar and cognition in
Pirahã. *Current Anthropology,* 46/4: 621–646.

(2009). *Don't Sleep, There are Snakes: Life and Language in the
Amazonian Jungle.* London: Profile Books.

(2012). *Language: The Cultural Tool.* London: Profile Books.

Falk, D. (1975). Comparative anatomy of the larynx in man and the
chimpanzee: Implications for language in Neanderthal. *American
Journal of Physical Anthropology,* 43: 123–32.

Fauconnier, G. (1994). *Mental Spaces.* Cambridge: Cambridge University Press.

(1997). *Mappings in Thought and Language.* Cambridge: Cambridge
University Press.

Fauconnier, G. and M. Turner. (2000). Compression and global insight.
*Cognitive Linguistics.* 11/3-4: 283–304.

(2002). *The Way We Think: Conceptual Blending and the Mind's
Hidden Complexities.* New York: Basic Books.

(2008). The origin of language as a product of the evolution of
double-scope blending. *Behavioral and Brain Sciences,* 31/5: 520–1.

Fitch, W.T. (2009a). *Musical Protolanguage: Darwin's Theory of Language Evolution Revisited.* Available online at http://languagelog.
ldc.upenn.edu/nll/?p=1136.

(2009b). Fossil cues to the evolution of speech. In R. Botha and
C. Knight (Eds.), *The Cradle of Language,* pp. 112–34. Oxford:
Oxford University Press.

Flaherty, M. (1999). *A Watched Pot: How We Experience Time.*
New York: New York University Press.

Floss, M. (2003). Did they meet or not. Observations on Châtelperronian and Aurignacian settlement patterns in eastern France. In
J. Zilhão and F. d'Errico (Eds.), *The Chronology of the Aurignacian
and of the Transitional Technocomplexes,* pp. 273–88. Lisbon,
Portugal: Instituto Português de Arqueologia.

Fodor, J. (1975). *The Language of Thought.* Cambridge, MA: MIT Press.

(1981). The current status of the innateness controversy. In *Representations,* pp. 257–316. Cambridge, MA: MIT Press.

(1983). *Modularity of Mind.* Cambridge, MA: MIT Press.

(1995). *The Elm and Expert: Mentalese and its Semantics*. Cambridge, MA: MIT Press

(1998). *Concepts: Where Cognitive Science Went Wrong*. Oxford: Oxford University Press.

(2008). *LOT2: The Language of Thought Revisited*. Oxford: Oxford University Press.

Fraisse, P. (1984). Perception and estimation of time. *Annual Review of Psychology*, 35: 1–36.

Freeman, N.H., S. Lloyd and C. Sinha. (1980). Infant search tasks reveal early concepts of containment and canonical usage of objects. *Cognition*, 8: 243–62.

Frye, D., P. Rawling, C. Moore and I. Myers. (1983). Object–person discrimination at 3 and 10 months. *Developmental Psychology*, 19: 303–9.

Galton, A. (2011). Time flies but space doesn't: Limits to the spatialization of time. *Journal of Pragmatics*, 43: 695–703.

Gamble, C. and G. Marshall. (2001). The shape of handaxes, the structure of the Acheulian world. In S. Milliken and J.D. Cook (Eds.), *A Very Remote Period Indeed. Papers on the Palaeolithic presented to Derek Roe*, pp. 19–27. Oxford: Oxbow.

Gavins, J. and G. Steen. (2003). *Cognitive Poetics in Practice*. London: Routledge.

Gazzaniger, M. (2006). Leon Festinger: Lunch with Leon. *Perspectives on Psychological Science*, 1: 88–94.

Geeraerts, D. (2009). *Theories of Lexical Semantics*. Oxford: Oxford University Press.

Gentner, D., M. Imai and L. Boroditsky. (2002). As time goes by: Evidence for two systems in processing space time metaphors. *Language and Cognitive Processes*, 17/5: 537–65.

Gibbs, R.W. (2008). *The Cambridge Handbook of Metaphor and Thought*. Cambridge: Cambridge University Press.

Gibson, J. (1986). *The Ecological Approach to Visual Perception*. Mahwah, NJ: Lawrence Erlbaum.

Goldberg, A. (1995). *Constructions: A Construction Grammar Approach to Verb Argument Structure*. Chicago: University of Chicago Press.

(2006). *Constructions at Work: The Nature of Generalizations in Language*. Oxford: Oxford University Press.

Gomes, C.M. and C. Boesch. (2009). Wild chimpanzees exchange meat for sex on a long-term basis. *ONE*, 4/4: e5116.

Goodwin, C. (2003). *Conversation and Brain Damage*. Oxford: Oxford University Press.

Glenberg, A.M. and M. Kaschak. (2002). Grounding language in action. *Psychonomic Bulletin and Review*, 9/3: 558–65.

Goldin-Meadow, S. (2003). *Hearing Gesture: How Our Hands Help Us Think*. Harvard: Harvard University Press.

Grady, J. (1997a). *Foundations of Meaning: Primary Metaphors and Primary Scenes*. Doctoral thesis, Linguistics Dept, University of California, Berkeley (available from UMI Dissertation Services: www.il.proquest.com/umi/dissertations/).

(1997b). THEORIES ARE BUILDINGS revisited. *Cognitive Linguistics*, 8/4: 267–90.

(1999). A typology of motivation for conceptual metaphor: Correlation vs. resemblance. In R.W. Gibbs and G. Steen (Eds.), *Metaphor in Cognitive Linguistics*, pp. 79–100. Amsterdam: John Benjamins.

Grady, J. and C. Johnson. (2000). Converging evidence for the notions of 'subscene' and 'primary scene', *Proceedings of the 23rd Annual Meeting of the Berkeley Linguistics Society*, pp. 123–36. Berkeley, CA: Berkeley Linguistics Society.

Gräfenhaim, M., T. Behne, M. Carpenter and M. Tomasello. (2009). Young children's understanding of joint commitments. *Developmental Psychology*, 45/5: 1430–43.

Green, R.E., J. Krause, A.W. Briggs, T. Maricic, U. Stenzel and M. Kircher. (2010). A draft sequence of the Neandertal genome. *Science*, 328: 710–722.

Green, D.J. and Z. Alemseged. (2012). *Australopithecus afarensis* scapular ontogeny, function, and the role of climbing in human evolution. *Science*, 338/6106: 514–517.

Gregory, R. (1998). *Eye and Brain* (fifth edition). Oxford: Oxford University Press.

Gries, S. Th. (2006). Corpus-based methods and cognitive semantics: The many meanings of *to run*. In S. Th. Gries and A. Stefanowitsch (Eds.), *Corpora in Cognitive Linguistics: Corpus-based Approaches to Syntax and Lexis*, pp. 57–99. Berlin: Mouton de Gruyter.

Haley, D. (Ed.) (1986). Sea otter. *Marine Mammals of Eastern North Pacific and Arctic Waters* (Second edition). Seattle, WA: Pacific Search Press.

Hampe, B. (2005). *From Perception to Meaning: Image Schemas in Cognitive Linguistics*. Berlin: Mouton de Gruyter.

Harnad, S. (1990). The symbol grounding problem. *Physica D*, 42: 335–46.

Hart, B.J., L.A. Hart, M. McCory and C.R. Sarath. (2001). Cognitive behaviour in Asian elephants: Use and modification of branches for fly switching. *Animal Behaviour* 62/5: 839–47.

Haviland, J.B. (1974). A last look at Cook's Guugu-Yimidhirr wordlist. *Oceania*, 44/3: 216–32.

Hawks, J. (2013). *Neandertal Ancestry and Founder Effects. John Hawks Weblog*. Available at: http://johnhawks.net/weblog/topics/introgression.

Hebb, D.O. (2002). *The Organization of Behavior: A Neuropsychological Theory* (new edition). Hove: Psychology Press.

Heine, B., U. Claudi and F. Hünnemeyer. (1991). *Grammaticalization: A Conceptual Framework*. Chicago: Chicago University Press.

Heine, B. and T. Kuteva. (2007). *The Genesis of Grammar: A Reconstruction*. Oxford: Oxford University Press.

Hespos, S.J. and R. Baillargeon. (2001). Reasoning about containment events in very young infants. *Cognition*, 78: 207–45.

Hofstadter, D. (1979). *Gödel, Escher, Bach: An Eternal Golden Braid*. New York: Basic Books.

Houghton, P. (1993). Neandertal supralaryngeal vocal tract. *American Journal of Physical Anthropology*, 90: 139–46.

Hublin, J.-J. (2009). Out of Africa: Modern human origins. *Proceedings of the National Academy of Sciences*, USA, 106: 16022–7.

Hulme, M. (2008). The conquering of climate: Discourses of fear and their dissolution. *The Geographical Journal*, 174/1: 5–16.

Hurford, J. (2007). *The Origins of Meaning. Language in the Light of Evolution I*. Oxford: Oxford University Press.

(2012). *The Origins of Grammar. Language in the Light of Evolution II*. Oxford: Oxford University Press.

Isenberg, N., D. Silbersweig, A. Engelien, S. Emmerich, K. Malavade, B. Beattie, A.C. Leon, and E. Stern. (1999). Linguistic threat activates the human amygdala. *Proceedings of the National Academy of Science, USA*, 96: 10456–9.

Jackendoff, R. (1987). *Consciousness and the Computational Mind*. Cambridge, MA: MIT Press.

(1992). *Languages of the Mind: Essays on Mental Representation*. Oxford: Oxford University Press.

(2010). Your theory of language evolution depends on your theory of language. In R. Larson, V. Déprez and H. Yamakido (Eds.), *The Evolution of Human Language: Biolinguistic Perspectives*, pp. 63–72. Cambridge: Cambridge University Press.

Jakobson, R. (1942). *Six Lectures on Sound and Meaning*. Boston, MA: MIT Press.

Jelinek, E. (1995). Quantification in Straits Salish. In E. Bach, E. Jelinek, A. Kratzer and B. Partee (Eds.), *Quantification in Natural Languages*, pp. 487–540. New York: Kluwer Academic.

Johanson, D.C. and M.A. Edey. (1981). *Lucy: The Beginnings of Humankind*. London: Penguin.

Johansson, G. (1973). Visual perception of biological motion and a model for its analysis. *Perception and Psychophysics*, 14: 201–11.

Johnson, C. (1999). Metaphor vs. conflation in the acquisition of polysemy: The case of *see*. In M. Hiraga, C. Sinha and S. Wilcox (Eds.), *Cultural, Typological and Psychological Perspectives in Cognitive Linguistics*, pp. 155–69. Amsterdam: John Benjamins.

Johnson, M. (1987). *The Body in the Mind: The Bodily Basis of Meaning, Imagination and Reason*. Chicago: University of Chicago Press.

Joormens, J., F. d' Errico, F.P. Wesselingh and colleagues. (2014). Homo erectus at Trinil on Java used shells for tool production and engraving. *Nature*, 10.1038/nature13962.

Julesz, B. (1981). Textons: The elements of texture perception and their interactions. *Nature*, 290: 91–7.

Julian, R. (2005). A John Dee Chronology, 1509–1609. *Renaissance Man: The Reconstructed Libraries of European Scholars: 1450–1700 Series One: The Books and Manuscripts of John Dee, 1527–1608*. Marlborough, Wiltshire: Adam Matthew Publications.

Kellman, P.J. and E.S. Spelke (1983). Perception of partly occluded objects in infancy. *Cognitive Psychology*, 15: 483–524.

Kendon, A. (1991). Some considerations for a theory of language origins. *Man*, 26/2: 199–221.

Kingdon, J. (2004). *Lowly Origin: Where, When, and Why Our Ancestors First Stood Up*. Princeton, NJ: Princeton University Press.

Klatzky, R.L., J.W. Pellegrino, B.P, McCloskey and S. Doherty. (1989). Can you squeeze a tomato? The role of motor representations in semantic sensibility judgements. *Journal of Memory and Language*, 28: 56–77.

Klein, R.G. (2009). *The Human Career: Human Biological and Cultural Origins* (third edition). Chicago: University of Chicago Press.

Kojima, S. (1990). Comparison of auditory functions in the chimpanzee and human. *Folia Primatology*, 55: 62–72.

Koestler, A. (1964). *The Act of Creation*. London: Hutchinson.

Koops, K., W.C. McGrew and T. Matsuzawa. (2010). Do chimpanzees (*Pan troglodytes*) use cleavers and anvils to fracture *Treculia africana* fruits? Preliminary data on a new form of percussive technology. *Primates*, 51/2: 175–8.

Kövescses, Z. (2010). *Metaphor: A Practical Introduction*. Oxford: Oxford University Press.

Kranjec, A., M. Lehet and A. Chatterjee. (2013). Space and time are mutually contagious in sound. In M. Knauff, M. Pauen, N. Sebanz and I. Wachsmuth (Eds.), *Proceedings of the Thirty-Fourth Annual Conference of the Cognitive Science Society*, pp. 829–33, http://cognitivesciencesociety.org/conference_past.html

Kubovy, M. (1988). Should we resist the seductiveness of the space:time:: vision:audition analogy? *Journal of Experimental Psychology: Human Perception and Performance*, 14/2: 318–20.

Lafon, J.-C. (1968). Auditory basis of phonetics. In B. Malmberg (Ed.), *Manual of Phonetics*, pp. 76–104. Amsterdam: North-Holland.

Lakoff, G. (1987). *Women, Fire and Dangerous Things: What Categories Reveal About the Mind*. Chicago: University of Chicago Press.

(1990). The invariance hypothesis: Is abstract reason based on image schemas? *Cognitive Linguistics*, 1/1: 39–74.

(1991). *Metaphor and War: The Metaphor System Used to Justify War in the Gulf*. An open letter to the Internet.

(1993). The contemporary theory of metaphor. In A. Ortony (Ed.), *Metaphor and Thought* (second edition), pp. 202–51. Cambridge: Cambridge University Press.

(2004). *Don't Think of an Elephant: Know Your Values and Frame the Debate*. White River Junction, VM: Chelsea Green.

(2008). The neural theory of metaphor. In R.W. Gibbs (Ed.), *The Cambridge Handbook of Metaphor and Thought*, pp. 17–38. Cambridge: Cambridge University Press.

Lakoff, G. and M. Johnson. (1980). *Metaphors We Live By*. Chicago: University of Chicago Press.

(1999). *Philosophy in the Flesh: The Embodied Mind and its Challenge to Western Thought.* New York: Basic Books.

Lakoff, G. and M. Turner. (1987). *More Than Cool Reason: A Field-guide to Poetic Metaphor.* Chicago: Chicago University Press.

Lalueza-Fox, C., A. Rosas, A. Estalrrich, E. Gigli, P.F. Campos and A. García-Tabernero. (2010). Genetic evidence for patrilocal mating behaviour among Neandertal groups. *Proceedings of the National Academy of Sciences,* USA, 108: 250–3.

Langacker, R. (2008). *Cognitive Grammar: A Basic Introduction.* Oxford: Oxford University Press.

Langacker, R.W. (1987). *Foundations of Cognitive Grammar* (Vol. I). Stanford: Stanford University Press.

(2013). *Essentials of Cognitive Grammar.* Oxford: Oxford University Press.

Langone, J. (2000). *The Mystery of Time: Humanity's Quest for Order and Measure.* Washington DC: National Geographic Press.

Larsen, C. (2003). Equality for the sexes in human evolution? Early hominid sexual dimorphism and implications for mating systems and social behavior. *Proceedings of the National Academy of Sciences,* USA, 100/16: 9103–4.

Leakey, M.G., F. Spoor, F.H. Brown, P.N. Gathogo, C. Kiarie, L.N. Leakey and I. McDougallet. (2001). New hominin genus from eastern Africa shows diverse middle Pliocene lineages. *Nature,* 410: 433–40.

Leakey, R.E. (1981). *The Making of Mankind.* Cambridge: Cambridge University Press.

LeDoux, J.E. (1995). Emotion: Clues from the brain. *Annual Review of Psychology,* 46: 209–35.

Lee, N., L. Mikesell, A.D. Joaquin, A.W. Mates and J.H. Schumann. (2009). *The Interactional Instinct: The Evolution and Acquisition of Language.* Oxford: Oxford University Press.

Legerstee, M. (1992). A review of the animate-inanimate distinction in infancy: Implications for models of social and cognitive knowing. *Early Development and Parenting,* 1: 59–67.

Le Poidevin, R. (2003). *Travels in Four Dimensions: The Enigmas of Space and Time.* Oxford: Oxford University Press.

Leslie, A.M. (1982). The perception of causality in infants. *Perception,* 11: 173–86.

(1984). Infant perception of a manual pick-up event. *British Journal of Developmental Psychology,* 2: 19–32.

Levinson, S.C. (2003). *Space in Language and Cognition: Explorations in Cultural Diversity*. Cambridge: Cambridge University Press.

(2006). On the human 'interaction engine'. In N.J. Enfield and S.C. Levinson (Eds.). *Roots of Human Sociality: Culture, Cognition and Interaction*, pp. 39–69. Oxford: Berg.

Lieberman, D.E. (2001). Another face in our family tree. *Nature*, 410: 419–20.

Lieberman, P. (2015). Review of *The Science of Language: Interviews with James McGilvray*, by Noam Chomsky. *Modern Language Review*, 110/1: 222–4.

Lieberman, P. and E. Crelin. (1971). On the speech of Neanderthal man. *Linguistic Inquiry*, 2: 203–22.

Linden, S.J. (2003). *The Alchemy Reader: from Hermes Trismegistus to Isaac Newton*. Cambridge: Cambridge University Press.

Loftus, E., J.W. Schooler, S.M. Boone and D. Kline. (1987). Time went by so slowly: Overestimation of event duration by males and females. *Applied Cognitive Psychology*, 1/1: 3–13.

Lozano, M., M. Mosquera, J. De Castro, M. Bermúdez, J.L. Arsuaga and E. Carbonell. (2009). Right handedness of *Homo heidelbergensis* from Sima de los Huesos (Atapuerca, Spain) 500,000 years ago. *Evolution and Human Behavior*, 30/5: 369–76.

Lucy, J.A. (1992). *Language Diversity and Thought: A reformulation of the linguistic relativity hypothesis*. Cambridge: Cambridge University Press.

Lurz, R. (2011). *Mindreading Animals: The Debate about What Animals Know, and Other Minds*. Cambridge, MA: MIT Press.

MacIntosh, J.J. and P. Anstey. (2014). Robert Boyle. In E.N. Zalta (Ed.), *The Stanford Encyclopedia of Philosophy*, http://plato.stanford.edu/archives/fall2014/entries/boyle/.

Mandler, J.M. (1988). How to build a baby: On the development of an accessible representational system. *Cognitive Development*, 3: 113–36.

(1992). How to build a baby II. Conceptual primitives. *Psychological Review*, 99: 567–604.

(1996). Preverbal representation and language. In P. Bloom, M.A. Peterson, L. Nadel and M.F. Garrett (Eds.), *Language and Space*, pp. 365–84. Cambridge, MA: MIT Press.

(2004). *The Foundations of Mind: Origins of Conceptual Thought*. Oxford: Oxford University Press.

Martin, A. and L.L. Chao. (2001). Semantic memory and the brain: Structure and processes. *Current Opinion in Neurobiology*, 11: 194–201.

Martínez, I., R.M. Quam, M. Rosa, P. Jarabo, C. Lorenzo and J.L. Arsuaga. (2008). Auditory capacities of human fossils: A new approach to the origin of speech. *Journal of the Acoustic Society of America*, 123: 3606–3606.

Martínez, I., M. Rosa, J.-L. Arsuaga, P. Jarabo, R. Quam and C. Lorenzo. (2004). Auditory capacities in Middle Pleistocene humans from the Sierrade Atapuerca in Spain. *Proceedings of the National Academy Sciences, USA*, 101: 9976–81.

McPherron, S.P., Z. Alemseged, C. Marean, J.G. Wynn, D. Reed, D. Geraads, R. Bobe and H. Béarat. (2011). Tool-marked bones from before the oldowan change the paradigm. *Proceedings of the National Academy of Sciences, USA*, 108/21: e116.

Meltzoff, A. and M. Moore. (1977). Imitation of facial and manual gestures by human neonates. *Science*, 198: 75–8.

Mithen, S. (1996). *The Prehistory of the Mind: A Search for the Origins of Art, Science and Religion*. London: Phoenix.

Miracle, A.W. Jr. and J. de Dios Yapita Moya. (1981). Time and space in Aymara. In M. J. Hardman. (ed), *The Aymara Language and Its Social and Cultural Context*. Gainesville, FL: University Presses of Florida, 33–56.

Moore, B.C. (1977). *Introduction to the Psychology of Hearing*. Baltimore, MA: University Park Press.

Moore, K.E. (2006). Space-to-time mappings and temporal concepts. *Cognitive Linguistics*, 17/2: 199–244.

Moore, K.E. (2013). *The Spatial Language of Time: Metaphor, Metonymy and Frames of Reference*. Amsterdam: John Benjamins.

Mounier, A., F. Marchal and S. Condemi. (2009). Is *Homo heidelbergensis* a distinct species? New insight on the Mauer mandible. *Journal of Human Evolution*, 56/3: 219–46.

Müller, M. (1861). The theoretical stage, and the origin of language. Lecture 9 from Lectures on the Science of Language. Reprinted in R. Harris (Ed.), 1996, *The Origin of Language*, pp. 7–41. Bristol, Avon: Thoemmes Press.

Nerlich, B., V. Evans and N. Koteyko. (2011). Low carbon diet: Reducing the complexities of climate change to human scale. *Language and Cognition*, 3/1: 45–82.

Newman, W.R. and L.M. Principle. (2002). *Alchemy Tried in the Fire*. Chicago: University of Chicago Press.

Núñez, R., B. Motz and U. Teuscher. (2006). Time after time: The psychological reality of the Ego- and Time-Reference-Point distinction in metaphorical construals of time. *Metaphor and Symbol*, 21: 133–46.

Núñez, R. and E. Sweetser. (2006). With the future behind them: Convergent evidence from Aymara language and gesture in the crosslinguistic comparison of spatial construals of time. *Cognitive Science*, 30: 401–50.

Paget, R. (1930). *Human Speech: Some Observations, Experiments, and Conclusions as to the Nature, Origin, Purpose and Possible Improvement of Human Speech*. London: Routledge and Kegan Paul.

Pansini, R. and J.R. de Ruiter. (2011). Observation of tool use and modification for apparent hygiene purposes in a mandrill. *Behavioural Processes* 88/1: 53–5.

Patel, A. (2008). *Music, Language and the Brain*. Oxford: Oxford University Press.

Peretz, I. (2006). The nature of music from a biological perspective. *Cognition*, 100: 1–32.

Pettitt, P.B. (2002).The Neanderthal dead: Exploring mortuary variability in Middle Palaeolithic Eurasia. *Before Farming*, 1: 1–19.

Peterson, D. (2011). *The Moral Lives of Animals*. London: Bloomsbury Press.

Piaget, J. (1962). *The Language and Thought of the Child*. London: Routledge and Kegan Paul.

Pierce, C.S. (1903). A syllabus of certain topics of logic. *EP*, 2: 272–3.

Pika, S., K. Liebal, J. Call and M. Tomasello. (2005). Gestural communication of apes. *Gesture*, 5/1–2: 41–56.

Pinker, S. (1997). *How the Mind Works*. New York: W.W. Norton and co.

Plutchik, R. (1980). *Emotion: Theory, Research, and Experience*. New York: Academic Press.

(2002). *Emotions and Life: Perspectives from Psychology, Biology, and Evolution*. Washington, DC: American Psychological Association.

Pöppel, E. (1994). Temporal mechanisms in perception. In O. Sporns and G. Tononi (Eds.), *Selectionism and the Brain: International Review of Neurobiology*, 37: 185–201.

(2009). Pre-semantically defined temporal windows for cognitive processing. *Philosophical Transactions of the Royal Society B*, 364: 1887–96.

Prinz, J. (2002). *Furnishing the Mind*. Cambridge, MA: MIT Press.

Pruetz, J. and P. Bertolani. (2007). Savanna chimpanzees, Pan troglodytes verus, hunt with tools. *Current Biology*, 17: 412–17.

Pulvermüller, F. (1999). Words in the brain's language. *Behavioral and Brain Sciences*, 22: 253–79.

Raichlen, D.A., A.D. Gordon, W.E.H. Harcourt-Smith, A.A. Foster and Wm.R. Haas Jr. (2010). Laetoli footprints preserve earliest direct evidence of human-like bipedal biomechanics. *PLoS ONE*, 5/3: e9769.

Rak, Y., A. Ginzburg and E. Geffen. (2007). Gorilla-like anatomy on Australopithecus afarensis mandibles suggests Au. Afarensis link to robust australopiths. *Proceedings of the National Academy of Sciences, USA*, 104/16: 6568.

Ratliff, F., and H.K. Hartline. (1974). *Studies on Excitation and Inhibition in the Retina*. New York: Rockefeller University Press.

Renfrew, C. (1990). *Archaeology and Language: The Puzzle of Indo-European Origins*. Oxford: Oxford University Press.

(2008). *Prehistory: The Making of the Human Mind*. London: Phoenix.

Reynolds, S. and A. Gallagher. (2012). *African Genesis: Perspectives on Hominin Evolution*. Cambridge: Cambridge University Press.

Roebroeks, W. and P. Villa. (2011). On the earliest evidence for habitual use of fire in Europe. *Proceedings of the National Academy of Sciences, USA*, 108: 5209–14.

Rosch, E. (1978). Principles of categorization. In B. Lloyd and E. Rosch (Eds.), *Cognition and Categorization*, pp. 27–48. Hillsdale, NJ: Erlbaum.

Ryle, G. (1949). *The Concept of Mind*. London: Penguin Books.

Sapir, E. (1921). *Language: The Scientific Study of Speech*. NY: Harcourt Brace and company.

Sandler, W., M. Aronoff, I. Meir and C. Padden. (2011). The gradual emergence of phonological form in a new language. *Natural Language and Linguistic Theory*, 29/2: 503–43.

Sandler, W., I. Meir, C. Padden and M. Aronoff. (2005). The emergence of grammar in a new sign language. *Proceedings of the National Academy of Sciences, USA*, 102/7: 2661–5.

Sandra, D. and S. Rice. (1995). Network analyses of prepositional meaning: mirroring whose mind – the linguist's or the language user's? *Cognitive Linguistics*, 6/1: 89–130.

Saussure, F. de. (1916). *Course in General Linguistics*. London: Harcourt.

Schacter, D.L., D.R. Addis and R.L. Buckner. (2007). The prospective brain: Remembering the past to imagine the future. *Nature Reviews Neuroscience*, 8: 657–61.

Schmelz, M., J. Call and M. Tomasello. (2012). Chimpanzees know that others make inferences. *Proceedings of the National Academy of Sciences,* USA, 108/7: 3077–9.

Schmid, H.-J. (2000). *English Abstract Nouns as Conceptual Shells: From Corpus to Cognition.* Berlin: Mouton de Gruyter.

Senut, B., M. Pickford, D. Gommery, P. Mein, K. Cheboi and Y. Coppens (2001). First hominid from the Miocene (Lukeino Formation, Kenya). *Comptes Rendus de l'Academie des Sciences, Series IIA – Earth and Planetary Science* 332/2: 137–44.

Seyfarth, R.M., D.L. Cheney and P. Marler. (1980). Monkey responses to three different alarm calls: Evidence of predator classification and semantic communication. *Science* 210: 801–3.

Shapiro, L. (2010). *Embodied Cognition.* London: Routledge.

Shipman, P. (2001). *The Man who Found the Missing Link: The Extraordinary Life of Eugène Dubois.* New York: Simon and Schuster.

Shinohara, K. (1999). *Epistemology of Space and Time.* Kwansei, Japan: Kwansei Gakuin University Press.

Shumaker, R.W., K.R. Walkup and B.B. Beck. (2011). *Animal Tool Behavior: The Use and Manufacture of Tools by Animals.* Baltimore, MA: Johns Hopkins University Press.

Siffre, M. (1964). *Beyond Time.* New York: McGraw-Hill.

Sinha, C. (1982). Representational development and the structure of action. In P. Butterworth and G. Light (Eds.), *Social Cognition: Studies of the Development of Understanding,* pp. 137–62. Brighton: Harvester Press.

(1988). *Language and Representation: A Socio-Naturalistic Approach to Human Development.* Hove: Harvester Press.

Sinha, C., V. da Silva Sinha, J. Zinken and W. Sampaio. (2011). When time is not space: The social and linguistic construction of time intervals and temporal event relations in an Amazonian culture. *Language and Cognition,* 3/1: 137–69.

Sørensen, B. (2009). Energy use by Eem Neanderthals. *Journal of Archaeological Science,* 36: 2201–5.

Sperber, D. and D. Wilson. (1996). *Relevance: Communication and Cognition* (second edition). Oxford: Blackwell.

Spivey, M., M. Tyler, D. Richardson and E. Young. (2000). Eye movements during comprehension of spoken scene descriptions. In

*Proceedings of the 22nd Annual Conference of the Cognitive Science Society*, pp. 487–92. Mahwah, NJ: Erlbaum.

Spoor, F., M.G. Leakey, P.N. Gathogo, F.H. Brown, S.C. Antón, I. McDougall, C. Kiarie, F.K. Manthi and L.N. Leakey. (2007). Implications of new early *Homo* fossils from Ileret, east of Lake Turkana, Kenya. *Nature*, 448/7154: 688–91.

Stanfield, R.A. and R.A. Zwaan. (2001). The effect of implied orientation derived from verbal context on picture recognition. *Psychological Science*, 12: 153–6.

Stanovich, K. (2011). *Rationality and the Reflective Mind*. Oxford: Oxford University Press.

Stern Jr., J.T. and R.L. Susman. (1983). The locomotor anatomy of *Australopithecus afarensis*. *American Journal of Physical Anthropology*, 60/3: 279–317.

Stockwell, P. (2002). *Cognitive Poetics: An Introduction*. London: Routledge.

Sweetser, E. (1988). Grammaticalization and semantic bleaching. In S. Axmaker, A. Jaisser and H. Singmaster (Eds.), *Proceedings of the 14th Annual Meeting of the Berkeley Linguistics Society*, pp. 389–405. Berkeley, CA: Berkeley Linguistics Society.

Talmy, L. (2000). *Toward a Cognitive Semantics* (two volumes). Cambridge, MA: MIT Press.

Tattersall, T. (2012). *Masters of the Planet: The Search for Our Human Origins*. London: Palgrave Macmillan.

Taylor, J. (2002). *Cognitive Grammar*. Oxford: Oxford University Press.
   (2003). *Linguistic Categorization* (third edition). Oxford: Oxford University Press.
   (2012). *The Mental Corpus: How Language is Represented in the Mind*. Oxford: Oxford University Press.

Taylor, L. and R. A. Zwaan. (2009). Action in cognition: The case of language. *Language and Cognition*, 1/1: 45–58.

Thierry, G., P. Athanasopoulos, A. Wiggett, B. Dering and J-R. Kuipers. (2009). Unconscious effects of language-specific terminology on preattentive color perception. *Proceedings of the National Academy of Science, USA*, 106/11: 4567–70.

Tomasello, M. (1999). *The Cultural Origins of Human Cognition*. Harvard, MA: Harvard University Press.
   (2003). *Constructing a Language*. Harvard, MA: Harvard University Press.

(2008). *The Origins of Human Communication*. Cambridge, MA: MIT Press.

(2011). Human culture in evolutionary perspective. In M. Gelfand (Ed.), *Advances in Culture and Psychology* (pp. 5–51). Oxford: Oxford University Press.

(2014). *A Natural History of Human Thinking*. Harvard, MA: Harvard University Press.

Tomasello, M. and J. Call. (1997). *Primate Cognition*. Oxford: Oxford University Press.

Tomkins, S. (1998). *The Origins of Humankind*. Cambridge: Cambridge University Press

Trevarthen, C. (1979). Communication and cooperation in early infancy: A description of primary intersubjectivity. In M. Bullowa (Ed.), *Before Speech: The Beginning of Human Communication*, pp. 321–47. Cambridge: Cambridge University Press.

Turing, A.M. (1950). Computing machinery and intelligence. *Mind*, 59: 433–60.

Turner, F. and E. Pöppel. (1983). The neural lyre: Poetic meter, the brain and time. *Poetry*, 142/5: 277–309.

Turner, M. (1996). *The Literary Mind: The Origins of Thought and Language*. Oxford: Oxford University Press.

(2014). *The Origin of Ideas: Blending, Creativity and the Human Spark*. Oxford: Oxford University Press.

Tyler, A. (2012). *Cognitive Linguistics and Second Language Learning: Theoretical Basics and Experimental Evidence*. London: Routledge.

Tyler, A. and V. Evans. (2001). Reconsidering prepositional polysemy networks: The case of over. *Language*, 77/4: 724–65.

(2003). *The Semantics of English Prepositions: Spatial Scenes, Embodied Experience, and Cognition*. Cambridge: Cambridge University Press.

Ungar, P. (2004). Dental topography and diets of *Australopithecus afarensis* and early *Homo. Journal of Human Evolution*, 46: 605–22.

Van Schaik, C., E. Fox and A. Sitompul. (1996). Manufacture and use of tools in wild Sumatran orangutans. *Naturwissenschaften*, 83: 186–8.

Vandeloise, C. (1994). Methodology and analyses of the preposition *in. Cognitive Linguistics*, 5/2: 157–84.

Varela, F. (1999). Present-time consciousness. *Journal of Consciousness Studies*, 6/2-3: 111–40.

Varela, F., E. Thompson and E. Rosch. (1991). *The Embodied Mind: Cognitive Science and Human Experience*. Cambridge, MA: MIT Press.

Verri, G., R. Barkai, V. Bordeanu, A. Gopher, M. Hass and A. Kaufman. (2004). Flint mining in prehistory recorded by *in situ*-produced cosmogenic10Be. *Proceedings of the National Academy of Sciences, USA*, 101: 7880–4.

Vigliocco, G., L. Meteyard, M. Andrews and S. Kousta. (2009). Toward a theory of semantic representation. *Language and Cognition*, 1/2: 219–48.

Villa, P. and W. Roebroeks. (2014). Neanderthal demise: An archaeological analysis of the modern human superiority complex. *PLoS ONE*, 9/4: e96424.

Watson, J. (1972). Smiling, cooing, and 'the game'. *Merrill-Palmer Quarterly*, 18: 323–40.

Watts, I. (2009). Red ochre, body painting, and language: Interpreting the Blombos ochre. In R. Botha and C. Knight (Eds.), *The Cradle of Language*, pp. 62–92. Oxford: Oxford University Press.

Watts, D. and J.C. Mitani. (2002). Hunting and meat sharing by Chimpanzees at Ngogo, Kibale National Park, Uganda. *International Journal of Primatology*, 23: 1–28.

Wertheimer, M. (1923 [1938]). Untersuchungen zur Lehre von der Gestalt II, in *Psycologische Forschung*, 4, 301–350. Published as: Laws of Organization in Perceptual Forms, in Ellis, W. (1938). *A source book of Gestalt psychology*, pp. 71–88. London: Routledge.

White, T.D., B. Asfaw, Y. Beyene, Y. Haile-Selassie, C.O. Lovejoy, G. Suwa and G. WoldeGabriel. (2009). *Ardipithecus ramidus* and the paleobiology of early hominids. *Science*, 326/5949: 75–86.

White, T.D., G. Suwa, S. Simpson and B. Asfaw. (2000). Jaws and teeth of *Australopithecus afarensis* from Maka, Middle Awash, Ethiopia. *American Journal of Physical Anthropology*, 1111: 45–68.

Whitehead, H. (2003). *Sperm Whales: Social Evolution in the Ocean*. Chicago: University of Chicago Press.

Whorf, B.L. (1956). *Language, Thought and Reality: Selected Writings of Benjamin Lee Whorf*. Cambridge, MA: MIT Press.

Wiener, M., P. Turkeltaub, and H.B. Coslett. (2010). The image of time: A voxel-wise meta-analysis. *Neuroimage* 49: 1728–40.

Wildman, D.E., M. Uddin, L. Guozhen, L.I. Grossman and M. Goodman. (2003). Implications of Natural Selection in Shaping 99.4% Non-synonymous DNA Identity between Humans and Chimpanzees: Enlarging Genus Homo. *Proceedings of the National Academy of Sciences*, USA, 100/12: 7181–8.

Wilkins, J. B.J. Schoville, K.S. Brown and M. Chazan. (2012). Evidence for early hafted hunting technology. *Science*, 338/6109: 942–6.

Williams, J.A. (2012). Lewis Carroll and the private life of words. *Review of English Studies*, 64/266: 651–71.

Wynn, K. (1992). Addition and subtraction by human infants. *Nature*, 358: 749–50.

(1995). Origins of numerical knowledge. *Mathematical Cognition*, 1: 35–60.

Yu, N. (2001). *The Contemporary Theory of Metaphor: A Perspective from Chinese*. Amsterdam: John Benjamins.

Zbikowski, L. (2001). *Conceptualizing Music: Cognitive Structure, Theory, and Analysis*. Oxford: Oxford University Press.

Zilhão, J., D.E. Angelucci, E. Badal-Garcia, F. d'Errico, F. Daniel, and L. Dayet. (2010). Symbolic use of marine shells and mineral pigments by Iberian Neandertals. *Proceedings of the National Academy of Sciences*, USA, 107: 1023–8.

Zilhão, J. and E. Trinkaus. (2003). Social implications. In 'portrait of the artist as a child'. In J. Zilhão and E. Trinkaus (Eds.), *The Gravettian Human Skeleton From the Abrigo Do Lagar Velho and its Archaeological Context*, pp. 519–41. Lisbon, Portugal: Instituto Português de Arqueologia.

Zwaan, R.A. (2004). The immersed experiencer: Toward an embodied theory of language comprehension. In B.H. Ross (Ed.), *The Psychology of Learning and Motivation*, pp. 35–62. New York: Academic Press.

Zwaan, R.A. and R.H. Yaxley. (2003). Hemispheric differences in semantic-relatedness judgments. *Cognition*, 87: 79–86.

# Index